Tim Wallace-Murphy studied medicine at University College, Dublin and then qualified as a psychologist. He is now an author, lecturer and historian, and has spent over 30 years following his personal spiritual path. He has written several bestsellers: *The Mark of The Beast* (with Trevor Ravenscroft), *Rex Deus: The True Mystery of Rennes-Le-Château* and *Rosslyn: Guardian of the Secrets of the Holy Grail* (with Marilyn Hopkins), which provided invaluable source material to Dan Brown for his best-selling novel, *The Da Vinci Code*, and more recently, *Cracking the Symbol Code*. He lives in Devon.

By the same author

The Mark of the Beast (with Trevor Ravenscroft)

The Illustrated Guidebook to Rosslyn Chapel

The Templar Legacy and the Masonic Inheritance within Rosslyn Chapel

Rosslyn: Guardian of the Secrets of the Holy Grail
(with Marilyn Hopkins)

Rex Deus: The True Mystery of Rennes-le-Château
(with Marilyn Hopkins and Graham Simmans)

Templars in America (with Marilyn Hopkins)

Custodians of Truth (with Marilyn Hopkins)

Cracking the Symbol Code

The Enigma of the Freemasons

WHAT ISLAM DID FOR US

TIM WALLACE-MURPHY

WATKINS PUBLISHING

LONDON

This edition published in the UK 2006 by
Watkins Publishing, Sixth Floor, Castle House,
75–76 Wells Street, London W1T 3QH

1 3 5 7 9 10 8 6 4 2

Designed and typeset by Paul Saunders

Printed and bound in Great Britain

British Library Cataloguing-in-Publication data available

ISBN-10: 1-84293-190-3
ISBN-13: 9-781842-931905

www.watkinspublishing.com

Contents

This book is respectfully dedicated to my
spiritual brother Rashied K Sharrief-Al-Bey of New York.
A beacon of tolerance and understanding from whom
I have learnt much.

Acknowledgements

No work such as this is ever produced without the help, encouragement and support of a number of people. Responsibility for the contents of this book rests entirely with the author, but I gratefully acknowledge the help and encouragement received from: Richard Beaumont of Staverton, Devon; Laurence Bloom of London; Richard Buades of Marseilles; Nicole Dawe of Okehampton; Sandy Donaghy of Newton Abbot; Jean-Michel Garnier of Chartres; the late Guy Jourdan of Bargemon; Georges Keiss of the Centre d'Études et de Recherches Templière, Campagne-sur-Aude; Michael Monkton of Buckingham; Dr Hugh Montgomery of Somerset; James Mackay Munro of Penicuick; Andrew Pattison of Edinburgh; Stella Pates of Ottery St Mary; Alan Pearson of Rennes-les-Bains; Amy Ralston of Staverton, Devon; Victor Rosati of Totnes; Pat Sibille of Aberdeen; Niven Sinclair of London; Alex Wood of Shaldon; Prince Michael of Albany, my editorial consultant, John Baldock, who has guided my hands so many times in the past, and, finally, Michael Mann and Penny Stopa of Watkins Publishing.

Introduction

THERE IS AN OLD CHINESE curse that proclaims 'May you live in interesting times', and interesting times are defined as times of turmoil. We certainly live in those times today when the Western countries are perceived as being at war with Islam, and Muslim fundamentalists respond with unpredictable waves of terror: the attack on the Twin Towers in New York, a suicide-bomber attack on a nightclub in Bali, bombed trains in Madrid and the attacks on the London Underground on 7 July 2005.

To understand how the relationship between Christianity, Judaism and Islam has degenerated to its present level of intolerance and distrust, it is necessary to go back in time to examine the common origin, history and development of all three of these great faiths and the changing relationships between them. We then discover that Islam has traditionally manifested an intrinsic and profound degree of toleration for the other great faiths. Within the Holy Qu'ran, Christians and Jews are described as 'the People of the Book' and have been treated with respect and toleration by the world of Islam throughout its long history. The People of the Book, are those faiths, such as Christianity and Judaism which, like Islam itself, are founded upon a written source of spiritual revelation.[1]

Furthermore, as we will also discover, Islam's contribution to the development of European culture has been profound.

With the dramatic destruction of Jerusalem by the Roman army in AD 70, most of the Jewish people, including the 24 families of the ma'madot, the hereditary high priests of the Temple that included the family of Jesus, had to flee for their lives.[2] The hereditary priests scattered all over the known world with many settling in Europe and some crossing the Jordan to settle in Arabia among other Jewish exiles. Muhammed grew up in an area inhabited by a considerable Jewish population descended from those who had fled to Arabia after AD 70. Impressive though Jewish influence was in that district, the influence of Coptic and Syrian Christianity was even stronger. However, these were Christians who would have been regarded as outright heretics by the Church authorities in Europe, for they believed that Jesus was human and not divine.[3] Muhammed, who was born in Medina in, or about, 570 CE, was absolutely convinced that he was a true 'messenger of God' in the respected and ancient spiritual tradition of Abraham, Moses, Elijah, John the Baptist and Jesus,[4] and no more perceived himself as founding a new religion than had Jesus before him. He believed that he was called upon to restore true monotheism by testifying to the ancient religion of 'the one true God'. According to the Prophet Muhammed, the One Truth had been revealed to both Jews and Christians but they had either distorted the message or ignored it.[5]

Unlike Christianity, which tried to suppress all rival religions, Islam from its very inception maintained a great degree of tolerance towards other faiths, so that members of all three great monotheistic religions of the world were able to live together in relative peace and harmony under the benevolent rule of Islam. The Jews, for example, who were being hounded to death or treated as second-class citizens in Christian Europe, enjoyed a rich cultural renaissance of their own[6] and, like the Christians, were allowed full religious liberty throughout the Islamic Empire. Volumes of study devoted to the initiatory wisdom of the traditional Jewish mystical stream known as the kabbalah were produced in the Jewish rabbinical schools in Moorish Spain, and most Spanish Christians were extremely proud to belong to a highly advanced and sophisticated culture that was light years ahead of the rest of Europe.[7] The Islamic mystery tradition was elaborated by the Sufi mystery schools of Andalusia which provided open and accessible sources of mystical teaching in an otherwise spiritually barren continent.[8]

The influence of Moorish Spain on the development of Western culture was indeed profound. For example, the well-attended and richly endowed colleges in Andalusia were later to provide a model for those of Oxford and Cambridge in England.[9] At a time when most European nobles, kings and emperors were barely literate, the Umayyad court at Cordova was the most splendid in Europe and provided a haven for philosophers, poets, artists, mathematicians and astronomers;[10] Islamic Spain also gave Europe an architectural and artistic heritage that is still a source of wonder to the modern world. It was in translation from Arabic, not the original Greek, that knowledge of the Greek philosophers crept cautiously back into the mainstream of Christian thought via schools in Spain.[11] Along with philosophy, mathematics and science came more recent advances in medicine, art and architecture. These were all fruits of spiritual insight, sacred gnosis that flowed from the Islamic mystical traditions and that were passed on to Christian Europe via the Rex Deus families who claim to be descended from the 24 high-priestly families in Jerusalem.

The contrast in attitudes to learning and religious toleration between Christian and Islamic cultures was made brutally obvious at the time of the Crusades. While Christian knights were butchering 'infidels' after the capture of Jerusalem, other, more enlightened, members of the same religion were sitting at the feet of Muslim scholars in Spain.[12] Spain was not the only cultural bridge between the Christian and Muslim worlds, Moorish incursions into Provence, the Arabic conquest of Sicily and, of course the Crusades and the long occupation of the Holy Land that followed, provided ample opportunities for cross-cultural fertilization.

In the troubled times we live in today, when the religion and culture of Islam is under apparently perpetual attack on all fronts, we need to remember how much we, in the intolerant Christian

West, owe to the spiritual insights of that great religious culture. Religious toleration, respect for learning, the concepts of chivalry and brotherhood are as relevant today as they have ever been. We were taught these principles by the people of Islam when, in Spain, they acted as Beacons of Light in the Dark Ages of European religious intolerance, narrow-mindedness, and persecution.

Part One

◊

THE INITIATORY TRADITION
AND THE ORIGINS OF JUDAISM
AND CHRISTIANITY

THE EARLIEST KNOWN EVIDENCE we have of man's desire to communi-
cate with the mysterious world of the Divine, are the numerous
Palaeolithic cave paintings which can be found throughout the world. It
was the Frenchman Norbert Casteret who found the first magnificent
European examples in the caves at Montespan and it is almost impossible to imagine his excitement when he found paintings of lions and
horses covering the walls of these subterranean chambers. Casteret had
stumbled upon the art and sacred symbolism of prehistoric cave men.[1]

The true nature of these fascinating cave paintings remained a matter
of speculation until, some years later, further cave paintings were discovered in the caves of Les Trois Frères in the Ariège in France. These
were paintings of men dressed as animals, Palaeolithic depictions of
men clad in Shaman's costumes.[2] In the opinion of Mircea Eliade, one
of the world's leading historians of man's spiritual development, 'It is
impossible to imagine a period in which man did not have dreams and
waking reveries and did not enter into "trance" – a loss of consciousness
that was interpreted as the soul's travelling into the beyond.'[3] Shamans
of the Palaeolithic era, just like their counterparts in hunter-gatherer
tribes in remote parts of the world today, believed that the phenomenal

world we live in rested upon another reality, the invisible world of the spirit.

Our Palaeolithic ancestors left us no written records as to the precise nature of the ritual practices they used to enhance their spiritual perceptions. However, it is with the rise of literate civilizations and the voluminous records they left us that we can begin to discern how early the practice of initiation into the spiritual world began. Bizarre though it may seem, it was again an 'accident' based upon curiosity and the age-old problem of greed that led to the discovery of the most ancient corpus of spiritual texts known to mankind – the Pyramid Texts of ancient Egypt.

The sacred knowledge contained within the Pyramid Texts became the vibrant heart that sustained and maintained the development of the civilization of ancient Egypt; one that was passed down through the hereditary priesthood by means of initiation into the ancient temple mysteries. These priestly initiates preserved, enhanced and transmitted this extraordinary body of knowledge from master to pupil down through the generations so that it could flow on, after the Exodus of the people of Israel from the land of Egypt, into a new religion and culture, that of the Jews. Ultimately it led, after much trauma, to the writing of the book that is revered by all three of the world's great monotheistic religions, the Tannakh, the Jewish scriptures that later became the biblical Old Testament.

Chapter 1

~

Ancient Egypt

EARLY ONE MORNING IN the winter of 1879, an observant and intelligent Egyptian workman standing near the pyramid of Unas at Saqqara, saw a desert fox silhouetted against the light of the rising sun. This wary animal was behaving in a rather bizarre and uncharacteristic manner. It moved, stopped and then looked directly at the workman as if inviting him to follow, then moved again before disappearing into a crevice in the north face of the pyramid. Intrigued by this, and scenting possible profit, for pyramids and tombs were renowned as repositories of treasure, the excited man followed the fox into the ancient structure and, after a difficult crawl through a tunnel-like passage, found himself in a large chamber within the pyramid.[1] Lighting a flaming torch, he found that the walls of the chamber were covered with turquoise and gold hieroglyphic inscriptions.[2] Later, after further investigation by the archaeologists, similar inscriptions were found in other nearby pyramids. These inscriptions are today known collectively as the Pyramid Texts.[3] They consist of over 4,000 lines of hymns and sacred formulae. Professor Gaston Maspero, the director of the Egyptian Antiquities Service was the first scholar of repute to view them *in situ*.

This seemingly 'accidental' discovery was of enormous importance, yet apparently brought about by an earthly incarnation of the ancient Egyptian god Anubis, a deified form of the jackal known as 'the Desert Fox'; his other divine incarnation was as Upuaut also known as the 'Opener of the Ways'. Thus, the modern four-legged incarnation of Upuaut had, both literally and figuratively, opened the ways not only to a more profound understanding of the spiritual beliefs at the time of Pharaoh Unas, the last ruler of the fifth dynasty, but also to an important understanding of the great depth that sacred knowledge or gnosis had attained in remote antiquity when the texts were actually composed. For, as Professor Maspero claimed, the bulk of the texts were the written expression of a much older tradition that dated back to Egypt's prehistoric past.[4] One that predates the events recounted in the Book of Exodus by over 2,000 years and the writing of the New Testament by nearly 3,400 years.[5] Professor I E S Edwards of the British Museum stated without reservation that, 'The Pyramid Texts were certainly not inventions of the fifth or sixth dynasties, but had originated in extreme antiquity; it is hardly surprising, therefore, that they sometimes contain allusions to conditions which no longer prevailed at the time of Unas...'[6]

Thus, two of Egyptology's greatest authorities agreed that the Pyramid Texts are the oldest collection of religious writings ever discovered. Yet, sadly, despite their immense importance, it was not until 1969 that the Professor of Ancient Egyptian language at University College London, Raymond Faulkner, published the first translation that was accepted as truly authoritative by most modern scholars and he again stressed that, 'The Pyramid Texts constitute the oldest corpus of Egyptian religious and funerary literature now extant.'[7] These hieroglyphic records within the pyramids at Saqqara are now accepted by Egyptologists and academics as the earliest collection of sacred knowledge, or 'esoteric wisdom' yet found.

Tep Zepi

The Pyramid Texts refer frequently to *Tep Zepi*, the so-called 'First Time', the legendary era of Osiris when Egypt was, according to tradition, ruled directly by the gods in human form. Gods who, according to myth and legend, gave the Egyptian people the blessed gifts of sacred knowledge as well as a complex and uncannily accurate knowledge of astronomy. This poses the question 'how did this highly sophisticated level of spiritual and astronomical knowledge arise in prehistoric Egypt?'. It also raises the important issue of 'when was the First Time and where did it take place?'. The author and Egyptologist, John Anthony West, advanced one theory that may help us answer the first question:

> Every aspect of Egyptian knowledge seems to have been complete at the very beginning. The sciences, artistic and architectural techniques and the hieroglyphic system show virtually no signs of 'development'; indeed many of the achievements of the earliest dynasties were never surpassed or even equalled later on... The answer to the mystery is, of course, obvious, but because it is repellent to the prevailing cast of modern thinking, it is seldom seriously considered. *Egyptian civilization was not a development, it was a legacy.*[8] [my emphasis]

If Egyptian civilization and its profound knowledge base were indeed a legacy, then whose legacy were they? As there is no evidence of any developmental period within Egyptian history, this inevitably leads us to the conclusion that this knowledge was either developed elsewhere, or that it arose from a much earlier Egyptian culture that is, as yet at least, undiscovered. This latter possibility, unlikely though it may be at first glance, still has to be considered as there are vast areas of Egypt buried by the sands of the desert or rendered incapable of excavation by the sprawling suburbs of Cairo and other cities.

Another, perhaps more plausible theory was advanced by William Matthew Flinders Petrie (1853–1942), namely the dynastic race theory. Flinders Petrie was the Professor of Egyptology at University College, London who is still revered as the father of modern Egyptology. In excavations of over 2,000 pre-dynastic graves at Nakada in 1893–4, Flinders Petrie and James Quibell examined over 2,000 graves of the pre-dynastic period and classified their finds as deriving from two distinct periods, Nakada I and Nakada II.[9] In the graves of the Nakada II period, Petrie found pottery fragments of a distinctly Mesopotamian character,[10] yet in all other excavations of Nile Valley sites of an earlier period, foreign artefacts were virtually nonexistent.[11] In 1956, one of Flinders Petrie's pupils, the English Egyptologist, Douglas Derry, argued that the evidence was suggestive of:

> ... the presence of a dominant race, perhaps relatively few in numbers but greatly exceeding the original inhabitants in intelligence; a race which brought into Egypt the knowledge of building in stone, of sculpture, painting, reliefs and above all writing; hence the enormous jump from the primitive pre-dynastic Egyptian to the advanced civilization of the Old Empire (the Old Kingdom).[12]

However, the sudden appearance of a large body of evidence of cross-cultural contact between Mesopotamia and Egypt, important though it may be, does not, as yet at least, prove that Egyptian culture and its spiritual foundations were Mesopotamian in origin. They might also have derived from the initiatory tradition of Zoroastrianism in ancient Persia. The fact is that, at present at least, we can only speculate. Egyptian spiritual tradition and its voluminous records, however, do allow us to trace its further development within Egypt itself.

Egyptian Initiatory Tradition

The English Egyptologist David Rohl has spent many years investigating the *Shemsa-Hor*, the followers of Horus, who are mentioned within the Pyramid Texts.[13] He suggests that the Shemsa-Hor were the immediate ancestors of the early Pharaohs.[14] The descriptions in the Pyramid Texts describing this elite group of initiates are the earliest documentary references yet found to a manner of transmission of sacred knowledge that has lasted from that time right down to the present day. According to Egyptian legend, this knowledge first arose in the mysterious 'time of the

Neteru' – the fabled era when the gods ruled Egypt immediately prior to the time of the earliest Pharaohs. It was then transmitted by a succession of priestly initiates who preserved, enhanced and transmitted this extraordinary body of knowledge from master to pupil down through the generations.

The English author, John Anthony West, in his book *Serpent in the Sky*, paraphrased the views of France's leading twentieth-century spiritual scholar of Egyptology, Schwaller de Lubicz, who recorded that Egyptian science, medicine, mathematics and astronomy were of an exponentially higher order of refinement and sophistication than most modern scholars will generally acknowledge. Furthermore, according to Schwaller de Lubicz, Egyptian civilization was based upon a complete and precise understanding of universal laws and it was by the inspired use of mythology, symbolic imagery and the sacred geometry of their architecture, that the Egyptians were able to encapsulate their knowledge of the basic pattern structures of the universe.

These sophisticated and incredibly high levels of sacred knowledge were passed down through successive generations of an elite, hereditary priesthood from master to pupil by the process of initiation into the Temple mysteries. Such sacred gnosis was not to be used for personal gain by the priestly and royal initiates, for while rank and royal birth undoubtedly carried considerable levels of economic and political privilege, the sacred knowledge of astronomy, agriculture, architecture, building, medicine, mathematics, navigation and metallurgy was to be used for the benefit of the entire community served by the priests, the Pharaohs and the aristocracy. Thus, protected by the deserts that surrounded it and sustained by divinely inspired gnosis, Egyptian civilization developed a degree of sophistication, stability, peace and complexity that has yet to be equalled or exceeded in many respects, much less fully understood. A vast body of esoteric knowledge was recorded within the Pyramid Texts as well as being encoded on temple walls elsewhere, such as the Edfu Texts, which are inscribed on the walls of the temple there, and the Books of the Dead (the funerary texts of ancient Egypt). The dualism that lay at the heart of Egyptian sacred knowledge was noted by the modern authors Bauval and Hancock when they wrote: 'The language of all these texts is exotic, laden with the dualistic thinking that lay at the heart of Egyptian society and that may have been the engine of its greatest achievements.'[15] The Edfu Texts, in particular, refer repeatedly to the 'wisdom of the Sages' and constantly emphasize that, to the Egyptian elite, their most valued gift was knowledge.[16]

According to Schwaller de Lubicz, the ancient Egyptians had their own unique and effective way of understanding the universe and man's place within it. They recorded and preserved this within a completely different knowledge system from that revered by modern man,[17] for this sacred 'way of knowing' could not be adequately transmitted by the normal vehicle of language but could only be taught or shown in myth and symbolism.[18] Schwaller de Lubicz began his important work on symbolism by stating that there are always two distinct and different ways of interpreting Egyptian religious texts, the exoteric and the esoteric; exactly the same principle that can be applied to many aspects of medieval Christian sacred art. The exoteric meaning is the standard explanation, which can be arrived at by a simple and direct interpretation of the hieroglyphic records or by the study of the appropriate textbooks on religion and history. In reality, this 'standard' version only exists to serve as a vehicle for a deeper, hidden, or esoteric meaning, which Schwaller described as the *symbolique* interpretation.[19] Two other French mystical writers, Pauwels and Bergier, commented on precisely this aspect of ancient symbolism and of the insight of the initiates who used it throughout the centuries that followed, when they stated simply that:

> They... wrote in stone their hermetic message. Signs, incomprehensible to men whose consciousness had not undergone transmutations... These men were not secretive because they loved secrecy, but simply because their discoveries about the Laws of Energy, of matter and of the mind had been made in another state of consciousness and so could not be communicated directly.[20]

While this form of esoteric knowledge has usually been either wilfully ignored by academics or is simply not recognized at all by the public at large, its symbolic remnants have been transmitted, in one form or another, down through all the great monotheistic religions of Judaism, Christianity and Islam that all sprang from common Egyptian roots.[21] Therefore it is no surprise to learn that the ancient Egyptian initiates were not the only ones to use symbols in this manner; symbolism is such an effective and instinctive form of communication, that it has been used, continually, for millennia, by sages and initiates of all the world's great religious traditions.

The Founding Father of the Jewish and Arab Peoples

The Prophet Abraham is revered as both the founder of the people of Israel and as the patriarch of the Arab peoples. Thus, in this seminal figure we have the direct spiritual and temporal founder of the monotheism that gave birth to the three great faiths of Judaism, Christianity and Islam. According to the account in the Old Testament, Abraham was born in the city of Ur. Yet, this bald statement may be a simple matter of camouflage created by Jewish scribes working in Babylon in the sixth century BCE to disguise the patriarch's true origins.

At the time, when the scriptures first took their present written form, the biblical Israelites and their Egyptian allies had just been defeated by the Babylonians and the scribes themselves were working in exile under the ever watchful eyes of their captors. It would have been deemed vitally necessary to play down any dynastic connections the Hebrew people had with Egypt. Yet, the account in Genesis has not been completely sanitized and still discloses certain facts about Abraham and his family that clearly demonstrate that he was not only an Egyptian but a very high-born one at that. For example, Abraham is quoted as describing his wife in the following terms: '... and yet indeed she is my sister; she is the daughter of my father, but not the daughter of my mother; and she became my wife.'[22] This clearly incestuous marriage to his sister has rarely been commented upon by modern biblical scholars, yet it is of supreme importance, for such marriages between siblings in that era in the Middle East were restricted to senior members of the Egyptian royal family. Therefore, it is almost certain that Abraham was a member of that select dynastic line. I am far from alone in reaching this conclusion, and certainly not the first to do so, for the eleventh-century biblical scholar Rabbi Solomon Isaacs, (1040–1105) also known as Rachi, wrote that, 'You should know that the family of Abraham was of a high line.'[23] Rachi's opinion flatly denies the accepted notion that Abraham was a nomadic shepherd and confirms his true social status.

The name by which the patriarch was originally known, Abram,[24] translates as 'exalted father', one of the ritual titles regularly used by the Pharaohs of Egypt. Furthermore, there is also the strange matter of a complete change of names for both Abram and Sarai, his wife, recorded in the Scriptures,[25] for this reinforces the fact of Abraham's Egyptian origin.[26] The term 'father of many nations' is applied to Abraham in the account in Genesis.[27] While his son Isaac became the root of the people of Israel, his son Ishmael by his wife's handmaiden Hagar, founded the Arab peoples. Abraham's wife's new name, Sarah, is the Egyptian term for 'princess'. It is also a matter of record that Sarah's handmaiden Hagar was also a relatively high-born Egyptian, being the daughter of one of the Pharaohs by one of his concubines.[28] To reinforce the point, the Bible also records the fact that the patriarch's son Ishmael took an Egyptian wife.[29]

Genesis also records a rather bizarre liaison between Sarah and the unnamed Pharaoh of that time;[30] this has given rise to much scholarly speculation in both Judaism and Islam, for both the Babylonian Talmud[31] and the Qu'ran[32] raise grave doubts about the true paternity of Abraham's son Isaac. Both these authoritative sources imply that the Pharaoh was the boy's real father, not the patriarch Abraham. So, arising from the biblical accounts we have two questions whose answers imply, even if they do not prove it outright, that the true origins of both the people of Israel and the Arabs is to be found in Egypt! Firstly: 'Was Abraham from Ur of the Chaldees, or was he an Egyptian?' Secondly, 'Do the people of Israel descend from the patriarch Abraham or the Pharaoh?'

These controversial ideas arise from clear and unequivocal statements in the book of Genesis and are further reinforced by the words of Melchizedek, the King of Righteousness, recorded later in the same account: 'Blessed be Abram, the most high of God, possessor of heaven and earth.'[33] Both Melchizedek, the priest king of Jerusalem, and Abraham use exactly the same telling phrase to describe the deity, *the Most High God*,[34] – one of the commonest terms used in the Egyptian records for the supreme god of the pantheon. It is also highly significant that Abraham adopted for himself and all his descendants the Egyptian custom of circumcision, ostensibly at the command of Almighty God himself.[35] Circumcision, despite the fact that it had been mandatory among the Egyptian royal family, hereditary priesthood and nobility since 4000 BCE, was a most unusual practice amongst other groups, religions or nations.[36]

However, even if one accepts the traditional interpretation of these accounts in Genesis, the meeting between Abraham and the Pharaoh undoubtedly signals the beginning of an ongoing cross-fertilization of spiritual ideas and experiences that took place between the descendants of Abraham and the land of Egypt that culminated in the foundation of Judaism. Two leading Jewish scholars of international repute, Sigmund Freud[37] and Ernst Sellin,[38] have both commented freely on the profound significance of Egyptian thought on the development of early Judaism.

Perhaps the crowning moment in Abraham's life came when, in obedience to God, he prepared to sacrifice his son Isaac as a burnt offering on the sacred site of Mount Moriah.[39] When God saw Abraham's total obedience to his demands, he sent an angel to intervene. The sacrifice was halted and a ram replaced the innocent boy as the burnt offering. From that time onward, human sacrifice of any kind, particularly the sacrifice of a child, which was common among the Canaanites, was held by the Jewish people to be an abomination in the eyes of the Lord. For his loyalty and absolute obedience to the will of God, Abraham was rewarded with the promise: ' ... and in thy seed shall all the nations of the earth be blessed because thou hast obeyed my voice.'[40]

Moses, Pharaoh of Egypt

For those who regard the Bible as 'the inerrant word of God' the problems of establishing a historical basis for Old Testament stories about the sojourn of the people of Israel in Egypt poses something of a dilemma. No valid basis for any realistic chronology of the events described can be found within the biblical accounts and this situation is further complicated by the slipshod way those narratives are written. No specific Pharaoh is named and, furthermore, despite the voluminous and detailed records of Egyptian history that have survived, no group can be irrefutably identified as 'the people of Israel'. The Egypt Exploration Society and the Palestine Exploration Society were both founded to establish the historical basis for the Bible by archaeological and documentary research. Yet, despite over 150 years of concerted effort, neither of these well-funded and superbly staffed organizations managed to do more than merely scratch the surface of this problem. It was other scholars, working from an equally devout perspective, who have helped to resolve some of the more important issues that have obscured this vital aspect of our spiritual and temporal history. To the devout of all three major monotheistic faiths, it may well come as a surprise that the identification and the true origin of the historical character named Moses in the Bible, is virtually established beyond doubt. Among scholars and Egyptologists there is no argument as to whether or not Moses was a Pharaoh or a foundling, simply a debate as to which Pharaoh he was.

This seemingly contradicts the biblical account, for the story of the infant Moses being found in the bulrushes by Pharaoh's daughter and his adoption by the Egyptian royal family[41] is the starting point for a chain of interlinked events that culminate in the Exodus of the 'people of Israel' from Egypt. Implicit in this account is the previously unquestioned assumption that, by the time of Moses, the people of Israel were an identifiable and distinct ethnic group –

a monotheistic nation subject to a covenant, or berit, with the God of Abraham. This belief is deeply entrenched in the minds of all devout followers of Judaism, Christianity and Islam. Yet, according to scholars of impeccable and international repute, nothing could be further from the truth.

Sigmund Freud (1856–1939) was not only a psychoanalyst of truly international reputation, but also a biblical scholar of considerable stature. He wrote that he could find no trace of the term 'Hebrew' prior to the Babylonian exile.[42] The modern Israeli biblical scholars, Messod and Roger Sabbah, assert categorically that there is no proof of the Hebrews' existence as a nation or tribe at the time of Moses in the manner described in the scriptures.[43] They then pose the following uncomfortable question:

> How could a people so impregnated with such a major part of the wisdom of Egypt disappear from the (Egyptian) historical record so mysteriously? More than 200 years of research in the deserts, tombs and temples have shown nothing![44]

For those who believe in the historicity of the Bible there is thus an insurmountable problem for, despite the detailed scriptural descriptions of the prolonged sojourn of the people of Israel in Egypt, no identifiable trace of these people can be found in the comprehensive and voluminous Egyptian historical records. Indeed, as Freud has pointed out, the term Hebrew as an indication of race is not found in any source other than the Bible, prior to the Jewish exile in Babylon. Furthermore, there is only one independent, archaeological, early reference to the people of Israel prior to that traumatic episode. The fact that the nation called 'Israel' had been established by 1207 BCE is confirmed by a stele recording their conquest by Pharaoh Mernephtah that reads, 'Israel is laid waste, his seed is not...' This is the first independent verification of the existence of the people of Israel and it does not occur until almost two centuries after the latest date given for the Exodus from Egypt.[45]

Prior to the late eighteenth and early nineteenth centuries, biblical stories were believed to be accurate historical accounts of real events. With the beginnings of critical biblical scholarship at that time, however, this conception began to undergo a rapid, radical and cumulative change. In the early years of the twentieth century, Dr Karl Abraham, a renowned Jewish biblical scholar published an article claiming that the Pharaoh Akenhaten may have been the biblical character known as Moses.[46] This received some degree of confirmation when Sigmund Freud published his final work *Moses and Monotheism* in 1939. Freud demonstrated that the story of Moses' birth in the Old Testament, was an amalgamation of the earlier mythology of Sargon (2800 BCE) and Egyptian legends of the birth of the Horus. Both mythological characters had been hidden in a reed bed to avoid their murder. Freud claimed that the story of Moses' origins was a fabrication created during the Babylonian Exile to disguise the fact that this leading 'Jewish' prophet was, in truth, a member of the Egyptian royal family. He also showed that the name Moses was a derivative of the common Egyptian name of *Mos* or child.

Karl Abraham and Freud were not the first to claim that Moses was born an Egyptian, for this assertion had been repeatedly made by earlier writers including the Egyptian historian and high priest of the third century BCE, Manetho; by the first century BCE Jewish historian Philo of Alexandria; by the Jewish historian of the first century CE, Flavius Josephus, and by Justin Martyr, an early father of the Christian Church who lived in the second century CE. Freud and Dr Abraham were followed by Robert Feather, the English author, who claimed that:

Detailed analysis of the Torah, the Talmud and Midrash led me to the conclusion that Moses was not only born and raised as an Egyptian, but was, in fact, a Prince of Egypt – a son of the Royal House of Pharaoh.[47]

Thus Karl Abraham, Sigmund Freud, Robert Feather and more recently, the popular English writer Maurice Cotterell,[48] have agreed that Moses was either the Pharaoh Akenhaten or one of his close entourage. These conclusions were reinforced by the Islamic scholar Ahmed Osman, a lawyer and author whose considerable forensic skill was deployed to prove that the most likely candidate who could be identified as Moses was Dr Abraham's original suggestion, the Pharaoh Akenhaten.[49]

The Egyptian Origins of the Jewish Religion

In his final work, *Moses and Monotheism*, Freud described the startling similarities between Atenism, the religion of Akenhaten, and Judaism, and went on to claim that Moses had simply transmitted his own religion of Atenism virtually unchanged to the new people of Israel. Furthermore, Freud claimed that the prayer *Schema Yisrael Adonai Elohenu Adonai Echod* (Hear, O Israel, the Lord thy God is One God), far from being a new and unique, post-Exodus Jewish invocation, was an exact replication of an Atenist prayer. He argued that, in translation the Hebrew letter **d** is a transliteration of the Egyptian **t**, and, in similar manner, **e** becomes **o**, thus this prayer when transcribed into Egyptian reads: 'Hear, O Israel, our god Aten is the only god.'[50] Perhaps this idea is not so startling as it may appear, for two millennia before Freud's birth, the priest and chronicler Manetho had remarked that Moses had discharged priestly duties in Egypt.[51] Akenhaten did just that as the supreme high priest in his temple to the Aten at Amarna.

Another traditional Egyptian practice was adopted under the leadership of Moses, the creation of the hereditary priesthood. The Bible recounts that this was based upon the tribe of Levi, in fact it was simply a continuation of the Egyptian priesthood, a hereditary caste who were the guardians of sacred knowledge. This 'new' Jewish hereditary priesthood simply continued the onward transmission of sacred wisdom, from master to pupil and on down through the generations, much as before. Yet another startling example of an Egyptian origin for the central aspect of Judaism can be found when we examine the basis for Jewish sacred Law – the Torah.

The Law of Moses is founded firmly upon the Ten Commandments which, according to the Bible, Moses received from Almighty

God on Mount Sinai. Yet, despite their divine origin, there are two different versions of the Ten Commandments in the Scriptures and one found in Deuteronomy reads as follows:

> I am the Lord thy God, which brought thee out of the land of Egypt, from the house of bondage. Thou shalt have no other gods before me. Thou shalt not make thee any graven image, or any likeness of any thing that is in heaven above, or that is in the earth beneath, or that is in the waters beneath the earth. Thou shalt not bow down thyself unto them, nor serve them: for *I the Lord thy God am a jealous God*, visiting the iniquity of the fathers upon the children unto the third and fourth generation of them that hate me.[52]
> [my emphasis]

Esoterically, the terms 'the land of Egypt' and 'the house of bondage' refer to the temporal world where we are enslaved by the ego. Escape from 'the land of Egypt' with its credence in a range of gods thus symbolizes a shift in consciousness. This passage also links Judaism to Atenism, for, according to Professor Flinders Petrie *The Aten was the only instance of a jealous God in Egypt*, and this worship was exclusive of all others, and claims universality.' [my emphasis][53] The Israeli scholars, Messod and Roger Sabbah, stress that Atenism abolished all the images and idols of other gods. This 'new' concept was of a god that was deemed to be the creator of the universe in a manner that was in complete accord with ancient Egyptian belief.[54] It therefore comes as no surprise to learn that the injunctions against the use of graven images laid out in Deuteronomy's version of the Ten Commandments simply replicate those in the Atenist code. The Egyptian Book of the Dead names the principles attested to by souls being assessed by the court of Osiris after death, in the following list:

I have done no falsehood against men

I have not impoverished (robbed) my associates

I have not killed[55]

This is transcribed in the Exodus account of the Ten Commandments, to become:

Thou shalt not kill

Thou shalt not steal

Thou shalt not bear witness against thy neighbour[56]

This simple comparison is another demonstration of the validity of the hypothesis that Judaism is a direct evolution from Atenism. A comparison of Psalm 104 in the Old Testament and Akenhaten's Hymn to the Aten further demonstrates the links between these two religions. Verse 24 of the psalm reads:

O Lord, how manifold are thy works!
In wisdom hast thou made them all:
the earth is full of thy riches.[57]

Allowing for problems in translation, almost identical phrasing and construction is found in the Hymn to the Aten:

How manifold are all your works,
They are hidden from before us,
O sole god, whose powers no other possesses
You did create the earth
According to your desire.[58]

The remarkable similarity of sacred terminology and ritual practice is both widespread and profound. In a brief work such as this I can only mention a few of the many examples that exist. The word for 'ark' or 'casket' is so remarkably similar in both Egyptian and Hebrew that it contributed to the claim by the nineteenth-century specialist in Semitic languages, Antoine Fabre d'Olivet: 'I regard the idiom of Hebrew sensed in the Sepher (the scriptural rolls of the Torah) as a transplanted branch of the Egyptian language.'[59]

The Ark, employed as a symbolic form of transport for the god

Aten in ceremonies at Amarna, was later used by the Jews of the Exodus to carry the tablets of stone inscribed with the Ten Commandments. The ten *Sephirot* or attributes of God found in the kabbalah, such as crown, wisdom, intelligence, mercy, power, beauty, victorious, glorious, foundation and royalty were, according to the Sabbah brothers, originally listed as attributes of the Pharaohs.[60] Akenhaten sacrificed animals at Amarna in an identical manner to Moses. Amarna itself was described as the Holy City and it is written that Akenhaten abandoned the sacred land of Karnak for *the Holy Land* of Akhetaten or Amarna. The 'Holy Land' – a telling phrase for Jews and Christians.[61] The ancient Egyptians ritually inscribed sacred texts above the entrances of their temples, a habit that is replicated today by the Jewish people where such texts known as mezuzoth can still be found high up near the doors of orthodox homes.[62]

Thus, early post-Exodus Judaism was undoubtedly, both ethnically and spiritually, Egyptian in origin. This salient fact has been recognized by scholars for many years yet, sadly, it has still to impinge itself upon public consciousness in the world at large. This blatant gap in the public's knowledge is perhaps one more contributory factor that has led misguided members of all three major world faiths to behave as antagonists rather than as brothers.

Chapter 2

~

The First Revelation of the Abrahamic Religion – The Writing of the Old Testament

I<small>T IS BIZARRE THAT WAR</small> and destruction have played such a formative role in the creation of the great monotheistic religions of the world. Not the wars apparently fought in the name of religion, that are usually found to be caused by the human greed for power or territory, but those that have resulted in the despoliation of one city above all others, namely the Holy City of Jerusalem.

The death of King Solomon, as recounted in the Old Testament, marked the end of the ancient kingdom of Israel. Tax increases imposed by his son and successor, King Reheboam[1] caused the country to split into two kingdoms, each named after their principal tribes. To the south was Judah, with Jerusalem as its capital; to the north was Ephraim, called Israel in the Bible, which later became Samaria. In 722 BCE, the Assyrians captured Samaria and the kingdom of Ephraim ceased to exist. This conquest of Samaria and the deportation of its people is one of the few important events described in the Bible during the so-called 'First Temple period' that can be clearly verified by external contemporaneous historical sources. We find, in the annals of Sargon II, King of Assyria: 'In the beginning of my royal rule, I have besieged and conquered the city of the Samarians... I have led away 27,290 of its inhabitants as captives.'² This event is still of traumatic significance to Jews throughout the world, for the spectre of the 'lost ten tribes of Israel' still haunts the collective memory of the Jewish people. Some 20 years later the Assyrians besieged Jerusalem in its turn, but the city did not fall. However, its freedom was not to last, for, in 598 BCE, a new conqueror, King Nebuchadnezzar of Babylon, invaded the land. Jerusalem fell in 597 BCE and 10,000 of its leading citizens, including the heir to the throne, were led away into captivity.³ Between 734 and 581 BCE, there were six enforced deportations of the people of Israel and, as a result, many others fled to seek safety in Egypt and other neighbouring lands.⁴

The Babylonian Exile

As a result of these traumatic events, the Diaspora of the Jews had begun in earnest and, from this time onwards, the majority of Jews would always live outside the Promised Land. They instinctively realized that, without a temple or a country of their own, their religion and culture were under serious pressure, for they faced imminent extinction as a people through absorption by the heathen among whom they found themselves. In response, they turned towards God. They had the sublime gift of the Torah and their other sacred writings, and around this spiritual core they created a new form of Judaism, one stripped of all territorial limitations and political loyalties and firmly founded upon piety and learning, religion and study.⁵

Thus, the apparent disaster of the enforced exile of the people of Israel in Babylon was turned to advantage in a manner that can only be described as divinely inspired. The Jews in exile in Babylon, not only transformed their religion and ensured their survival as a people, but, as the intervening centuries have shown, they commenced a process that, ultimately, transformed the world. Out of their sacred writings, the priests and scribes created the literary and spiritual masterpiece that Christians call the Old Testament – the scriptural basis of the world's three great monotheistic faiths. The exiles had The Law, the Book of Deuteronomy (which had been discovered in rather peculiar circumstances just before the fall of Jerusalem), some records of their past, their oral traditions, and the sayings of the prophets. With a passionate sense of purpose they founded their faith on what they had, explained the realities of their present travails and then projected their vision not only into the future, but retrospectively into the newly created and carefully embroidered accounts of their past. Thus, it is apparent that many of the pivotal figures of biblical history, such as Saul, David, Solomon,[6] Elijah and even Joshua, had lived and died without the benefit of the Scriptures to guide them. What had guided these spiritual giants of Jewish history was the mystical and initiatory heritage of their Egyptian ancestors, now being incorporated into the new Scriptures being written in Babylon. The process that began in exile in Babylon did not reach completion until the second century BCE. The Hebrew Bible, on which the Christian Old Testament is based, consists of three major parts: The Torah or Pentateuch, The Neviim or Prophets and The Ketuvim or Sayings. Parts of Daniel, Ezra and Jeremiah are written in Aramaic, the rest is written in Hebrew.[7]

There is now a general consensus among modern biblical scholars on the authorship of the Scriptures. Contributions from the earlier sources and traditions can be identified according to either the manner in which they describe God, or the bias or emphasis that discloses their probable origins. During the exile in Babylon and thereafter, the scribes blended all their varying sources into one viable, if sometimes contradictory, whole, and used their underlying beliefs about Jewish history and mythology to give them a compelling narrative style. According to the modern scholarly documentary hypothesis, four major sources can be discerned: identified as J, who refers to God as Yahweh or Jehovah; E who refers to God as the Elohim; D, the assumed author of Deuteronomy; and P, the Priestly source.[8] Beyond the world of academia, even most Christians, with the possible exception of those of a fundamentalist faith, and some orthodox Jews, accept this hypothesis, or one of its several variants, instead of the old idea that the Pentateuch was written by Moses.

The gifted scribes, scholars and priests who compiled the Scriptures were spiritually inspired in what they wrote. Nonetheless, they had their own personal axes to grind, for the new scriptures stressed the role and importance of the entire hereditary priestly caste and within that group laid special emphasis upon the members of 24 *ma'madot*, or hereditary high-priestly families who took turns in serving in the temple in Jerusalem and who all had to be descendants of Zadok the high priest at the Temple in the time of King David.

One important aspect of projecting their spiritual understanding retrospectively was that a plausible and apparently valid explanation was devised to explain the traumatic event of the Exile. The people of Israel were suffering because they had individually and collectively, signally and repeatedly, failed to keep the covenant with God. The recurrent idolatry and backsliding that was detailed in the new scriptures was used to explain God's anger with his chosen people, resulting in the disaster of conquest and exile. Thus, the people of Israel had brought ruin on themselves – the Exile was divine punishment for their sinful past. This explanation not only explained disaster in spiritually valid terms, but allowed the majority of Jews to regain their self-respect. It was an explanation that meant that given due repentance and a return to righteousness, there would be a renewal of God's blessing and protection.[9] Jews were now vigorously encouraged to come closer to Yahweh by observing the Torah. The newly discovered sacred writings of Deuteronomy listed a number of obligatory laws, including the Ten Commandments, which were now elaborated into the complex and scripturally sanctioned legislation of the 613 commandments or mitzvoth of the Pentateuch.[10] Judaism was, thereby, transformed into a highly legalistic code that now impinged on every aspect of its adherents' behaviour.

The development and use of the synagogue can also be traced back to the Exile, for in Babylon the Jews were bereft of their central shrine of the Jerusalem Temple. They needed a new focal point for their activities, one that would bind them together in religious observance, serve as a centre of dissemination for the new Scriptures and, just as importantly for their racial survival, reinforce their national and cultural identity. With no temple that they could attend, ritual sacrifice in the proper manner could not take place and, as a result, for their communal worship they were forced to rely on prayer and the reading of the new religious texts.

It was in Babylon that the Jews began to speak in Aramaic, the local Semitic language that closely resembles, but is still distinct from, Hebrew.[11] They continued speaking Aramaic when they returned to Jerusalem and Judea and it became the common tongue, one that was later used by Jesus. Hebrew was reserved for the sacred texts and ceremonial and ritual occasions and although it is now commonly held to be the language of the people of Israel, it was not known by that name before its use in the prologue to Ecclesiasticus (written circa 130 BCE).

Jewish Initiatory Tradition

It is clearly apparent from the Scriptures that the Jews treasured their own mystical and initiatory religious traditions and deliberately stressed their importance in the inspired writings composed during the Exile. The role of the priest-king David and the initiatory wisdom of his son, King Solomon, were revered and the initiatory concept of ascending degrees of holiness pervaded Jewish life and the very precincts of the temple itself.

Furthermore, the mystical vision of the prophets was extolled time and time again, particularly Elijah and Elisha. In addition to this, Norman Cantor, John Allegro and Professor Morton Smith, all suggest that the Jews learned more than Aramaic and synagogue worship while in exile in Babylon and that Jews brought a volatile brand of esoteric religion back from Babylon to complement the more sedate biblical religion we recognize today.[12] Later, a distinctive trend of charismatic Judaism developed that had Galilean roots,[13] as well as a many-faceted mystical trend of truly Egyptian/Hebraic roots. From the second century BCE the Devir, or Holy of Holies, built to house the Ark of the Covenant – God's throne on Earth – became the focus for mystics who visualized ascending directly to God's heavenly palace and approaching his celestial throne. Thus, we read of Jewish mystics preparing for this mystical ascent by special, initiatory disciplines.[14] Other mystical speculations found within the Talmud focus on the *maaseh bereshith*, or the work of creation described in the first chapter of Genesis, and the *maaseh merkabah*, or the divine chariot in the account of Ezekiel's vision. Needless to say, these mystical doctrines were carefully guarded and it was forbidden to expound them except to a few chosen disciples in the traditional Egyptian manner.

There are also 'the Psalms of ascents' in the Bible and a form of initiatory mysticism known as the 'Ascents tradition' was passed down orally for centuries before gaining written form in the kabbalah during the medieval era. This form of mysticism described ascents to the higher heavens, or the ascent through the various degrees of Neoplatonic enlightenment or gnosis in another variation of the Merkabah tradition known as Hekaloth.[15] The kabbalah itself is said to derive from Aaron, the priestly brother of Moses and can justly claim to be Judaism's oldest mystical tradition. The teaching was passed down from master to pupil in an oral tradition that only finally assumed written form in the twelfth century CE. One of its better known tenets is the idea of the Zaddik or the Righteous One[16] who, as Ezekiel puts it, will not suffer for someone else's sin. He will not die. 'The man who has sinned... is the one who must die. A son is not to suffer for the sins of his father, nor a father for the sins of his son.'[17] In the *Sefer–ha Zohar*, or Book of Splendour, it is written that Noah was a righteous one of whom it was said: '"The Righteous One is the Foundation of the World," and the Earth is established thereon, for this is the Pillar that upholds the world. So Noah was called "Righteous... and the embodiment of the world's Covenant of Peace".'[18]

Thus, at the heart of this new form of Judaism was a subtle blending of the new legalistic approach with the age-old and revered prophetic and initiatory tradition that inspired a religion of imperative command and deep and abiding moral commitment. This was made manifest in the difference of approach in worship in the pre- and post-Exilic eras. Worship during the First Temple period is recorded in the Scriptures as having been noisy, joyful and tumultuous; by contrast, in the Second Temple period, worship tended to be much quieter and of a more sober nature. In exile, the people of Israel had become acutely aware that their own sins were responsible for the destruction of Jerusalem, and this was reinforced by the new festival of Yom Kippur, the Day of Atonement. This was the one day in the year when the high priest entered the Devir, or the Holy of Holies, as the representative of his people pleading on his knees before the Throne of God for forgiveness for the sins of the entire nation.[19]

The combined result of the composition of the sacred Scriptures, the unquestioned, absolute and exclusive monotheism, the codifying of the 613 strictures of the Law, the institution of the synagogues and the new religious vision of the priests and scribes was summed up superbly by Karen Armstrong:

> Yaweh had finally absorbed his rivals in the religious imagination of Israel; in exile the lure of paganism lost its attraction and the religion of Judaism had been born.[20]

Mythologized Biblical History

Thus, while the majority of Jews, Christians and Muslims are familiar with the biblical accounts of the Exodus of the people of Israel from Egypt and all that followed such as the 40 years wandering in the wilderness and the subsequent conquest of the Promised Land, they are usually blissfully unaware that these Scriptures were written over seven centuries after the events they describe. Modern historians have analyzed these dramatic accounts with mixed results and tend to view their contents with extreme caution or even outright scepticism. Indeed many leading Israeli scholars describe the Exodus as pure mythology. A leading Jewish-American, Norman Cantor, suggested that this account of the enslavement of the people of Israel in Egypt was a deliberate fiction:

... perhaps the whole Egyptian sojourn was fabricated in later centuries for some ideologically conditioned or socially advantageous purpose.[21]

Later in the same work he carried this line of thought to its rational conclusion, one considered as blasphemous by those who believe the Bible is the 'inerrant word of God':

Such is the biblical story whose verification defies the course of historical and archaeological science. *It is a romantic fantasy.*[22] [my emphasis]

Sigmund Freud described the immediate post-Exodus era, that of the conquest of the Promised Land, as one that is, '... particularly impenetrable to investigation.'[23] Even the devout Roman Catholic historian, Paul Johnson, who generally accepts the Scriptures as a true historical record, wrote:

Some other sites mentioned in Exodus have been tentatively identified. But plotting these wanderings on a map, though often attempted, and undoubtedly entertaining, can produce nothing more than conjecture.[24]

The Dead Sea Scrolls scholar, John Allegro, was even more explicit:

We are in a shadowy half-world, where the hard facts of history fade off into mythology, and where the clear dividing line we like to draw between fact and fiction has no place... .[25]

However, despite his doubts about the historicity of the Exodus, John Allegro clearly recognized the essentially *spiritual* truth that lies behind this fascinating fable when he claimed that:

During the desert wandering under Moses, following their providential escape from Egypt, the Israelites were welded into a nation, allowed to know the secret name of God, and given the inestimable gift of the *Torah*, or Law.[26]

The prolonged wandering in the wilderness is often described as an allegory for the Israelites search for 'spiritual truth' that culminates in God granting them the Torah and allowing them to enter the 'Promised Land'.

Also, within the early Scriptures, there are many clear indications that stress the Egyptian and Gnostic roots of emergent Judaism. The psalmists record, for example, that God spoke to them in a pillar of cloud[27] which was later interpreted to mean the fount of revelation or the very seat of Wisdom herself.[28] This interpretation implied that 'Wisdom' was a separate divine entity from the Lord God of Israel. In the *Apocrypha* we find that God's relationship to Wisdom is again defined with cloud symbolism: 'In the high places did I fix my abode, and my throne was in a pillar of cloud.'[29] Thus, gnosis, or sacred wisdom, was as important to the 'new' hereditary priesthood instituted by Moses as it was to their Egyptian ancestors. The importance of Wisdom is shown in its description as God's helper in the act of creation, with the words: 'She built her house, she has set up her seven pillars (of Wisdom).'[30] Wisdom is also described as 'the consort of God', a rather strange phrase for any truly monotheistic priesthood or people.

The conquest of the Promised Land recounted in the Scriptures, was apparently confirmed by the work of the archaeologist, Albright, who conducted a series of excavations at the city of Jericho from 1935–1965. When he found evidence for the collapse of the city walls and claimed this as proof of the historical accuracy of the Bible, his announcement was greeted with delight by fundamentalists of all faiths.[31] This ecstatic euphoria was short-lived, however, for further excavations made by another archaeologist, Kathleen Kenyon, some years later, demonstrated unequivocally that the ruins excavated by Albright were from a much earlier period than the alleged conquest of Jericho by Joshua and, therefore, could not be ascribed to his conquest of the city.[32]

The modern state of Israel is probably the most comprehensively excavated country in the world, yet archaeologists have discovered little or no substantive evidence of conquest by the people of Israel at the time of their alleged occupation of that land. The English biblical scholar and historian, Robin Lane Fox, wrote: 'There is no sign of foreign invasion in the highlands, which would become the Israelite heartland.'[33] Furthermore, the Bible records a multitude of events that completely contradict the alleged monotheism of the people of Israel with numerous accounts of pagan idolatry that took place from time to time.

One of the earliest references to the one true God is that to Melchizedek's god, El Elyon, the 'God Most High'[34] on whose account Abraham gave Melchizedek tithes. El Elyon, or El, the title of the Canaanite god Ba'al of Mount Zaphon, was the generic west-Semitic word for God. Similarly, Elot, the Semitic word for goddess, with the feminine plural Elohim, is frequently found in the Bible.[35] The Bible records that Israelites participated in the fertility rites of Ba'al, worshipped many Syrian deities, and venerated the goddess of fertility, Asherah, who was described as El's consort in the Jerusalem Temple.[36] Asherah, who was known variously as 'She who walks in the Sea', 'Holiness' and Elath 'the Goddess', was described as the wife of Yahweh as he assimilated to himself the father god imagery of El.[37] A later king of Israel, King Manasseh, erected an altar to Asherah in the Temple,[38] an altar which was later broken up by Josiah.[39]

Eventually, the mixed multitude that had fled from Egypt amalgamated with, and began to dominate, the Semitic tribes in Canaan. Gradually shedding their polytheistic and pagan practices and uniting around their belief in Yahweh, who took on aspects of the worship of the Canaanite god Ba'al or Melchizedek's El Elyon,[40] this strange group eventually became known as the people of Israel. Karen Armstrong states this succinctly when she writes:

The Bible makes it clear that the people we know as the ancient Israelites were a confederation of various ethnic groups, bound principally together by their loyalty to Yahweh, the God of Moses.[41]

King Solomon's Temple

The design of Solomon's Temple, as described in the Old Testament, conformed closely to earlier Egyptian, Canaanite and Syrian models[42] and consisted of three square areas, leading to a relatively small, cube-shaped room known as the Devir, or the 'Holy of Holies' that housed the Ark of the Covenant.[43] Yet, despite all the scriptural proscriptions against graven images, the temple contained carved cherubim ten cubits high[44] and depictions of palms and flowers. It also housed a bronze altar as well as a huge bronze basin that represented Yam, the primal sea of Canaanite myth,[45] this was supported by bulls also cast in bronze, plus two 40ft-high freestanding pillars that symbolized the fertility of Asherah.[46] Standing before the Temple, in line with the ancient Egyptian wisdom tradition, were two freestanding pillars, each 35 cubits high, called Joachin and Boaz.[47]

At the time of Solomon, the people continued to worship Yahweh in the high places they had inherited from the Canaanites at Beth-El, Shiloh, Hebron, Bethlehem and Dan, and frequently attended pagan ceremonies at these shrines. Indeed, it is recounted that Solomon himself venerated pagan deities and built a high place to Chemosh, the Moabite god, and Moelch, the god of the Ammonites.[48] Even the worship of Astarte of the Sidonians was allowed in Israel during this era. So despite being credited with building the first temple to Yahweh in Jerusalem, even King Solomon himself can hardly be extolled as a pure monotheist. It was not until the period of the Babylonian exile (597–539 BCE) when the Scriptures first took definitive written form, that the Israelites finally decided that Yahweh was their sole God and that there were no others.[49] Prior to that time, the issue is somewhat confused for a people claiming to be exclusively and uniquely monotheistic.

The various biblical reports of the Temple of Solomon contain further strange anomalies. The account in Kings makes no mention of priests,[50] but, yet another in Chronicles details their precise duties at the time of King David and strongly implies that these practices continued thereafter.[51] Samuel Sanmell, the biblical historian explains this strange contradiction by claiming that:

> The ordinary view of modern scholars is that in Chronicles the ecclesiastical organization which arose in the latter part of the post-exilic period was anachronistically read back into the times of David and Solomon, thereby giving the sanction of antiquity to the ecclesiastical system of the post-exilic period. This ecclesiastical organization provided for twenty-four *ma'madot*, priestly teams who took turns in serving in the Temple in Jerusalem.[52]

Sanmell is correct when he states that the scriptural accounts of the reigns of David and his son Solomon were written at least four centuries after the events they describe, for, as I have described, the Old Testament only began to take its present form during the Babylonian exile and was not completed until several centuries later. Thus it was only in the post-Exilic era that Judaism developed into a rigidly and exclusively monotheistic system with a clearly established and powerful priestly caste and became a highly legalistic religion based upon the 613 strictures of the Law.

The Torah

It was after the exile in Babylon that the Torah became the very heart of both religious and secular life and it was this enthronement of the Law that saved Judaism from becoming just another priestly religion, concerned only with matters of ritual and religious practice and, instead, transformed it into one embracing every aspect of life in a manner that allowed Israel to develop into a theocratic nation.[53] However, the identity of the people of Israel was no longer limited by any territorial boundaries, for God's rule extended to the Diaspora, even though his special home was in the Devir within the Temple in Jerusalem.

God's instructions to his chosen people were contained in the ever developing Scriptures. Writings which, formidable in bulk and sometimes impenetrable in their obscurity, gave rise to an ever increasing army of scribes and priests to interpret them. These voluminous commentaries, such as the Mishna and Talmudic studies, filled great libraries and gave rise to endless debates and arguments. As a result, the entire Jewish world, both in the Promised Land and in the Diaspora, was luxuriant with internal conflicts that spawned a welter of sects and divisions that coexisted, more or less peacefully, under the broad spiritual umbrella of Judaism. As the Persian Empire was tolerant of its subject's religious beliefs, these developments proceeded without outside interference. In 333 BCE, when Alexander the Great's army conquered the region, Judea was again granted considerable autonomy and the high priest remained both the religious and political leader of his people. At first, the only extra burden imposed upon the newly conquered Jews, was the extremely high level of taxation imposed by the conquerors.

Later, under the rule of the Selucid king, Antiochus IV, these already high taxes were doubled and the king deposed the last true Zadokite high priest in 175 BCE and appointed his own nominee in his place. The deposed high priest's son built a rival temple at Leontopolis in Egypt while the majority of the Zadokite priests of the *ma'madot* withdrew from the Temple in Jerusalem and formed their own sect in the wilderness near Qumran. There, they developed a new form of worship based upon strict rules of purity and a fanatical devotion to the Torah under the inspired leadership of one of their number whom they called the Teacher of Righteousness.

In response to the defilement of the Temple and the increasing burden of taxes, the country rose in revolt under the leadership of the priest Mathias and later under that of his son Judas Maccabeus. This was a war fought on two fronts: firstly against any Jews who were willing to obey Greek laws and secondly against the Greek invaders. The Maccabean revolt ultimately led to victory. The Temple in Jerusalem was purified and rededicated at the first celebration of the new feast of Hanukkah, the Festival of Light. In 143 BCE a great assembly in Jerusalem named Simon Maccabeus as the hereditary high priest and ethnarch. The Hasmonean Era had begun and for the first time in centuries, the people of Israel had their own priest-kings. The new kingdom prospered at first and, under Alexander Jananeus, it became comparable to that ruled by the legendary King Solomon. Sadly, as the Hasmonean dynasty was riven by internecine strife, eventually civil war broke out and the Roman Empire was sought as an ally by one of the warring factions. Ultimately, this led to the rule of a man described as 'a friend of Rome,' the complex, politically gifted and brutal man known to history as Herod the Great.

Chapter 3

~

Judaism at the Time of Jesus

THE JEWISH STATE OF JUDEA became a puppet state of Rome in 63 BCE following Pompey's intervention in the civil war between the Pharisees and the Jewish rulers, Hyrcanus and Aristobulus.[1] In 43 BCE, Herod the Great seized the throne and was confirmed as *King of the Jews* by Rome some four years later when, as Strabo, the Roman historian, records, Herod 'was so superior to his predecessors, particularly in intercourse with Romans and in his administration of the affairs of state, that he received the title of King'.[2]

At first, Herod was a brave and resourceful king, a capable administrator and a supremely able politician who brought order and stability to this much troubled land. He was a prolific builder who completely rebuilt the Temple in Jerusalem, founded the port of Caesarea, and built fortresses as far south as the Jordan and in Damascus to the north. An Idumean who wore his Judaism lightly, he built temples to pagan gods: one at Caesarea, another in Sebaste and the third in Panias.[3] He also built a temple to the ancient Canaanite god Ba'al at Sia, gave considerable financial help to those building pagan temples at Berytus and Tyre,[4] and, in addition, helped restore the temple of Pythian Apollo in Rhodes.[5] He built the Antonia for Mark Antony, a building that later became the residence of the Roman proconsuls and was eventually occupied by Pontius Pilate.

The flaws within the Gospel accounts about Herod are easily established for he was undoubtedly one of the best-documented characters in that era. In respect of his cruelty, it is a matter of record that he behaved murderously towards any members of his family that he perceived as a threat to his power.[6] Indeed, the Emperor Augustus said of him, 'I would rather be Herod's pig than his son'[7] – a brutally honest comment from the most powerful ruler on Earth on the subject of one of his most trusted subordinates. The Gospel account of his 'slaughter of the innocents'[8] maligns him unjustly, however. The Jewish historian Flavius Josephus's failure to mention this event in his exhaustive litany of Herod's cruelty, casts considerable doubt on the Scriptural account. Furthermore, there is no mention of this massacre at all in the Talmudic literature of the time, a body of work that is hardly enamoured of the dubious charms of King Herod. When we consider these facts in the light of the startling differences between the various Gospel accounts of the birth of Jesus, they do not merely give us grave cause to question this brutal tale, they lead us to conclude that, as it is not recorded by the severest critics of King Herod, it simply did not happen.

In the early decades of Herod's reign, the Romans, who interfered as little as possible with the internal affairs of conquered provinces, granted the Jews a large measure of autonomy and the people were allowed full freedom of religious worship, thus the relationship between the Romans and the Jews was apparently fruitful.[9] Herod's commendable political skills even managed to keep the lid on the seething hotbed of nationalist discontent that had been the ever-present backdrop to affairs of state since the time of Antiochus IV (169 BCE), long before the arrival of the Romans.

The Rebellious Jews

After the death of Herod, this nationalistic and religious fervour bubbled to the surface repeatedly in violent confrontations with the *Kittim* the hated Roman occupiers. One major rebellion, called Varus's War in the Talmud, was a major revolt that started during the feast of Pentecost and spread like wildfire from Jerusalem into Judea, Galilee, Perea and Idumea. Varus, the Roman governor of Syria, promptly put his legions into the field, burnt Emmaus and Sephoris and enslaved the survivors of those cities.[10] Using the standard Roman punishment for sedition, he ruthlessly crucified 2,000 Jews for rebellion.[11] This was merely the first in a series of violent episodes that signalled the ever-present Jewish discontent with the Romans. As the Romans and their puppet-kings steadily increased taxation, the heady mix of religious fervour and political agitation gathered momentum.

Biblical Israel was, as I mentioned earlier, a theocracy; the Torah was the only law the Jews respected and, for them, any Roman law was an imposition. In a theocratic state, it was impossible to make a religious statement without it also being a political one and, by the same token, it was frankly impossible for the Romans to impose any legal constraints upon the people without them being perceived as a form of religious infringement. This was the turbulent and potentially violent reality that pervaded Judea, not the gentle, peaceful, rural atmosphere implied by the Gospels.

Robert Eisenman, the Dead Sea Scrolls scholar and Director of the Center for the Study of Judaeo-Christian Origins at California State University, suggests that the apparently peaceful Hellenized country where the Galilean fishermen cast their nets, the New Testament scenes depicting Roman officials and soldiers as 'near saints', and the vindictiveness of the Jewish mob described in the Gospels, all have to be understood in the light of the fact that these allegedly 'divinely inspired' accounts were written in subservience to the ever-present and brutal realities of Roman power.[12] In this he is merely echoing Flavius Josephus who made the same point over 2,000 years ago by claiming that all historical accounts of that period suffered from two major defects: 'Flattery of the Romans and vilification of the Jews, adulation and abuse being substituted for the real historical record.'[13]

Jewish Sects at the time of Jesus

Reading the Gospels gives the distinct impression that there were only two major religious factions within Judaism at the time of Jesus, namely the Sadducees and the Pharisees, with a brief and relatively uninformative mention of the Samaritans. Indeed, it is strongly implied that apart from the Sadducees and Pharisees, Judaism at that time was a fairly unified religion. Contemporary historical documents, however, tell a very different story. Josephus, describes four main sects within Judaism at that time, the Essens, the Sadducees, the Pharisees and those of the group he called the 'fourth philosophy'.[14] The Essens, or Essenes, were the spiritual and lineal descendants of the 24 families of the *ma'madot* who had withdrawn to Qumran in protest against the defilement of the Temple by Antiochus and the later appointment of non-Zadokite high priests by the Maccabeans.[15] They and their followers, who were numerous, held their goods in common, lived austere lives, maintained ritual purity and believed that the soul was immortal. They were possessed by a fanatical insistence on 'doing Torah', that is, living life in strict accordance with the law of God. For them, the Temple in Jerusalem had been defiled; the new spiritualized Temple was the purified Essene Community.[16] A Temple of God formed of dedicated and devout men. Josephus described them in the following terms: 'They exceed all other men that addict themselves to virtue, and this in righteousness.'[17]

The Sadducees, to the contrary, did not believe in the immortality of the soul but, nonetheless, still insisted that the Law of Moses had to be obeyed without the slightest deviation.[18] This deeply conservative group, which was drawn from the property-owning class, had been deeply influenced by Greek culture and preached cooperation with the Imperial power of Rome. The Sanhedrin, the religious court composed of high priests, was controlled by the Sadducees and this body exercised jurisdiction in all cases, whether religious or civil, that involved an infraction of Jewish law. In addition, there was also the political Sanhedrin who acted as intermediaries between the Roman administration and the people. They were charged with policing cases of sedition and insurrection under Roman law and handing over the accused to the Roman procurators. However, all the procurators who governed Judea tended to abuse their power and rendered the lot of their Jewish subjects miserable and bitter.[19] The historian, Isadore Epstein, delineated the major differences between the Sadducees and Pharisees thus:

> The Pharisees desired that all the affairs of the State should be governed on strict Torah lines, with no concern for any other consideration. The Sadducees, on the other hand, maintained that whilst it was well to recognize the Torah as the basic constitution of the State, it was impossible to carry on a Government, which, under changed conditions, necessarily demanded close relations with heathen powers without making political expediency and economic interest the final arbiter of things.[20]

According to Epstein, the Pharisees were the only party truly suitable to deal with the needs of the times. They believed that oral law had been revealed in spiritual teaching to Moses when he received the Ten Commandments and, contrary to the nit-picking reputation accorded to them in the Gospels, were liberal in their attempts to interpret this. In fact they tried to interpret its meaning and modify its observance to make it relevant to the lives of ordinary people, an attitude that gained them considerable support. In this attempt, they were vehemently opposed by the Sadducees. Thus, in certain respects, the attitude of the Pharisees was an inspired and popular response to the demanding, anachronistic, legalism of the Sadducees.[21]

Within the Dead Sea Scrolls there is another, more scathing, description of the Pharisees that portrays them as 'seekers after smooth things', only too ready to make accommodation with foreigners, which, to their more Zealot opponents, made them look like collaborators.[22] From the time of the Maccabeans to the fall of Jerusalem in 70 CE, the Sadducees and Pharisees were active political and religious rivals competing for control of the state.[23] Josephus also mentions a fourth sect among the Jews that he describes as having 'an inviolable attachment to liberty which causes the nation to go mad with this distemper and makes them revolt against the Romans'.[24] Within the Essene tradition, though not necessarily belonging to that sect, was another group of visionaries whose ideas are enshrined in the body of literature known as the Apocalypse.[25] Then, in apparent contrast to the Essenes and the Apocalyptists, were the Zealots who were out to fight against the Roman oppressors and make an end of foreign tyranny. These ardent patriots combined a devotion to the Torah with an intense love of their country and were ready to fight and die for both.[26] To all of these vigorous sects we must add the various mystical groups listed earlier.

Therefore, despite what is written or implied in the Gospels and the Acts of the Apostles, Judaism at that time embraced at least 24 parties or sects that were not regarded as heretical, but as integral parts of the Jewish religion.[27] To complicate the matter still further, any devout Jew could sit at the feet of a teacher in any one or several of these groups, at different times, in order to gain spiritual knowledge and seek the path to righteousness – all without any apparent contradiction.

Josephus lists frequent acts of rebellion against the Roman occupation, many inspired by leaders or prophets of the apocalyptic tradition of Judaism. This visionary tradition spoke of God's intervention in the final battle of the righteous against the forces of evil. This was an important facet of messianic teaching that was also common within other aspects of mainstream Judaism. Within both the Zadokite/Essene and the Pharisaic traditions, two messiahs were awaited, not one: a priestly messiah and a kingly messiah. Both traditions believed that until the elect of Israel adhered strictly to the covenant with God, the final redemption of the Chosen People and the eternal triumph of good over evil could not take place.[28] Therefore the priestly messiah was expected to purify the elect and then the kingly messiah was to lead them to victory in the final war against evil. The Scriptures had prophesied the coming of the messenger of the covenant who would 'purify the sons of Levi'[29] and spoke of the return of Elijah as reconciler.[30]

John the Baptist

When we come to study the enigmatic figure of John the Baptist, it is appropriate to note that the Gospel records that John's own followers believed that he was Elijah come again.[31] The devout Catholic historian, Paul Johnson, describes how the example of the Essenes led to the creation of a number of Baptist movements in the Jordan valley. Indeed, he describes the whole area between the Lake of Genasseret and the Dead Sea as 'alive with holy eccentrics', many imbued with Essene teaching.[32] Most scholars are now convinced that John the Baptist was a one-time Essene who saw his mission as the creation of a purified 'elite within an elite' – the necessary prelude to the coming apocalypse.[33] Josephus delineates both his mission and subsequent execution as follows:

Herod had put him [John surnamed the Baptist] to death, though he was a good man and had exhorted the Jews to lead righteous lives, to practise justice towards their fellows and piety towards God, and in so doing to join in baptism. In his view this was a necessary preliminary if baptism was to be acceptable to God. They must not employ it to gain pardon for whatever sins they had committed, but as a consecration of the body implying that the soul was already cleansed by right behaviour. While others too joined the crowds about him, because they were aroused to the highest degree by his sermons, Herod became alarmed. Eloquence that had so great an effect on mankind might lead to some sort of sedition... John, because of Herod's suspicions, was brought in chains to Machareus... and there put to death.[34]

The reason Josephus gives for John's execution is entirely credible. However, the version given in the Gospels is also highly plausible in the light of John's connection with the Essenes, who constantly railed against 'fornication'. Josephus's opinion on the matter of John's beliefs and his view of baptism is, perhaps, more important. According to the biblical scholar, John Dominic Crossan, Josephus's view demonstrates that John's baptism was not a ritual act that removed sin, but was, on the contrary, a physical and external cleansing, that symbolized that a spiritual and internal purification had already taken place prior to the baptism of the disciple or pupil.[35] The historian Joan Taylor clarified this initiatory process:

> People placed themselves in the position of disciples of John [the Baptist] in order to learn how to be purified effectively both inwardly and outwardly. Once they felt fairly confident of their righteousness, by John's definition, then they came for immersion... Not all the people became his disciples. *Once people were immersed, however, they would already have accepted John's teaching and therefore become his disciples before this.*[36] [my emphasis]

The Christian Church has always vehemently denied any teaching role to John the Baptist in his relationship with Jesus. Yet, despite this, most modern scholarship supports the view that Jesus was the pupil of John the Baptist, thereby confirming a tradition that has been kept alive for 2,000 years by the descendants of the *ma'madot*, namely the Rex Deus families and their spiritual heirs, the Templars and the Freemasons.

Jesus the Nazorean

The teacher-pupil relationship between John and Jesus shows that, for whatever reason, the Church has been a trifle 'economical with the truth' in a manner that impinges directly on the belief that Jesus is divine. For, if Jesus was indeed a disciple of John the Baptist, then he must have been a sinner who had been restored to righteousness in order to qualify for baptism; a disturbing concept for those who have been taught that Jesus is Divine. Jesus was a devout Jew who became a pupil of John the Baptist and underwent purification from sin and baptism, therefore it is impossible to accept that *he* ever thought of himself as divine. For him and for all other Jews, that would have been the ultimate blasphemy. The author A N Wilson reached an identical conclusion and stated that Jesus was a Galilean *hasid*, or holy man, a healer in the prophetic tradition. Wilson writes:

> I had to admit that I found it impossible to believe that a first-century Galilean holy man had at any time of his life believed himself to be the Second Person of the Trinity. It was such an inherently improbable thing for a monotheistic Jew to believe.[37]

Trying to arrive at any realistic understanding of the teachings of Jesus is extremely difficult, for he made little impact outside the New Testament. The Gospel stories, with one or two notable exceptions, tell us more about the viewpoint of the authors than they do about Jesus himself, and while they are documents of great spiritual import, sadly they have little historical validity. Therefore we have to attempt to reconstruct Jesus' teaching, not only from the canonical Scriptures but also from the apocryphal Scriptures and the relevant documentation found among discoveries at Qumran and Nag Hammadi.

Furthermore, all of these sources must be carefully assessed against the framework of Jewish custom and practice during the late Second Temple era. We must also never forget that Jesus was a devout Jew teaching other Jews. Indeed, Karen Armstrong recounts one episode that highlights this often-forgotten perspective when she remarks: 'Certainly Jesus' disciples did not think that they had founded a new religion: they continued to live as fully observant Jews and went every day in a body to worship at the Temple'[38] – a comment based upon a passage from the Acts of the Apostles.[39] Furthermore, according to the second-century philosopher Aristides, one of the earliest apologists for Christianity, the worship of the first Jerusalem 'Christians' was fundamentally more monotheistic than even that of the Jews. Thus the teachings of Jesus were certainly *not* regarded by either his disciples or his apostles as being either the foundation of a new form of religion or an indictment of Judaism. The significant difference between them and their fellow Jews was their fanatical adherence to Jesus' interpretation of the Torah, strengthened by their faith in the messianic nature of his role.

The Church's use of the title 'Jesus of Nazareth' is grossly misleading, for Nazareth did not exist at that time. His true title is Jesus the Nazorean, indicating his membership of an initiatory sect of the Essenes. His reverence for the ancient mystical and initiatory tradition is made explicit in a passage from the Gospel of Thomas discovered among the Nag Hammadi Scrolls in Egypt in 1945, which records Jesus as saying: 'He who will drink from my mouth will become like me. I myself shall become he, and things that are hidden will be revealed to him.'[40] Thus, Jesus initiated the elite among his followers into the Nazoreans by a form of baptism. The truth of this was discovered by Professor Morton Smith when he found fragments of the Secret Gospel of Mark in the monastery of Mar Saba in Israel,[41] a document that was, most probably, originally known as the Gospel of the Hebrews.

We can safely accept the reported sayings of Jesus when they are uncontaminated by pro-Roman bias or are consistent with mainstream Jewish belief. For example, Jesus is quoted as saying, 'Go not into the way of the Gentiles and into any city of the Samaritans enter ye not: but go rather to the lost sheep of Israel.'[42] As this is entirely consistent with Essene teaching, it can be taken as authentic. Another saying attributed to him, 'Go ye therefore and make disciples of all nations, baptizing them in the name of the Father and of the Son and of the Holy Spirit',[43] must be rejected for no-one of the Essene tradition would instruct his disciples to preach to the Gentiles. More importantly, the use of the phrase, 'In the name of the Father and of the Son and of the Holy Spirit' would be anathema to any Jew and certainly did not come into general use until after Christian doctrine had attained a substantial degree of development.

The crucial period to understand is the one marked by Jesus' entry into Jerusalem and his crucifixion less than one week later.

The staging of his triumphal entry into the holy city a week before Passover, as recounted in the Gospels,[44] gave advance warning to the Romans and their Sadducee allies that potential rebellion was brewing. One Gospel records that he was hailed with the words 'Blessed is the King',[45] which would sound to Roman ears like an open call to insurrection. A warning that must have been amplified when Jesus upset the tables of the moneychangers in the Temple, shortly after he entered the city.[46] All this when the city was already bursting at the seams with the full complement of Sadducees, Pharisees, Zealots, Hassidim and assorted apocalyptic fundamentalists imbued with nationalistic and religious fervour.

The Roman Procurator at that time was hardly the ideal choice to deal with these potentially explosive circumstances. Pontius Pilate had a well-earned reputation for corruption, violence and numerous executions without the formality of a trial.[47] The Temple guards, acting on orders issued by the political Sanhedrin, arrested Jesus and handed him over to Pilate's none-too-tender mercies.[48] Despite what is written in the Gospels, there was no night-time Sanhedrin trial of Jesus for blasphemy, for that would have been illegal at that time. Neither was there an appearance before Herod. It is impossible to conceive that there was any prevarication on Pilate's part. Why indeed should he concern himself with the life of one man when he had the precedent of his predecessor Varus who had crucified 2,000 Jews for sedition? Jesus could not have been arraigned by the Jews for blasphemy, for his teaching was in accord with Judaic tradition. He was tried and executed by Pontius Pilate[49] to nip any potential insurrection in the bud. Crucifixion was a Roman punishment for sedition, rebellion and mutiny. The Jewish penalty for blasphemy was death by stoning, as we shall see later.

Part Two

✧

THE FOUNDATION OF
CHRISTIANITY

IT MAY COME AS A SURPRISE to many devout Christians to discover that their faith is based less upon the teachings of Jesus than it is on the views of the man known as St Paul, who is described by some historians as 'the Father of Christianity'. Paul's teaching began a process that began to distance Christianity from the strict monotheism of the Jews and that of Islam which came later, thereby creating tensions between the monotheistic faiths whose intolerant results so distort the world we live in today.

The Christian Church undoubtedly acted as the saviour of Europe from the Barbarian invasions that followed the fall of the Roman Empire, but it exacted a high price for this, instituting a strict regime over its congregations, absolute control and censorship over education and a fanatical grasp over all forms of worship, denying the validity of all other faiths and suppressing them without mercy.

Chapter 4

~

The True Teachings of Jesus

THE GOSPELS OF MATTHEW, Mark and Luke are described as synoptic because in content, language and order they have so much in common. There is now complete agreement among biblical scholars that these Synoptic Gospels are all founded primarily on one earlier lost common source, commonly referred to as 'Q', that may well have been based, in whole or in part, on the testimony of eyewitnesses. Furthermore, a consensus has been reached about Q's content and style that has resulted in an accurate recreation of this vital document. Professor Burton L Mack, Chair of New Testament Studies at the Claremont School of Theology in California declares that:

> The remarkable thing is that the authors of Q did not think about Jesus as the Messiah or the Christ, nor did they understand his teachings to be an indictment of Judaism. They certainly did not regard his crucifixion as a divinely inspired, or saving event. Nor did they believe that he had been raised from the dead to rule over the world. They thought of him as a Jewish prophet whose teaching made it possible to live an attainable and righteous life in very troubled times. As a result they neither gathered to worship in his name, honoured him as a god – which to them, as devout Jews

would have been the ultimate blasphemy – nor celebrated his memory through hymns, prayers or rituals.[1]

Yet the Christian Gospels, substantively based on information from Q, nonetheless speak of Jesus as a divine figure. However, any scholarly examination of Jesus' allegedly 'divine' status, that is not blinkered by faith but is, on the contrary, informed by a reasonable knowledge of Judaic practice and belief in the second Temple era, reveals the a priori impossibility of the claimed deity of Jesus. The doctrine of a divine human being is diametrically opposed to the Jewish concept of God. It must be stressed that Jesus was born, raised and taught as a Jew and, as we have seen, his followers regarded themselves as a Jewish movement. Any Jew, especially those who sought acceptance by other Jews, who presented himself in such a manner would be stoned to death as a blasphemer.

However, the deification of humans was common practice throughout the Roman Empire, which leads to the inevitable con- clusion that the deification of Jesus was an intrusion from Roman, pagan or heretical sources. It most certainly was not fundamental to the integrity of Jesus' message. The mere idea of Jesus' deification was staunchly resisted by the original Apostles and the Jews who be- lieved that he was the Messiah.[2] As a source, the New Testament is undoubtedly of immense spiritual import, but little factual validity, furthermore, one that has been edited and redacted numerous times, usually for doctrinal reasons so that the end result is highly flawed. This becomes blatantly obvious when we study what is known about the immediate family of Jesus in the Scriptures and compare that with the later pronouncements of the Church.

The Family and Marriage of Jesus

When, in the second century, in its divinely guided wisdom, the Church decided that Mary the mother of Jesus was a virgin, that Jesus was her only child and, furthermore, that he was celibate, it opened a theological 'can of worms' that has never been successfully closed. As the Gospels make abundantly clear, Jesus was a member of a rather large family that included James, Joses, Simon and Judas Thomas and several unnamed sisters.[3] This was not the only awkward problem that Church theologians had to overcome, there was another: the question of Jesus' marital status. Jewish custom at that time demanded that all males, especially rabbis, marry and produce a family and therefore, as a rabbi, Jesus was obliged to take a wife. Furthermore, as he was of the direct line of David and the heir to the throne, it was incumbent upon him to produce an heir. The few exceptions to this obligation to marry are clearly delineated as such in the New Testament and other sacred commentaries. The prime example of this being that of Jesus' brother James, who was described by the early Church fathers and theologians as a Nazorite who was 'dedicated to Holiness from his mother's womb'[4] and who, as a result, was celibate. The Professor of New Testament theology at the École Biblique in Jerusalem, Father Jerome Murphy O'Connor, stated in one BBC radio broadcast, that:

> Paul was certainly married... Marriage was not a matter of choice for Jews, that's why you have so few in the early centuries who weren't married and that's why... Paul... *must have been married* because this was a social obligation whose social fulfilment was obvious.[5] [my emphasis]

Neither the Church nor Fr. Murphy-O'Connor have applied this compelling argument to the case of Jesus, despite the fact that there is no mention in the New Testament that Jesus was unmarried, a situation that would undoubtedly have provoked considerable comment at the time. However, there are still traces of Jesus' marital status and clues as to the identity of his wife detectable in the Gospels. A N Wilson, suggests that, 'The story of the wedding feast at Cana contains a hazy memory of Jesus' own wedding',[6] and the Muslim scholar, Professor Fida Hassnain makes the following comment on that feast:

> The question arises who is the guest and who is the bride? I would suggest Mary is the host for she orders the procuring of the wine

for the guests, which Jesus deals with. One wonders whether it is *his* own marriage with Mary Magdalene, and whether the whole episode has been kept under camouflage... I believe that Mary Magdalene behaved as the chief consort of Jesus, and he also took her as his spouse.[7]

The story of that wedding and the 'miracle' of turning water into wine can be found in the Gospel of John.[8] After the miracle, Jesus orders the servants to distribute the wine and Jewish custom dictates that only the bridegroom or the groom's mother had the authority to give orders to the servants at a wedding feast,[9] indicating, in this instance, that this was Jesus' own wedding. I have delineated in detail the evidence for the marriage of Jesus in several earlier works.[10] The Catholic theologian, Margaret Starbird, who set out to refute heresy of Jesus' marriage as described in *The Holy Blood and the Holy Grail*, published instead a detailed exposition of the conclusive evidence proving the marriage of Jesus to Mary Magdalene and their founding of a dynasty in *The Woman with the Alabaster Jar*.[11]

After the Crucifixion

The question as to who was to succeed Jesus as leader and teacher of the original disciples is another area where Holy Mother the Church has somewhat muddied the waters of truth. One of the early documents suppressed by the Church, the Gospel of Thomas, vanished from sight for over 1,500 years until a copy was rediscovered at Nag Hammadi in 1945. In it we find that:

> The disciples said to Jesus:
> We know that you will depart from us.
> Who is to be our leader?
> Jesus said to them:
> Wherever you are, you are to go to James the righteous,
> For whose sake the heaven and earth came into being.[12]

The phrase 'For whose sake the heaven and earth came into being' has distinct echoes of the kabbalistic description of Noah of whom it was written, 'The Righteous One is the Foundation of the World'. Yet another reference to Jesus' appointment of James as the disciples' new leader occurs in the Pseudo-Clementine *Recognitions*,[13] and another early Church father and historian of Christianity, Epiphanius, describes James as, 'The first to whom the Lord entrusted his Throne upon Earth'.[14] Even the New Testament acknowledges this when it delineates James as 'the first bishop of Jerusalem'.[15] Robert Eisenman summarized this situation:

> James was the true heir and successor of his more famous brother Jesus and the leader at that time of whatever the movement was we now call 'Christianity', not the more Hellenized character we know through his Greek cognomen Peter, the 'Rock' of, in any event, the Roman Church.[16]

Logically we are forced to pose the question: 'Who would have known Jesus' teaching best and been deemed sufficiently trustworthy to carry it forward unaltered?' Surely the answer must be his own brother, James the Just, who already had a well-earned reputation for righteousness.

The long-standing tradition that Jesus appointed Peter to lead the disciples after the Crucifixion was a fabrication created by Church leaders, over half a century later, to justify the claimed supremacy of Rome and reinforce its power over all other centres of Christianity. This deliberate creation of the Petrine foundation myth forced the Church to marginalize the role of James in order to diminish his worth in the eyes of their flock and so, in Church literature, he became known as 'James the Less'.

The First 'Church' in Jerusalem?

It will come as no surprise to learn that despite its later marked divergence from the initiatory teachings of Jesus, the structure of the early Church was largely shaped by Essene teaching, tradition and practice.[17] The early Christians are known to have used a book known as the Didache, or 'the teaching of the Lord', and the similarities between the Didache and the Community Rule found amongst the Dead Sea Scrolls is quite startling. Yet, the Church has made a determined attempt to date the Community Rule to an earlier era. Both describe 'the two ways', the way of light and the way of darkness, and any comparative study leaves no doubt as to which is the parent document. The first 'Christian Church' in Jerusalem, described in the Acts of the Apostles, was led by a triumvirate of elders known as 'the Pillars', James the brother of Jesus, Simon-Peter and John.[18] This tri-partite leadership was clearly based upon Essene practice. Reinforcing this Essene connection, the Dead Sea Scrolls scholar, Robert Eisenman, equates James the Just with the 'Teacher of Righteousness' of the Essenes.[19]

James the Righteous

James was not only a member of the *ma'madot* but also a hereditary high priest; the Christian historian Epiphanius described his function as follows:

> I find that he also exercised the Priesthood according to the Ancient Priesthood, [the Rechabite or Nazorite one – possibly even the one Hebrews is calling the 'Priesthood after the Order of Melchizedek']. For this reason he was permitted to enter the Holy of Holies once a year, as the Bible lays down in the Law commanding the High Priests. He was also allowed to wear the High Priestly diadem on his head as the aforementioned trustworthy men – Eusebius, Clement and others have related in their accounts.[20]

Hegesippus, another early father of the Church, describes how James was brought to the Temple by the Scribes and Pharisees to pacify the Passover crowd hungering after the Messiah. But James, who was at the centre of agitation at the Temple in the years leading up to the war against Rome,[21] had a different intent, for far from quietening the crowd, he fanned the flames of revolt.[22] Josephus in *The Antiquities of the Jews*, delineates the beliefs and actions of the 'fourth philosophy', those zealous for freedom and liberty, and merges his earlier descriptions of the Essenes in *War of the Jews* with that of this ultra-nationalistic group, thereby confirming that the Essenes and the Zealots had become almost indistinguishable from one another. It is also indicative of this trend that Josephus only used the term Zealots when referring to those people in opposition to the illegally appointed high priest Ananus who eventually murdered James.

So, Jesus had entrusted the leadership of his disciples to his brother James, the leader of a group of deeply religious, national-istic Jews. Could there have been any major or significant differ-ence between the teachings of Jesus and those of James? No! Major or significant deviations are inconceivable. Then how and why is the version of Jesus' teaching reported in the canonical Gospels so different from the Torah-based, ultra-orthodox practices revered by James the Righteous and the Essenes? To understand how Jesus' teaching was so distorted, we need to examine the character of a man who started by persecuting Jesus' followers, was then 'miraculously' converted, joined James and the others only to betray them.

Saulus or St Paul

Paul Johnson, the staunchly Catholic historian of Christianity, called Saul of Tarsus, or St Paul as he is better known, 'the first and greatest Christian personality... who some accuse of invent-ing Christianity.'[23] To others among the followers of James, now known as the Ebionites, he was 'an apostate of the Law', the 'spouter of wickedness and lies' and 'the distorter of the true teachings of Jesus'.[24] The controversial figure of St Paul was indeed a very strange and complex man. From his own writings, which are accepted as the earliest Christian primary sources we possess, we learn that he was both a Roman citizen and a Pharisee who spent some time persecuting the followers of Jesus after the Crucifixion.[25]

There are also several other matters which pass unnoticed by devout Christians that give us an insight into Paul's background which are both revealing and pertinent to his motivation. Paul was a member of the Herodian royal family and disclosed this when he wrote: 'Greet those who belong to the household of Aristobulus. Greet Herodian my relative.'[26] Aristobulus was the son of Agrippa I's brother, Herod of Chalcis, whose son was known as Herodian or 'the Littlest Herod.' These links to the royal family explain how Paul wielded power in Jerusalem as a member of the Temple guard authorized by the high priest to persecute the followers of Jesus. Any group of nationalistic zealous Jews, such as the followers of Jesus, was a prime target for Temple authorities bent on suppressing rebellion against their Roman masters. The English author A N Wilson suggests: 'It does not seem unreasonable to suppose that he [Paul] was in the same position in the Temple guard when Jesus was arrested.'[27] Josephus records that the Antipater, the father of Herod the Great, was awarded hereditary Roman citizenship for services to Caesar,[28] so Paul as a member of the Herodian family[29] was born into this highly privileged position that he exploited to the full. Paul's Roman citizenship is, however, merely stated in the New Testament and never explained. Now we know why.

In Paul's epistle to the Philippians, he mentions Epaphroditus, a senior advisor of the Roman Emperor Nero;[30] a connection he stresses with the words: 'Greetings, especially those in Caesar's household.'[31] Paul, or Saulus, as the Romans and royal family called him, had important and influential contacts in very high places indeed. Relationships that tell us how a supposedly simple Jewish tent-maker, travelled the world with consummate ease, had several 'miraculous' escapes from prison and yet was treated as the welcome guest of people of considerable power and political influence.

These strong Herodian and Roman pro-establishment links explain why Paul stripped Jesus' message of all nationalistic fervour and substituted so many calls to obey lawful authorities.[32] Paul's message of subservience to 'lawful' i.e. Roman, authority and his preaching of a New Covenant, denied the validity of the Torah and totally negated the teaching of James and the original disciples of Jesus in Jerusalem. For example, James's zealous and intrinsically Jewish stance had a powerful political dimension in his agitation at the Temple where he actively promoted a pro-Torah, nationalistic, anti-Herodian and anti-Roman policy that led to a head-on collision with the Jewish political and religious establishment in Jerusalem, the Saducee high priests and their important ally, Paul's relative King Agrippa II.

Following Saul's miraculous conversion on the road to Damascus, he changed not only his religion but also his name. Then, after an inexplicable three years spent in Arabia,[33] Paul joined the Ebionite community in Jerusalem to learn the 'true Way' taught by Jesus.[34] Following that, Paul began a mission that took him to many cities of the eastern Mediterranean, yet, within a remarkably short time he was subject to scathing criticism by James and the disciples in Jerusalem. It is clear that there was a fundamental difference between the Way, as interpreted by James and the Ebionites on the one hand, and that preached by Paul on the other. A rather sanitized and diplomatic version of this conflict can be found in the account of the 'Council of Jerusalem' found in the Acts of the Apostles which implies that Paul's version of the message was deemed acceptable and valid.[35] However, in the light of the Ebionites absolute dedication to the Torah, their strict prohibition against mixing with Gentiles, and their rigorous adherence to the dietary laws of Judaism, the glossed-over account in Acts is absolutely incredible, especially when we read Paul's beliefs expressed so clearly in his epistles.

Robert Eisenman has found records within the Dead Sea Scrolls and related documents that have enabled him to reconstruct a more accurate version of these differences. The dispute hinges on Paul's persistent preaching to the Gentiles and his repeated denials of the validity of the Torah. In the documents studied by Eisenman, this led to a dramatic confrontation between a man called the Liar and those of his persuasion on one side, and the Teacher of Righteousness and the disciples on the other. The underlying text refers to treachery and factional strife arising within the community.[36] The Qumran Community Rule states that:

> Any man who enters the Council of Holiness walking in the Way of Perfection as commanded by God and, whether overtly or covertly, transgresses one word of the *Torah* of Moses on any point whatsoever... shall be expelled from the council of the community and return no more. No Man of Holiness shall associate with him in monetary matters or in approach *on any matter whatsoever.*[37]

This is precisely the fate that befell Paul. After his expulsion from the Community, even Barnabas deserted him, as he recounts in the Epistle to the Galatians.[38] Paul's repudiation of the Law, his novel idea that salvation is by faith alone and not by doing Torah, is made apparent in the same letter.[39] Paul Johnson records that after this dispute, the mission of St Paul steadily lost ground to that of the evangelists duly accredited by James the Just in Jerusalem. [40]

Paul himself confirms this practice of official accreditation, by trying to dismiss it when he writes, 'Or do we need, like some people, letters of recommendation to you...'.[41] Paul Johnson claims that if it had not been for the destruction of Jerusalem by the Romans in 70 CE, Paul's evangelical efforts would have been forgotten altogether.[42] From now on, few, if any, Jewish disciples have anything more to do with Paul. His only named collaborators after his expulsion are Judeo-Greeks, such as Timothy[43] and his relative the Herodian Princess Drusilla.[44] All his epistles written after his expulsion are bitter, whining and resentful. For example: 'Am I not free? Am I not an apostle? Have I not seen Jesus our Lord?... Even though I may not be an apostle to others, surely I am to you!'[45] Later he writes: '... and for this purpose I was appointed a herald and an apostle – I am telling the truth I am not lying...'[46] Read Paul's epistles one after another and it is impossible to miss the self-pity and resentful defensiveness that emerges; then, perhaps, you will perceive St Paul in a very different light.[47]

Because of his anti-Torah teaching, Paul was regarded by James and the Ebionites as a false prophet. Iraneus, the Bishop of Lyon, once quoted an Ebionite document that described Paul as 'an apostate of the Law.'[48] Indeed, the family and original disciples of Jesus viewed Paul with considerable contempt and in Paul's letters we can discern that this distrust and dislike were mutual. Paul's position was summed up by two simple phrases from one of his epistles: 'Everyone who accepts circumcision is obliged to do the whole Law. Whosoever is justified by the Law are set aside from Christ.'[49] As far as James and the original brethren in Jerusalem were concerned, Paul had adopted a two-faced approach, summed up by Paul himself, as being simultaneously a 'Law-Keeper to those who keep the Law' and a 'Law breaker to those who do not.'[50] This bitter quarrel did not cease with Paul's expulsion from the community, it ended with an act of truly murderous intent.

Paul's Arrest by the Romans

According to the account in the Acts of the Apostles,[51] Paul was arrested, supposedly because he had incensed the mob at the Temple by preaching the Gospel. The real reason for this arrest was to protect this member of the Herodian family and friend of Rome, for the mob wished to murder Paul following his unsuccessful attempt to kill James the Righteous. In this murderous assault, James was thrown headlong down the Temple steps. Paul's attempted murder of James is recorded in the Pseudo-Clementine *Recognitions* and is also part of the subject matter of the *Anabathmoi Jacobou* – the Ascents of James, a lost work about James from which Epiphanius quotes several passages. A detailed and meticulous scholarly study of this event is found in Robert Eisenman's masterwork, *James the Brother of Jesus*.[52]

When Paul warned the arresting officer of yet another plot to kill him,[53] he was escorted to Caesarea under a large military escort of 200 soldiers, 70 cavalrymen and 200 spearmen,[54] yet few have questioned why such an expenditure of military resources is committed to his removal at a time of potential rebellion. This is not the usual fate of a blasphemer who would normally be handed over to the Jews to be stoned to death. Paul's political 'clout' may also explain this and his comfortable status during his two-year 'imprisonment' at Caesarea at the behest of the Roman governor Felix.[55] Felix was married to a Jewess named Drusilla, the third daughter of Agrippa I, sister of Agrippa II and both a relative and follower of Paul. Drusilla had divorced her first husband to marry Felix.[56] Felix, in his turn, was also well connected, being the brother of Pallas, one of Emperor Nero's favourites.

The Murder of James the Righteous

The confrontation between James and the religious and political establishment in Jerusalem finally came to the boil when King Agrippa appointed a new Saducee high priest, Ananus. He ordered that the Sanhedrin be convened to put James on trial for blasphemy. The Mishna Sanhedrin lists the acceptable procedures that existed for the execution of men deemed popular with the people and recommends that the priests gather around the condemned man, jostle him and cause him to fall from the temple wall, then stone him and beat out his brains with clubs.[57] Thus James the Just was cast down from the temple wall, stoned and then given the coup de grâce with a fuller's club.

James' judicial murder took place despite his popularity with the mass of the people and the fact that 80 Pharisees had petitioned Rome on his behalf and volunteered to die with him.[58] Jerome (340–420 CE), who was the first to translate the Bible into Latin, wrote that, 'James was of such great Holiness and enjoyed so great a reputation among the people that the downfall of Jerusalem was believed to be on account of his death.'[59] Both the third-century Christian theologian, Origen, and Eusebius, Bishop of Caesarea, recorded that they saw a copy of Josephus different from the one we have, probably the Slavonic version, which states baldly that the fall of Jerusalem was a consequence of the death of James, *not the death of Jesus*, a very significant admission by two respected early fathers of the Church.[60]

It was after the murder of James that the Ebionites and other members of the *ma'madot*, now under the leadership of James's 'cousin' Simeon, left Jerusalem and crossed the Jordan into Pella.[61] After their flight to Pella, leadership of the Ebionites remained among the descendants of the family of Jesus, known as the *Desposyni*, for more than 150 years.[62]

In Jerusalem and Judea, reaction among the Jewish population was sharply divided. The Zealot faction advocated immediate rebellion against the Roman occupation, the collaborative Sadducee faction, 'Hellenizers' and the Herodians, and by 66 CE, the move to war came into the open. Saul, the well-known kinsman of Agrippa, then revealed his true colours, for Josephus records that when the war broke out in 66 CE and the Zealots occupied Jerusalem:

> The men of power [the Sadducees], perceiving that the sedition was too hard for them to subdue... endeavoured to save themselves, and sent ambassadors, some to Florus [the Roman Procurator]... and others to Agrippa, among whom the most eminent was Saul, and Antipas, and Costobarus, who were of the king's kindred.[63]

Surely this Saul, the kinsman of Agrippa and friend of Nero, is the man also known as Saul of Tarsus, or St Paul. The idea of this delegation was to ensure prompt military action by the Romans and suppress the rebellion before it got out of hand, a concept consistent with Paul's instruction to his converts to 'obey lawful authorities.' This stratagem failed and the insurrection became unstoppable and the Jews repeatedly defeated the Romans. At this point, a deputation was sent to the Emperor Nero then residing near Corinth at Achia. Josephus once more provides the details:

> Cestius sent Saul and his friends, at their own desire, to Achia, to Nero, to inform him of the great distress they were in... [64]

Nero appointed Vespasian as general in command of the legions in Palestine, and after four years of prolonged and bitter fighting, Jerusalem was besieged and fell to the Romans amid scenes of unprecedented carnage and brutality. Its surviving inhabitants were slaughtered, crucified or sold into slavery and the city and the Temple were razed to the ground. In this manner the heart was brutally ripped out of Jewish culture, religion and traditions. Despite the scriptural prophecies, the forces of darkness had triumphed over the sons of light. Now everything had changed, not only for the Jews but for the entire world. Paul's teaching was now virtually unopposed and the stage was set for the rise of Christianity.

Chapter 5

~

The Foundation of Christian Europe
and the Dark Ages

THE HOLY CITY OF JERUSALEM was left a smoking charnel
house, the Temple destroyed, the streets choked with putrefy-
ing corpses and the ruined city walls delineated by a ring of Jewish
rebels, crucified after their failed attempts to escape. Many of the
citizens who survived were paraded through the streets of Rome in
chains, behind a procession of their conquerors bearing the treas-
ures of the Temple commemorating the victory of Rome. The triumph culminated with the execution of the leaders of the revolt,
and the rest of the captives were dispatched to the slave markets,
to end their days in servitude, the arena, or in the galleys and mines
of the empire.

The range of consequences that flowed from the failed Jewish
revolt of 66–73 CE are so complex that they are almost impossible
to fully comprehend. With the passage of time, its far-reaching
results have moulded the development of European culture and
profoundly influenced the history of the peoples of the Middle East.
However, the historian Neil Faulkner pin-points one development
of immense significance:

The defeat of apocalyptic hope and the physical destruction of the
Judaeo-Christian sect cleared the way for Pauline Christians to

de-nationalise Jesus, cauterise his revolutionary message and re-package him as a 'saviour-god' dispensing opiate for the masses.[1]

Emerging Christianity, in order to survive, had to conform to the realities of Roman Imperial power. Paul's teaching, 'obey lawful authorities', proved to be a crucial element in this strategy as it produced a subservient and law-abiding congregation of believers. Similarly, all Jewish religious or cultural activity had to be drastically recast in line with the ever-present realities of Roman power.[2] Mainstream Judaism had to learn from its previous experience in Babylon and once again had to change substantially in order to avoid being crushed by the brutal and pragmatic power of the Roman Empire.

The Transformation of Judaism

Most Pharisees had traditionally preached a degree of accommodation with the Romans and one in particular, Rabbi Yohanen ben Zakkai, had been absolutely opposed to the extremism of the Zealots. After the fall of Jerusalem, he and his companions were the only Jewish leaders to retain a degree of political credibility with the Romans and the surviving Jews in Judea. Rabbi Yohanen asked permission from the new Emperor Vespasian to found a school at Jamnia where Jews could study the scriptures, pray, and restructure their religion. The school, the Rabbi insisted, would be a centre of spirituality and not a hotbed of revolutionary fervour. As a result, Judaism was stripped of its messianic and intensely nationalistic zeal.[3]

The rabbis instructed their fellow Jews to experience God in their neighbour and held that the mitzvah, 'Thou shalt love thy neighbour as thyself', was 'the greatest principle of the Torah'.[4] The rabbis at Jamnia altered the emphasis, but not the substance, of their religion and created a form of worship and ritual that was acceptable to the Romans. Again, drawing on their people's earlier experience of exile in Babylon, they drew on established tenets of belief and the vast store of scriptures and exegesis their predecessors had accumulated since then, and continued to speak of Jerusalem in the present tense even though the Temple had been destroyed. For them, Jerusalem and the Temple still symbolized the reality of God's mystical presence on Earth and this eternal truth was now the heart of Judaism.[5]

The Dispersal of the *ma'madot*

Led by Simeon, the Ebionites and surviving members of the *ma'madot* returned from Pella and took up temporary residence near Mount Sion in the ruined city of Jerusalem.[6] However, this was a short-lived move, for successive Roman emperors, Vespasian, Titus, Domitian and Trajan, endorsed the existing orders to the main force of occupation, the Tenth Legion, to find and execute any Jew who claimed to be a descendant of King David.[7] This was not a new experience for them, for *ma'madot* traditions recount that more than 30 years earlier, the children of Jesus had been parted and sent to places of safety to ensure their survival.[8] Jesus' son, James, had been entrusted to the care of Judas Thomas Didymus, Jesus' twin brother, and sent to the safe custody of King Abgar of Edessa.[9] Jesus' pregnant wife, Mary Magdalene, had fled to Egypt where she gave birth to a daughter called Sarah before eventually seeking refuge in Southern France.[10]

Now it was time for all the *ma'madot*, especially those who were descendants of the Davidic line, to run and hide in order to avoid Roman persecution. They dispersed throughout the Middle East, as well as to Jewish enclaves within France, England, Spain Italy and Northern and Eastern Europe. Keeping strictly to their Cohenite marital practices in order to preserve their sacred blood-lines, they also began to transform the public face of their religious practices in order to ensure their own survival. They discarded their fervent nationalistic anti-Roman stance and apparently deny-ing their Jewish origin, outwardly practised the prevailing religion of their place and time. Passing down their own teaching in secret within the families, they laid even greater emphasis on behaviour and were still intent on creating an 'elite within the elite'. They now dedicated their lives to the principles of a sacred brotherhood founded firmly on the Gnostic principles of justice and truth. Thus, they strove to preserve the spiritual core of their initiatory message and its insistence on 'doing Torah' without fear of persecution by the Romans or any other temporal power. One early father of the Church, Epiphanius, recorded their true beliefs about Jesus:

> Beside a daily ritual bath, they have a baptism of initiation and each year they celebrate certain mysteries... In these mysteries they use unleavened bread and, for the other part, pure water... They say that Jesus was begotten of human seed... that he was not begotten by God the Father, but that he was created... and they too receive the Gospel of Matthew and this they use... to the exclusion of all others. But they call it the Gospel according to the Hebrews.[11]

The historian Karen Armstrong, confirmed their view of Jesus as human and not divine, when she wrote, 'After all, some of them had known him since he was a child and could not see him as a god.'[12]

The Early Christians

After the fall of Jerusalem, those who claimed to follow the teachings of Jesus fell into two main groups: the original disciples, now known as the Ebionites, who followed the teachings of Jesus that they had received directly from the original Apostles or from the brothers of Jesus and the people who had walked and talked with him when he was alive. Their theological opponents, the so-called Christians, followed the teaching of Paul who, according to his own writings, had never met the living Jesus. Paul's claim to authority was solely based on visionary instruction that he claimed came directly from the man he called 'the risen Lord'. The Pauline Christians were relatively settled in various locations, but squabbled among themselves. The battle for supremacy among them was eventually won by the group centred in Rome whose theological views eventually began to predominate and shape the beliefs and structure of this 'new' religion.

There is no doubt that Paul's epistles are the earliest primary documentation of the Christian faith and his letters to the communities he served date from about 47 CE, more than 30 years before the first of the canonical Gospels was written.[13] Prior to the writing of the Gospels, these were the only documents circulating among Paul's converts. The biblical scholar, Robert Eisenman writes:

> In using the letters of Paul as our primary source material, we are on the firmest ground conceivable, for these are indisputably the earliest reliable documents of Christianity and can be dated with a high degree of certainty. They are patently earlier than the Gospels or the Book of Acts, which precede them in the present arrangement of the New Testament and which are themselves in large part doctrinally dependant upon Paul. Acts to some extent is dependant on Paul's letters for historical information as well.[14]

The almost complete doctrinal dependence of the Acts of the Apostles, as well as much of the theological content of the Gospels upon the work of Paul, is not obvious because in the New Testament, the Gospels come first, followed by Acts and then by the Epistles. This order of presentation is usually taken to reflect the chronological order of composition, a mistake that distorts the relative theological importance of the Scriptures concerned. Thus, it is extremely difficult to penetrate and expose the original content of Jesus' teaching from the New Testament Scriptures because the activities, influence and teaching of Paul overshadow and virtually exclude the contribution of the real Apostles and their view of the true doctrine of Jesus. In a New Testament dominated by Pauline thinking, we can only catch fleeting, inadequate and misleading glimpses of the very substantial Nazorean movement to which the true Apostles really belonged.[15]

The Writing of the Gospels

There is now a consensus about the probable dating of the composition of the four canonical Gospels. Mark is now agreed to have been the first to appear and was apparently written between 70 and 80 CE, after the fall of Jerusalem, when Paul's thinking predominated without any effective opposition. The Gospel according to Matthew made its appearance about ten years later with the Gospel according to Luke and the Acts of the Apostles first seeing the light of day sometime in the first decade of the second century. The Gospel of John, now held to be transcribed from an earlier oral transmission, is variously dated from 100–120 CE.[16]

It would be completely wrong to imply that at first there was any real degree of unanimity of belief among the numerous 'Christian' groups which were now scattered among the cities and towns of the Mediterranean littoral, for these, by and large, consisted of a variety of disparate and squabbling sects founded on differing traditions that largely depended on who evangelized them. Gradually, Pauline theologians began to consolidate their hold over the emerging Christian Church using the traditional Pauline means of falsehood and calumny to strengthen their case. The tone of the doctrinal debates was such that it gave rise to the term *odium theologicum*, a form of venomous abuse that centred on character assassination rather than on their intellectual quality or spiritual truth.

For example, in order to legitimize its claim to spiritual supremacy, the Roman Church used a completely unjustifiable assertion that both St Peter and St Paul had been martyred in Rome, despite contemporary evidence that Peter had been crucified in Jerusalem and the uncomfortable fact that no evidence exists to even suggest that Paul was executed either by his Roman friends or anyone else. The fabricated Petrine foundation myth, classed as 'tradition' by the Church, was then used to justify the spurious claim to 'apostolic succession' that asserted the primacy of the Bishop of Rome over all Christians. Subject to occasional waves of persecution that were brutal in the extreme, but usually brief, nonetheless, Christianity grew steadily in numbers and in influence.

Constantine the Great (circa 274–337 CE) became Emperor of Rome after his victory in the civil war at the Battle of the Milvian Bridge in 312 CE. Almost immediately afterwards he passed the Edict of Milan granting the Christian Church freedom from persecution, religious toleration and restoration of its property rights,[17] which were, by then, very considerable indeed. It was in the interests of all who sought the favour and protection of the new ruler, to use any means possible, including flattery, imitation and corruption,[18] and as Christianity was now the emperor's favoured religion, it grew in power and influence. However, Constantine was not a Christian, in fact he was an adherent of the Mithraic cult of Sol Invictus[19] who simply wished to use the disciplined, law-abiding traditions of the Christians and their beliefs as a socially cohesive force in healing the bitter divisions within the empire brought about by the recent civil war.[20] While Christianity was now both legalized and encouraged, it did not become the officially preferred state religion for another 70 years.

Constantine, however, was disappointed, for among the most divisive factors within the empire were the on-going doctrinal disputes within Christianity. In fact the state was in grave danger of being torn apart by the increasingly vituperative theological disputes within the Church.[21] Not surprisingly the most bitterly disputed question arose from the ever-present debate about the true nature of Jesus, or Christ as he was now more commonly called. To the Pauline Christians, Jesus was not merely divine, he was 'the only begotten Son of God'. To the Arians, on the other hand, God the Father was the 'One True God' and although Jesus was divinely guided, he was not God, either essentially or necessarily. According to Arius (d. 336 CE), it was possible for Jesus to have sinned. The Arian 'heresy' caused uproar within the Church and demonstrated the heights of absurdity that could be reached by theologians in their attempts to defend and clarify the blasphemous concept confected by Paul, that Jesus, that ultra-orthodox Jewish rabbi, was God. The only way to put a stop to this increasingly bitter internecine strife was to come up with a working definition that clarified in precisely what sense Jesus was God. Constantine placed political stability far higher than the truth of religious dogma in his ordering of priorities and, to impose his imperial will on these squabbling clerics who threatened to tear his Empire apart, he convened the first ecumenical council of the Church at Nicea in 325 CE.[22]

The Council of Nicea

The Council of Nicea accomplished a very necessary political objective in what was, for that time, a novel manner. The decisions of the carefully chosen delegates were promulgated as official Church doctrine which was to have devastating long-term effects. Firstly the Church and State were now officially confirmed as being in line with one another and, secondly, the teachings of Arius were condemned as heretical.[23] Constantine also officially incorporated Mithraic mythology and practice into Christianity, including the myth of a holy birth in a grotto attended by shepherds, an apocalyptic judgement day, the concept of a 'Holy Trinity', first suggested by another sun-worshipper, the Pharaoh Akenhaten in Egypt, the resurrection of the body and the second coming of a god, only this time it was not Mithras who was to come again, but Jesus. Sunday, the day previously dedicated to Sol Invictus was now to be the official Sabbath instead of Friday dusk until Saturday sun-down. The Creed of Nicea, not to be confused with the later Nicene Creed, stated that Jesus was divine and the equal of God the Father in every way.

Lastly, laying firm foundations for the many centuries of repression that were to come and sowing the seeds of future antagonism towards Jews and Muslims, the council decreed that anyone who did not accept the divinity of Jesus was to be excommunicated. One of the emperor's final actions neatly illustrates the freedom of conscience accorded to the delegates when he imposed criminal sentences of exile on all the bishops who refused to sign the council's decrees. One year later, he published a letter addressed to the newly defined heretical sects informing them that their places of worship were to be confiscated.[24] In 333 CE, the emperor initiated further punitive action against heretics by writing a decree that stated:

> ... if any teatise composed by Arius is discovered, let it be consigned to the flames... in order that there be no memorial of him. Whatever be left... if anyone shall be caught concealing a book by Arius, and does not immediately bring it out and burn it, the penalty shall be death; the criminal shall suffer punishment immediately after conviction.[25]

Thus was created the first official Church/State establishment in Europe, founded firmly on the spiritual bedrock of fear and repression; it set the scene for much of what was to come. For the next five centuries, the vexed questions about the true nature of Jesus continued to bedevil the Church. Theologians who followed the Pauline heresy were faced with an almost impossible task for, as they were incapable of accepting that Jesus was a divinely inspired teacher but nonetheless a man, they had to constantly struggle to prop up the Pauline fantasy that Jesus was God.

The Pope Consolidates His Power

After the Council of Nicea, it became part of the doctrine of the Church that the Bishop of Rome, and the hierarchy that served under him, were God's representatives on Earth and that their pronouncements were made with divinely approved authority. In this manner, the position held by James the Just, the first 'Bishop' of Jerusalem was completely negated. James, the hereditary high priest at the Temple in Jerusalem, had humbled himself in the Holy of Holies as the representative of his people, praying to God for forgiveness. Now, the position had changed; the pope was the representative of God before the people and claimed to rule over them all in God's name. James had served his people, the pope ruled his. The English writer, Laurence Gardner, records that Pope Sylvester informed a group representing the *Desposyni*, the descendants of the Messiah, that they and their teachings had no place in the new Christian order.[26] The pope informed the delegation that the teachings of Jesus had been superseded by Church doctrine which now had been amended in conformity to imperial desires. Despite the fact that at the Council of Nicea Jesus had been elevated to co-equal status with God the Father, the pope informed them that salvation rested not with Jesus, but with the Roman Emperor Constantine the Great.[27]

The Concept of Heresy

Constantine himself soon made it abundantly clear that the benefits he had granted to the Christian Church, 'must benefit only adherents of the Catholic Faith',[28] that is those who accepted without reservation the doctrine enunciated in the new creed as well as the supreme ecclesiastical authority of the bishop of Rome. He stated: 'Heretics and schismatics shall not only be alien from these privileges but shall be bound and subjected to various public services.' Other emperors who succeeded him continued with a similar policy to ensure that membership of any heretical sect incurred a degree of infamy and a loss of civil rights.

St Augustine of Hippo (354–430 CE) defined heresy as, 'the distortion of a revealed truth by a believer or an unbeliever.' 'Revealed truth' was defined as, 'what the Church itself had declared to be revealed truth.' The hierarchy used this circular argument to establish a total monopoly on all access to the sacred.[29] The Church has always seemed to believe that heresy exists wherever and whenever any man exercises his God-given gift of free will in matters of faith. Before he was elected to the papacy in 2005 and took the name Benedict XVI, Cardinal Joseph Ratzinger was in charge of the *Congregation of the Doctrine of the Faith*, the modern equivalent of the Inquisition. In 1990 he claimed that: 'The freedom of the act of faith cannot justify the right to dissent.'[30] To show how little has changed over two millennia, the New Catholic Catechism, published in 1990, states that: 'The task of giving an authentic interpretation of the Word of God... has been entrusted to the living teaching office of the Church alone.'

Further specific legislation against heresy was promulgated in the 380s[31] and by the time of Emperor Theodosius in the late fourth century, they had multiplied until there were over 100 separate laws against heresy. Theodosius I (d. 395 CE), who debarred all heretics from public office and conducted purges against them,[32] was also responsible for the exile and expulsion of Nestorius, the patriarch of Constantinople. The patriarch had asserted that to argue about whether Jesus was either God, or more simply the 'Son of God', was totally irrelevant as everyone knew that he had been born to a human father and mother like everyone else. Exiled with Nestorius was a large group of Greek classical scholars who left Europe taking their books and manuscripts into exile with them. Thus, all the benefits from centuries of Greek intellectual speculation and learning, philosophy, mathematics, and science were wiped from the memory of European man as if they had never existed.[33] This vast body of learning was lost to Western civilization for many centuries, but was preserved in the later Islamic Empire and, thanks to the efforts of Jewish and Islamic scholars, eventually resurfaced in Europe at the Renaissance.

The Church Tightens its Grip

The descendants of the *ma'madot*, now known as Rex Deus, the last truly authoritative group that could give the lie to the Church's dogmatic and blasphemous assertion that Jesus was God, were now scattered and silent. A silence that was necessary for survival, for the Church tolerated no rivals and campaigned vigorously throughout the empire for the destruction or closure of all the temples and centres of worship of rival faiths, hijacking these sacred sites for its own use wherever possible. The mystery temples of classical Greece were rendered defunct and their revered oracles silenced for all time.[34]

The Church slammed all the doors that gave access to the spiritual and cultural heritage of the various tribes and peoples of the empire. In its relentless march towards absolute power and authority, it feared any access to the realms of either sacred or secular knowledge that it did not control.[35] Who knows what might happen if people were encouraged into education, intellectual adventure and inquiry in the traditional Roman or Greek manner of old? Education was soon to be solely restricted to the clergy and, as a result, taking holy orders eventually became the essential prerequisite for basic literacy.

Even with the clergy, however, the Church tightly controlled what they learned. The great works of the philosophers of ancient Greece were condemned as 'pagan' and a little neo-Platonism to support theology was all that the Church required from that ancient and revered centre of learning. Thus the Church revealed its real aims and objectives, absolute power and control over kings, emperors and princes; over territories, peoples and individuals; over this life and entrance to the next. With the Church's stranglehold on all forms of education, the superstitious populace remained quiescent in a state of ignorance and fear and with the effective end of the Arian faith in the fifth century, a period of calm and unity of religious belief appeared to pervade the intellectual and spiritual desert that was Europe in the Dark Ages.

With the collapse of the Western Roman Empire (476–9 CE), the Church was the only surviving institution with a clear sense of purpose and the skills necessary for survival. By extending its influence over the barbarian tribes, the Church became the major lawmaker in the declining empire, and the clergy, who were the final arbiters against whose decisions there was no appeal, codified the traditional laws of the tribes of Europe. The Church scribes recorded the oral legends, myths and stories of the tribes, adding their own dogmatic gloss, but omitting all that was offensive to accepted doctrine, retaining this, adding that, subtly changing the histories and forming the mould for a new, essentially Christian, culture. Tribal myths and legends were reduced to stories; mere fiction stripped of all power and validity.

Thus the Church distorted the histories of entire cultures, and increased its grip not only on the current reality of the tribes, but also on their past and their ancient cultural heritage,[36] reinforcing this process by the incorporation of pagan festivals into the Christian calendar. Easter replaced the festival of Astarte, the Phoenician goddess of love and fertility; The feast of St John the Baptist replaced the summer solstice; the 25th of December, birthday of Mithras, the Persian god of light, became amalgamated with the winter solstice and was celebrated as the birthday of Christ or 'Christmas'. However, even in the well-named Dark Ages, there were glimmers of hope, little points of light battling against the seemingly all-pervading darkness imposed by the Church's monopoly on education and salvation.

Celtic Christianity

One source of the light of learning could still be found in Ireland, the seat of the Celtic Church. The first evangelization of the British Isles had taken place only four years after the Crucifixion when evangelists accredited by James the Just founded the Church in Britain. According to St Gildas, writing in 542 CE[37] and the early Christian historian Freculpus,[38] this evangelical effort spawned a distinctive religion known as Celtic Christianity which developed a form of monasticism characterized by spiritual purity and simplicity. Priests were encouraged to marry and have families, for the priesthood was, like that in the early Jerusalem Church, a hereditary office.[39] Rejecting all the trappings and benefits of temporal power, the simplicity and humility of the Celtic monks stood in stark contrast to the pomp and circumstance of the priesthood in the rest of Europe. In Ireland education was treasured and the monks possessed large and well-used libraries.

The Celts evangelized much of Western Europe,[40] crossing from Scandinavia in the north to Switzerland in the east and the seventeenth-century historian, Thomas Fuller, described these footloose Irish missionaries as the 'wandering scholars'. The quality and range of their learning was such that Professor H Zimmer claimed: 'It is almost a truism to state that whoever knew Greek on the continent of Europe in the days of Charles the Bald (823–77 CE), Holy Roman Emperor and King of the Franks, was an Irishman or had been taught by an Irishman.'[41] They became known as the 'snail men' because they left a silver trail of knowledge behind them wherever they went.

Their efforts were soon swamped by the pervasive and repressive attitudes of the corrupt Church in Rome, but all was not yet lost in the Dark Ages. Far beyond the reach of Rome there was a country in the Middle East which was to give birth to a deeply spiritual man, steeped in the prophetic tradition, who founded a religion of great spiritual purity that was imbued from the beginning with a respect for learning, and whose tolerance for other faiths was to be exemplary, the Prophet Muhammed.

Part Three

◇

THE FOUNDATION OF THE
WORLD OF ISLAM

Aᴛ ᴛʜᴇ ʙᴇɢɪɴɴɪɴɢ ᴏꜰ ᴛʜᴇ seventh century the third of the world's great
monotheistic faiths was born in a little-known part of Arabia; a
religion that spawned a highly sophisticated civilization that was to have
a profound influence on the ultimate development of European culture,
and ultimately, through the conversion of millions of people, would
make its effects felt throughout the world. In dramatic contrast to the
Christian Church's intolerant world-view, one that brooked no competition and repressed dissent within its own ranks with increasing ferocity,
Islam was, from its very inception, a bastion of tolerance, social justice
and incredible piety. Unlike Christianity, which by now was well established in Europe, this religion, born among the Arab peoples, never
developed a hierarchy of priests corrupted by power and wealth. The
simplicity of its faith was such that all its adherents sought to do was
submit themselves to the will of God as disclosed by the Holy Qur'an.
Within the growing empire of Islam, knowledge and education were
revered and encouraged, and the followers of all the major monotheistic faiths – Jews, Christians and Zoroastrians alike – were treated
with respect and tolerance as 'The People of the Book'.[1]

Chapter 6

~

The 'Seal of the Prophets'

THE CLIMATIC CONDITIONS of the deserts of Arabia gave birth to a way of life for most of the Arab peoples that was both primitive and harsh, one that condemned them to seemingly perpetual isolation on the periphery of the known world, largely ignored by the great civilizations of the seventh century. The nomadic Bedouin tribes who inhabited the desert had to live in fierce competition with one another to gain even the bare necessities of life. This gave rise to an ideology called *muruwah*, which stressed the vital importance of courage in battle, patience and endurance in suffering and, above all, absolute and unequivocal dedication to the welfare and needs of the tribe.[2] The Bedouin worshipped the fixed stars and planets, angels and a wide-variety of inferior deities who were perceived as capable of interceding on their behalf before 'the most high God', al-Lah.[3] The term 'most high God' has distinct overtones of the God worshipped by both Abraham and Melchizadek as recorded in the Bible.

In the city of Mecca in the Hijaz, stood the Kabah,[4] a huge block of stone said, at that time, to be the seat of the Nabatean god Hubal. This was a revered centre of annual pilgrimage for the Arab tribesmen, and for the duration of this pilgrimage, or haj, all hostilities between the various tribes were banned. Mecca was therefore a place of peaceful contact between the tribes and developed into a thriving centre of trade, becoming the hub of a series of caravan routes to nearby Yathrib and to more distant destinations such as Egypt, the Yemen and Syria.[5] However, apart from trade links to Mecca, Yathrib and the Yemen, the civilizations of Byzantium, Persia, Iraq, Syria and Palestine regarded Arabia as a barbaric place but, enhanced by the growth and power of these lands, a degree of intellectual and spiritual life arising from both Jews and Christians alike began to affect the Arab people.[6]

Centuries before, a large number of Jewish families had fled to Arabia and settled there after the fall of Jerusalem in 70 CE; these early settlers were later joined by others fleeing from Judea after the failure of the Bar Kochba revolt in 135 CE. While they became assimilated into the Arab lifestyle, in outward respects at least, and lived in a mainly polytheistic environment, nonetheless, they preserved much of their own culture, remaining absolutely steadfast in their religion and unwavering not only in their monotheism but also in the sure and certain knowledge that they were the chosen people.

By the time of the birth of Muhammed in or around 570 CE, there were Jewish tribes living at Fadak, to the north of Mecca;[7] there were more Jews living in Wadi al-Quara and Tayma,[8] and the Khaybar Jewish community resided about 100km to the north of Yathrib. Almost half the population of Yathrib, now the city of Medina, were Jewish, including the tribes of the Banu Nadir, the Qurayza, Qaynuga' and descendants of the *ma'madot*, the hereditary high-priestly families of Jerusalem, now known as the Kahinan.[9] In addition to these direct family links to the true teachings of Jesus, there were a variety of apocryphal writings associated with James the Just and the Ebionites circulating among both Jews and Christians in Arabia.[10] In contrast to these well-established Jewish communities, many of the northern tribes on the borderland between the Persian and Byzantine empires had converted to Nestorian Christianity[11] which, as I have indicated earlier, firmly believed that Jesus was both a man and a prophet but not divine. Around Mecca and Yathrib, the influence of Christianity was even stronger, not Christianity of the Pauline variety however, but that of the Monophysite heresy which taught that in the person of Jesus there was only one single, human nature.[12]

In about the year 610 an Arab merchant of the thriving city of Mecca in the Hijaz, underwent a deep spiritual experience. Each year, the merchant Muhammed ibn Abdalla of the Quraysh tribe, took his family to Mount Hira outside Mecca during the month of Ramadan, a common practice among the Arabs of the Peninsula. Muhammed spent this time of spiritual retreat praying to the High God of the Arabs, al-Lah, and distributing food and alms to the poor who came to visit him during this sacred period.[13] Like most of his fellow countrymen, Muhammed believed that al-Lah, the High God of the Arab pantheon, whose name simply means 'the God', was the identical deity to that worshipped by the Jews and the Christians. The Arab people were uncomfortably aware that al-Lah had never sent them either a prophet or a scripture of their own, despite the fact that he had had his shrine in their midst since time immemorial. For although the Kabah, the massive cube-shaped shrine in the heart of Mecca which was clearly of great antiquity, was dedicated to the Nabatean deity Hubal, by the seventh century most Arabs had come to believe that originally it been dedicated to al-Lah.[14]

Muhammed recounts that he was forcibly awoken from his sleep on the 17th night of Ramadan in 610 CE, and immediately felt himself enveloped by a divine presence. Much later when he described this ineffable experience, he recounted that an angel had appeared to him and given him a curt command: 'Recite!' (iqra). Like the Hebrew prophets of antiquity who were often reluctant to utter the Word of God, Muhammed refused and protested, 'I am not a reciter!' For him, as for most of the Arabs of that era, a reciter was a kahin, an ecstatic fortune-teller who claimed to recite in-spired oracles. But then, Muhammed reported, the angel enveloped him in an overpowering embrace once more, and with such force that he felt as if all the breath was being squeezed from his body. Just when he realized that he could bear this powerful embrace no longer, the angel released him and commanded him again to

'Recite!' Once again Muhammed refused and the angel embraced him a third time, squeezing him until he felt that he had reached the limits of his endurance. Then, at the end of this third terrifying embrace, Muhammed heard the first words of a new sacred scripture pouring from his mouth:[15]

> Recite in the name of thy Sustainer, who has created – created man out of a germ-cell! Recite – for thy Sustainer is the most Bountiful, One who has taught [man] the use of the pen – taught him what he did not know![16]

Immediately he recovered his senses, Muhammed felt terrified and rushed from the cave with the intention of throwing himself off the mountain to his death. Before he could do so, however, he heard a voice from heaven which declaimed: 'Oh Muhammed! Thou art the Apostle of God and I am Gabriel.'[17] Then Muhammed, according to the English author Karen Armstrong, had 'that overpowering apprehension of numinous reality which the Hebrew prophets called *kaddosh*, holiness, the terrifying otherness of God'.[18]

However, unlike the prophets of biblical Israel, Muhammed had no religious tradition to sustain him in this time of spiritual crisis and confusion, and no past history of religious scripture to put these strange events into any form of comprehensible context. In terror he fled into the arms of his wife who suggested he consult her cousin, Waraqa ibn Nawfal. Waraqa, who was a Christian and well versed in the scriptures, was in no doubt as to the truth of what had just happened; Muhammed had indeed received a true revelation from God. The God of Abraham and of Moses and the prophets had now appointed Muhammed as an Apostle of God and the divine envoy to the Arab people.

The Prophet, who had suffered periods of self-doubt after his first visionary experiences, soon became convinced of the innate truth of the revelations that had been granted to him and 'knew' that he was indeed a 'messenger of God' in the time-hallowed tradition of Abraham, Moses, Elijah, John the Baptist and Jesus.[19] Furthermore, despite the fact that this was the first revelation to the

Arab people, Muhammed no more thought of himself as the founder of a new religion than had Jesus before him. He was convinced that he was restoring the one true monotheism that had existed since ancient times, and that he was simply the last in a long line of prophets who testified to the same religion of 'the one true God'. Indeed, he regarded himself as 'The Seal of the Prophets'. According to the Prophet, the One Truth had been revealed to both Jews and Christians but they had either distorted the message or ignored it.[20]

The Holy Qur'an

Later, Muhammed dictated these visions to scribes who recorded them as the Holy Qur'an which, in its *suras*, or chapters, preaches pure and unalloyed monotheism through beautiful yet simple instructions to submit to God's will. When one considers that Muhammed himself thought he was re-establishing a religion of great antiquity, it comes as no surprise to note the strong similarities and parallels between the Judaism of the Ebionites and the teachings of the Qur'an. Indeed, during his visionary sessions, Muhammed had a deep mystical experience in which he was magically transported to Jerusalem and then ascended through the seven heavens – a replication of the fruits of the Jewish Hekkaloth tradition. Whatever truth may lie in either of these approaches, the indisputable fact remains, nonetheless, that however many times God chose to reveal his will for mankind, when these revelations are authentic, they will always be the same after making due allowance for differences in both language and culture.

In distinct contrast to the Torah, which in the Jewish tradition is said to have been revealed in its totality to Moses in one fell swoop on Mount Sinai, the new revelation was given to Muhammed, line by line and verse by verse over a long period of time, some 23 years in all.[21] Each revelation was an intensely painful spiritual experience. In later years the Prophet confessed that: 'Never once did I receive a revelation without the feeling that my soul was being torn away from me.'[22] Sometimes the meaning of the revelations was abundantly clear, at others disturbingly inarticulate. He said, 'Sometimes it comes unto me like the reverberations of a bell, and that is the hardest upon me; the reverberations abate when I am aware of their message.'[23] During these sessions Muhammed was in a state of trance, sweating profusely even on the coldest days, with his head between his knees. The revelations continued and, little by little, the Qur'an developed in a manner that is unique in the annals of religion. As each part was revealed, Muhammed, who could not read or write, recited it aloud so that it could be learnt by heart and later written down.

Some years after the revelations began, Muhammed started to preach to his fellow tribesman of the Quraysh in Mecca, for at first he thought that these were the only people to whom he had a mission[24] and he believed that he had a duty to warn the Quraysh of the dangers of their materialist situation. The early verses of the Qur'an all encourage Muhammed's fellow tribesmen to be aware of God's benevolence and learn that their newfound wealth and prosperity depend entirely upon the goodness of God. The revelations reminded these tribesmen that their present material success depended entirely on the veneration accorded to the Kabah by the Bedouin tribes and that the Kabah was, in its turn, a gift from al-Lah. Should they fail to mirror God's benevolence to them by their actions towards others, they would not be in accord with the divine order of life. For Muhammed, an atheist was not someone who refused to believe in God, it was one who knew what was owing to God and refused to be properly grateful.

Islam

The Prophet decreed that new converts should bow down in ritual prayer (*salat*) five times a day, an external gesture signifying an internal humility towards God. In time, this religion became known as *Islam*, a form of existential submission to al'Lah. A Muslim was anyone, male or female, who surrendered their whole being, body, soul and spirit, to the Creator of all. This, in practical terms, signalled the foundation of a pious, just and equitable society in which the poor, the sick and the vulnerable would be treated with respect and dignity. By the standards of Islam, it is wrong to accumulate wealth for wealth's sake but good to share a reasonable proportion of one's wealth with the poor. The principle of alms-giving, or *zakat*, and prayer, or *salat*, became two of the five essential pillars, or *rukn*, of Islam. Ritual fasting, or *saum*, during the month of Ramadan was, at first, a matter of recommended voluntary self-denial but after a time this too became one of the obligatory 'pillars of Islam'.[25]

Theological speculation of any kind was dismissed as *zanna*, or self-indulgent guesswork about matters that would be forever beyond the understanding of any mere mortal. This concept was markedly different from the practice within Christianity which stridently proclaimed the Church's views on such abstruse theological matters as 'The Holy Trinity' or 'The Incarnation' and then proceeded to persecute anyone who had the temerity to disagree with their official pronouncements. Islam has far more in common with Judaism, where God's covenant with his people translates into a moral imperative, a divine call to good actions and charitable behaviour.

The suras teach Muslims to glimpse the Divine in the 'signs' of nature; the Qur'an urges all true believers to view the world as an ongoing epiphany; one in which they need to be constantly aware in order to perceive the transcendental, divine reality that unites everything in the diverse and complex world of God's creation. The new scripture instructed Muslims to use their God-given powers of reason to decipher these 'signs' or divine messages, an instruction that imbued all Muslims with a healthy attitude to both intellectual endeavour and curiosity; one that led to a remarkable development of the study of natural science that was fully in keeping with God's will. This was in stark contrast to the Christian Church's innate distrust of intellectual adventure and speculation that ultimately led to the perception that science was a danger to the Christian faith.

Most of the early biographies of the Prophet Muhammed describe with awe, the shock and sense of transcendent wonder felt by his early followers when they heard the Qur'an recited for the first time. Frequently, converts describe these events by likening them to a divine invasion of their spirit, one that tapped deeply buried yearnings and, in consequence, released deep, pent-up spiritual feelings. Many were instantly converted and claimed that only God himself could be responsible for the extraordinary beauty of the language. One young man of the Quraysh, Umar ibn al-Khattab, is reported as saying, 'When I heard the Qur'an, my heart was softened and I wept and Islam entered into me.'[26] The English historian of religion, Karen Armstrong, claims that 'without this experience of the Qur'an, it is extremely unlikely that Islam would have taken root'.[27]

Muhammed's Mission

Muhammed preached in Mecca, warning the citizens against social indifference and the perils of their newfound materialism. He also vehemently opposed the prevalent polytheism on which they thought their newfound wealth depended.[28] From that time onward, the first 'pillar of Islam' was to be the shahadah, the profession of faith: 'I bear witness that there is no god but al-Lah and that Muhammed is his messenger.'[29] This threatened the basis of Mecca's wealth and trade and, as a result, the Prophet along with his small band of followers, were forced to move to Yathrib in fear of their lives. The date of this move, or Hegira, in 622 CE marks the beginning of the Muslim calendar. Yathrib itself was soon re-named as Medinat-al-Nabi, the city of the Prophet, now known as Medina.[30]

Muhammed thought that the large Jewish population of Medina would be highly receptive to his message. He was wrong; while they were receptive at first, later they tended to deride him. For them, the age of prophecy was long over and while they still cherished expectations of the coming of the Messiah, no Jew, or Christian for that matter, would have deemed it possible that, in their day and age, anyone could now be a prophet in the Old Testament tradition. Not all the Jews rejected Muhammed, however, some were friendly and gave him a deep insight into the Jewish

Scriptures that enabled him to distinguish between Judaism and Christianity and begin to perceive how the revelations in the Scriptures had been added to in both faiths by rabbinical studies and Christian dogma. Despite his rejection by many Jews, the Holy Qur'an still insists that all the People of the Book[31] were not necessarily in error and that, fundamentally, all religions based upon revelations from God were, essentially, one. Thus, the Prophet never expected Christians or Jews to convert to Islam, because they too had received authentic revelations from God. The revelations of the Qur'an were not held to cancel out or devalue previous scriptural sources, but to confirm and complete them. The Holy Scriptures of Islam, therefore, do not condemn other religious faiths as false or even as incomplete, but, on the other hand, do stress that each prophet has confirmed the revelations of his predecessors and developed those insights according to the will of God.[32]

The world of Islam does not start its calendar from the beginning of the Prophet's revelations, but from the date of the Hegira to Medina, for it was only then that Muslims began to implement God's plans and make Islam a political and temporal reality as well as a spiritual one by converting the Arabian tribes from their old pagan beliefs to Islam. The Qur'an instructs all Muslims to create a just society and the new followers of Islam took this duty very seriously indeed. Faced by enemies in Mecca and elsewhere, Muhammed spent the last ten years of his life in a struggle against opposing forces and, as a result, converted people at phenomenal speed and vastly expanded the territory he controlled. By the end of his life, most of the Arabian tribes had joined him. He conquered the city of Mecca two years before he died and instituted the haj, or pilgrimage to that city as the fifth pillar of Islam. A sacred duty every Muslim is bound to make at least once in his life, if circumstances allow.

The Death of the Great Prophet

Muhammed died unexpectedly after a short illness in the month of June in the year 632 CE, without having nominated a successor. Despite the shock, Islam stood firm; Muhammed had not only been the divinely chosen vehicle for a new revelation, but his military success had laid down a solid political and temporal foundation on which his successors could build. The Prophet was succeeded by Abu Bakr who reigned from 632–4, and was so close to Muhammed that by many he was regarded as the Prophet's alter ego. This was the leader responsible for arranging for the first written version of the Holy Qur'an. His authority was such that he was able to forge what had been a loosely connected group of disparate tribes into a cohesive and devout community. He took the title of caliph, from the Arabic *khalifa,* or representative, as did the others that followed him.[33] He, in his turn, was succeeded as caliph by another of the Prophet's early converts, Umar ibn al-Khattab (634–44 CE), a man renowned for his piety, humility, courage and strength of will. With his generals Khalid ibn al-Walid, Amr ibn al-As and Sad ibn Abu Waqqas, the new caliph can be regarded as the true founder of the Islamic Empire. His success in war gave him immense authority over the proud chieftains of the Arab tribes and his statesmanship was seemingly limitless. Umar consolidated Islam's hold over the conquered territories by a variety of reforms which included the distribution of land, a pension scheme, *dhimmi* taxes (a poll tax on non-Muslims), and added a new title to that of caliph, *amir al-mumminin,* or Commander of the Faithful. Umar was followed as caliph by a profoundly virtuous and pious man, Uthman ibn Affan. Sadly he was neither a good administrator nor a military leader and he was eventually murdered.

By 665 CE, a little over 20 years after the Prophet's death, the empire of Islam stretched from Kabul in the east to Tripoli in the west; from the southern shores of Arabia to the greater part of present-day Turkey in the north. It continued to spread until it stretched from the Atlantic coast of North Africa right across the Middle East to the borders of the Chinese Empire.

Chapter 7

~

The Consolidation of the Empire and the Development of Islamic Culture

THE MOST FORMIDABLE expansion of the Islamic Empire took place after the accession of the first Umayyad Caliph Uthman (644–56 CE). His reign was followed shortly afterwards by that of the Caliph Imam Ali, but the Umayyads regained definitive control of the caliphate after 661. Their power base was Syria, and Damascus became their capital. The empire spread with formidable speed due to the military genius of the Umayyad generals and the warlike prowess of the Arab tribesmen. However, while these vast territorial gains were undoubtedly made by the sword, the spread of Islam as a religion was not. The newly subject peoples who became the followers of Islam in such vast numbers were attracted to that religion by its spiritual purity and the relevance of its message to their daily lives. Forcible conversion was against all the fundamental principles of choice that Islam espoused. Indeed, the People of the Book, Jews, Christians and Zoroastrians, were treated with such respect and tolerance within the Islamic world that they readily became willing subjects of the caliphate. The reason is not hard to understand, for their legal status under the rule of Islam was infinitely better than that accorded to them by their previous rulers: the Byzantines in Syria, Palestine and Egypt, the Sassanids in Persia or the Visigoths in Spain.

The division of the Muslims between Sunni and Shiite, happened early on; the Sunnis regard the first four caliphs as 'the four rightly guided caliphs', while the Shiites regard the first three as usurpers and accuse Caliph Uthman, the third caliph, of nepotism and misappropriation of state funds. The Shiites regard the fourth Caliph Imam Ali (the Prophet's cousin and son-in-law) and his descendants as infallible imams (leaders of the community of the faithful) and hold them in almost as much reverence as the Prophet himself. However, unlike later factions within Christianity, the conflicts that occurred between Sunni and Shiite were almost all about power and territory and not about their religious differences.

Under the benevolent rule of Islam, Jews, who had often been previously barely tolerated, now found themselves protected, gaining religious liberty, physical security, economic freedom and enjoying a marked degree of autonomy for their communities. So they, and the numerous and large Christian communities, willingly accepted their new colonial masters. Indeed, some traditions claim that the towns of Caesarea and Hebron were delivered to the Muslim armies by their Jewish inhabitants. For the Jewish people, perhaps the greatest gift they received from their new conquerors was the fact that the centuries-old prohibition against Jews residing in Jerusalem, first imposed by the Romans and maintained by the Byzantine Christians, was finally lifted and several families were able to take up residence in the Holy City.[1]

Jewish Sanctuaries within the Islamic Empire

The largest concentration of Jews in the new empire was to be found in Iraq and Iran. Preceding the Muslim conquest, the Jews there had been particularly badly treated so they also were well-pleased with their new legal status and delighted with the ties they could now establish and maintain with the other Jewish communities throughout the empire. Long-standing Jewish traditions from a variety of sources stress the excellent relations that were forged between the first Umayyad caliphs and the leaders of these communities.[2]

There were some restrictions, however, for laws ensured that churches and synagogues could not be built any higher than the local mosque. Furthermore, Muslim houses were to be no lower than the houses of their non-Muslim neighbours. Restrictions were also in place to prevent mixed marriages and inter-faith sexual liaisons. Grave punishment was meted out for sexual intercourse between members of differing religious faiths, and mixed marriages were strictly forbidden except where the non-Muslim partner converted to Islam.[3]

The creation of the new Islamic Empire had some significant effects on the economic structure of the conquered peoples. In Palestine during the seventh century, for example, as throughout most of the East, the Jewish economy was essentially an agricultural one. The *dhimmi*, the new poll and land tax, imposed by the Arab conquerors, led to many Jews leaving the land and seeking their fortune in the far more lucrative world of commerce.[4] By the end of the eighth century this resulted in the growing prominence of Jews in all caravans connecting the East to the West. As traders, the Jews had certain inbuilt advantages over people of other faiths: they operated under a unified legal code, benefited from having supportive Jewish communities strategically placed along the trade routes and, above all, had a fluent mastery of the two major international languages, Arabic and Hebrew. These Jewish merchants became important cultural agents, bringing the teachings of their religious school, or yeshiva, in Baghdad to all the communities of the Diaspora and contributing to its increasing authority.[5] In fact the Islamic Empire was an important vehicle that brought a high degree of unification to Jewish communities throughout the Diaspora;[6] one that ensured that the vast majority of the Jewish settlements scattered throughout the world, indeed some claim as many as 90 per cent, were now united under the rule of one political state. Indeed, the later establishment of the Abbasid capital at Baghdad, which I detail later, ensured that the largest and wealthiest Jewish communities were always close to the seat of real political power.[7]

Tolerance and Dissent

In the predominantly Christian countries of Iraq, Syria and Egypt, the coming of Islam resulted in the granting of religious freedom that put an end to Byzantine intolerance of many of the so-called heretical sects. This soon resulted in a renaissance of minority churches, the rebuilding of many monasteries, and ultimately led to the recruitment of many Monophysite Christians as officials within the administration of the new state.[8] Baghdad had long been an important Christian city and was home to the Nestorian patriarch and contained monasteries belonging to the Nestorian, Jacobite and Melekite obediences. It was also, as mentioned above, the intellectual capital of Judaism with its Talmudic schools and the presence at court of the exilarch.[9]

The government of the empire by the Umayyad dynasty developed in an atmosphere of continual conflict, political, ideological and familial, that created warring factions among the Arab peoples. It was also beset by the difficulty of finding solutions to the ever-present problems of power within the wider Islamic community: relations between the conquerors and the conquered, and the creation of a body of law and regulation that would give them effective control over the entire Islamic world that was now swollen by conquest to dimensions as vast as those of any empire in antiquity.[10]

The unity of the disparate peoples in this vast and growing empire was enhanced by a variety of factors, the most important of which arose from their faith in Islam assisted by others that sprang from the innate political skill of the caliphs and their advisors. The fundamental basis for union could be found in the principles that are the very foundation of Islam itself: 'There is no God but God; He is one, without associate, and Muhammed is the messenger of God'; God is one, God is eternal, He begets not, He was not begotten, none is equal to him. Caliph Abd al-Malik (685–705 CE) used these inscriptions on the first uniform coinage issued by the empire in 695 CE.[11] This coinage, consisting of the gold dinar and the silver dirham, was another factor in the growing unity that was developing among the conquered peoples of the empire. It facilitated long-distance trade, simplified the collection of taxes and brought in its train a growing commercial prosperity.

This vast collection of peoples were further united by a common language, for the Holy Qur'an had to be read or recited in its original form, so all new converts had to learn Arabic. This led to a rapid rise in literacy and, as the Qur'an instructed the faithful to seek for signs of God's activities in the world, to the encouragement of natural science. So the empire of Islam rapidly acquired a degree of sophistication and learning that was not to be equalled, much less excelled, by the Christian West for nearly nine centuries. Under the Umayyads, Arab armies continued to extend the territorial limits of the caliphate, and in 711, led by General Tariq, the Muslims of North Africa crossed the Straits of Gibraltar while others crossed the Indus at about the same time, thus taking Islam into both Spain and India.[12]

Jostling for Position

The intellectual freedom that was so central to the ideals of Islam tended to produce a trend of philosophical and political doctrines that was far from favourable to the Umayyads. Many devout Muslims who stressed the inaccessibility and Oneness of God, were vehemently opposed to the immorality of their Umayyad rulers and, emphasizing the divinely ordained responsibility to create 'good government' in line with the teachings of the Holy Qur'an, they began to preach rebellion against rulers who were perceived as unjust and immoral.[13] Thus the overstretched Arab Empire was now becoming the victim to a variety of forms of rekindled local patriotism and dissatisfaction arising from a deep and abiding faith; a heady mixture wherein a growing number of Arabs sought to escape the high levels of taxation that supported the caliphate and recover some measure of political independence.

These circumstances allowed a certain Abu'l Abbas (749–54 CE) to exploit his relationship with the Prophet and gather a group of malcontents around him in the East. This motley group comprised Persian soldiers, heavily taxed Iranian landowners and sincere believers who reproached the Umayyads with spilling the blood of the faithful.[14] The Abbasid family could trace its origins back to al-Abbas ibn Abd al-Muttalib ibn Hashim, the uncle of the Prophet. This claim of descent from the Prophet's uncle was a far closer and more legitimate relationship than the Umayyads had been able to establish, and the principle of heredity, both spiritual and genealogical, was of vital importance in establishing authority among tribal peoples. Thus, the Abbasids fomented bloody revolution by channelling the general dissatisfaction with Umayyad rule, gathering support from disparate groups. The old Umayyad caliph, Marwan II, was killed near Mosul in 751 CE and Abu'l Abbas started his reign with the massacre of the remaining members of the Umayyad family.[15]

However, all was not completely lost for the Umayyads, for Syrian troops sent among the Berbers found an Umayyad, Abd-al-Rahman, who had miraculously escaped the slaughter of 750, and welcoming him as a saviour, crossed the straits of Gibraltar with him. Accompanied by his freed slave, Badr, this scion of the Umayyad family entered Cordova in 756 and proclaimed the restoration of his family dynasty and assumed the title of Emir as Ab-ar-Rahman I and reigned from 756–88.[16]

The Founding of Baghdad

In order to position themselves among their principal supporters and to distance themselves from the old regime, the Abbasids moved their capital from Syria to Iraq. In 756 CE, Caliph Al-Mansur (754–75 CE) began the construction of his new capital, Baghdad, which soon became not only the political centre of the empire but also the hub of a network of important caravan routes linking East and West. Situated in a commanding position over the two principal waterways of Iraq, the Euphrates and the Tigris, at a point where both rivers were navigable to the sea, Baghdad retained its commercial prominence until, many centuries later,

European mariners discovered the sea routes to the Far East. And, for reasons explained earlier, the new capital quickly assumed a pre-eminence in the sciences, literature and the arts that it would maintain long after the city had lost its political power.[17]

During the early years of the ninth century, Baghdad became the political centre of the vast Arab Empire, the home of wealthy merchants and learned scholars who all came to live and flourish in the shadow of an enlightened caliphate. People from all over the Muslim world looked to Baghdad and the culture of Iraq for artistic inspiration. Under the rule of the caliphs al-Mansur, his son al Mahdi (775–85 CE) and then his nephew Harun al-Rashid (786–808 CE) – the caliph of *A Thousand and One Nights* – the subjects of theology, law, history, geography, poetry and architecture flourished as never before. When Harun's son, al-Mamun (813–33 CE) became caliph after defeating his brother Amin, the Abbasid empire reached its cultural peak. Al-Mamun, a highly educated man in his own right, established the 'House of Science', otherwise known as the 'House of Wisdom' (*bait al-hik-ma*) to preserve and disseminate the accumulated learning of Greek Antiquity.[18] Thus, Baghdad became the epicentre of an empire and a vibrant culture that was undoubtedly the most sophisticated in the known world outside of China.

Intellectual Life

Thus it was the muslims, and not the Christians, who rekindled the flames of classical Greek science. The learned men of Baghdad knew that the world was round, and could measure a degree of longitude many centuries before their European Christian counterparts. They revived the astronomy of the Chaldeans, encouraged Jewish alchemists and men of medicine and translated the works of Galen, the second-century Greek physician, into Arabic. Tabari, the Arab historian and theologian, in writing his *Annals of the Prophets and Kings*, studied for more than 15 years in the Greek and Persian libraries of the Islamic Empire. The quality of Islamic art and architecture was of such renown that architects and mathematicians from as far away as Constantinople and Sammara came to the empire's centres of learning.[19]

At this time, Persian thought was also reborn and although its metaphor and imagery are Arabic and its metaphysical inspiration Greek, nonetheless, Persian national genius had reawakened. Firdousi (b. 941 CE), the Persian poet, wrote the 60,000-verse epic the *Book of Kings*, a complete history of Persia. The legend of Sinbad the Sailor which gained popularity at that time, was Persian, as was the poetry of writers such as Akhtal in the eighth century and Abu Nuwas in the ninth, that was sometimes bitter, oft-times cynical, frequently sensual and erotic, but always humorous.[20]

At the same time, flourishing astrological, astronomical, and medical culture could be found in the palaces, the observatories, the public hospitals and the House of Wisdom, there also developed a popular Islamic culture that was both vigorous and attentive to philosophical debate.[21] This development of Islam consisted, in the main, of an increase in depth and a reasoned reflection on the basic elements of faith of such quality that it still exerts a profound influence on Islam to this day.

During the second half of the eighth century, at a time when Muslim civilization was at its highest state of development, the Abbasids established a lasting domination. With Spain and parts of North Africa hived off as semi-independent or independent territories, the empire gained in solidity and consolidation what it had apparently lost in territorial extent. Trade continued with Spain and North Africa but, on the other hand, wars fought against the Christian territories of Byzantium and Europe became wars of prestige.[22]

The abrupt halt to the tide of conquest dried up the spoils of war and thus the Abbasids had to concern themselves with everyday economic matters to maintain the ever more complex services of the state; hence the interest they took in the factories of the state (*tiran*). To further these aims, profitable trade links between Asia, particularly China, and the Mediterranean which had been the chief objective of the Sassanid dynasty in Persia were re-forged. Arab and Jewish merchants exploited the caravan routes and the seas; Samarkand was linked with Canton, Kabul with the Ganges, Pelisium and Baghdad with India and the Comoro Islands. Silks bought from the Chinese could be found everywhere from the Pamirs to Kairwan and even among the Christian nations of Europe.[23] However, trade and warfare against the Christian states were mere sideshows when compared to the enlightenment spread into Dark Age Europe by the culture of Islam through that beacon of intellectual and spiritual light, Moorish Spain.

Chapter 8

~

A Beacon of Light for the European Dark Ages – Moorish Spain

THE WARLIKE ARABS WHO had been the driving force behind the rapid expansion of the Islamic Empire proved as skilful in shipbuilding and naval warfare as they had been in building cities and fighting on land. They mounted seaborne expeditions against Cyprus in 648; in 655 they won a decisive naval victory in the 'battle of the masts' and less than 20 years later, a large Muslim fleet appeared under the walls of Constantinople in the first of several naval sieges of that great city. They were frustrated in these early attempts to capture Constantinople by the Byzantine's secret weapon, Greek fire, that strange amalgam of naphthalene against which wooden ships were particularly vulnerable.[1] However, despite their failures at the eastern end of the Mediterranean, the naval and military might of the growing empire of Islam was to score a signal victory far to the west where the sea was at its narrowest, at the Straits of Gibraltar.

Visigothic Spain

Visigothic Spain was in a state of political turmoil when King Witzia (d. 710 CE) sought to strengthen his power at the expense of both the Church and the nobility, only to be violently overthrown in 710 CE. Many of the nobles, however, were as opposed to his successor, the usurper Roderick (d. 711 CE), as they had been to Witzia himself.[2] While it is feasible to suggest that both Byzantine and Jewish merchants in Spain may have sent for help to combat Visigothic persecution,[3] Musa ibn Nusair, the governor of the Islamic province of Ifriqiya, which comprised North Africa and the Maghreb, seized the opportunity created by the political chaos in Spain to invade. He dispatched his most able general, Tariq ibn Zihad, in April 711 with an army of 7,000 Berbers.[4] Tariq landed at Gibraltar, the name derives from the Arabic *Jebel al-Tariq*, or the Rock of Tariq, and pushed inland. In a lightning campaign which met little resistance, he captured Malaga, Grenada and Cordova and then, on 19 July 711 at the Battle of the Rio Barbate, he destroyed the Christian army led by Roderick who was killed in battle. The defeated and demoralized Christians fled in disarray to the north, and Tariq occupied and looted the rich royal city of Toledo. Musa himself landed in Spain in June accompanied by 18,000 Arab troops and proceeded to conquer Seville and Mérida before joining forces with Tariq outside Toledo.[5] Resistance to the Muslim invasion was sparse and ineffective. The flight of the Christian armies was panic-stricken, and this incredibly rapid conquest of the greater part of Spain by the forces of Islam that took only two or three years at most, was typical of the way in which the Muslim armies combined prudence with audacity.[6]

For the Jews of Spain, the Arab invasion was a godsend. The Visigoths had prohibited all manifestations of Judaism and had even cruelly separated children from their parents in order to bring them up in the Christian faith. Thus, the Jews not only welcomed the Muslims as saviours but also actively collaborated with the invaders who rewarded them by leaving the defence of some conquered towns and cities to Jewish garrisons. After the Muslim conquest, many Jews who had previously left Spain to avoid persecution by the Visigoths now returned from North Africa where they had previously sought sanctuary.[7]

For the next few years, the constantly changing and fluid boundaries between the Christians in the north and the Muslims in the south of Spain led to the creation of a variety of independent cultural entities. There were the new Islamic converts, or *muwalladun*; there were Christians who lived under Arab rule and who became known as the Mozarabs, from the Arabic word *mustarib*, 'Arabized' and, in centuries to come, Muslims living under Christian rule, the Mudejar. The entire territory of Muslim Spain became known as al-Andalus, a name which, according to Heinz Halm, the twentieth-century German historian, was derived from the Gothic word for 'landless', *landahlutz*.[8]

Forays into the Lands of the Franks

The new conquerors extended the range of their military activities when, in 719 CE, they crossed the Pyrenees and invaded and plundered parts of the Frankish Empire. Some year later the Muslim armies conquered Carcassonne and ravaged territory on the far side of the Rhône as far as Autun in Burgundy. One Governor of al-Andalus, Abd-al-Rahman al-Gafiqui, ranged as far as the Loire and sacked Tours. In October 732, however, at the famous Battle of Poitiers, he was defeated and killed by a Frankish army under the command of Charles Martel (688–741 CE), the grandfather of Charlemagne, known thereafter as Charles the Hammer.[9] The pivotal Battle of Poitiers, which the Christians later called 'the salvation of the West', was only one battle among many, for frontier disputes continued for many years and after 791, Muslim troops once again captured Carcassonne and Narbonne.[10]

In the early years of the Moorish occupation, the scarcity of the Muslim ruling class in respect of their conquered peoples posed potentially serious problems to the new rulers. Several waves of settlers and soldiers were brought to Spain from Islamic countries to compensate, and given lands vacated by the Christians who had fled to the north. They were generally settled according to their tribal groups, which proved to be a grave mistake that led to bitter inter-tribal jealousy, conflict and, ultimately, to civil war. This was only one important factor in an already fundamentally unstable political situation reflected in the fact that 19 different governors ruled Cordova in the 30 years between 716 and 747.[11] The situation began to be resolved under the governor Yusef al-Fihri (747–56 CE) who installed members of his own family in key positions in many leading cities, thus stabilizing the situation throughout al-Andalus. This stability was not to last, however, for after 750, discontented southern Arabs who were hostile to Yusef's rule, demanded that Prince Abd al-Rahaman ibn Muawiya (756–88 CE), who had miraculously survived the massacre of the Umayyad family, be given ultimate power throughout Spain.[12]

The Creation of the Spanish 'March'

The potential for expansion of Moorish Spain was severely limited in the East by an astute statesman and brilliant warrior of the Rex Deus line, Charles the Great, otherwise known as Charlemagne (742–814 CE). The grandson of Charles Martel, Charlemagne first succeeded to the throne jointly with his brother Carloman. After the death of Carloman, Charlemagne reunited his divided kingdom and began a series of successful wars to expand it until, eventually, as Holy Roman Emperor; he ruled a territory that stretched from the Danube to the Mediterranean. He made several forays into Moorish Spain and while he was unsuccessful in the north, in the south he captured several important areas collectively known as the Spanish Marches which acted as a bulwark against further Moorish incursions eastwards into Christian territory. Behind this line of defence, he consolidated the empire's hold on Septimania, an area that had once been settled by the seventh legion of the Roman army, now the Languedoc/Rousillion area of southwestern France.

Jewish Septimania

Not long before the Moorish invasion of Spain, Jews fleeing persecution instituted by the Visigoths, settled in Septimania. This considerable and prosperous Jewish community eventually came to live under the guidance of their own nasi, or prince, whose appointment was first authorized by Pepin the Short, King of the

Franks (747–68 CE) and father of Charlemagne, after the capture of Narbonne in 759.[13] Perhaps this proposed installation of a Jewish prince in Christian Europe was an act of gratitude in recognition of the fact that the Jews of Narbonne delivered the city to the Franks in return for a promise of self-government under their own king, a matter recorded in several Hebrew and papal documents.[14]

After the capture of Narbonne, the Jews of Septimania were clearly perceived as a highly privileged group, richly endowed with freehold estates granted to them by the Carolingian kings.[15] Their protection was assured by Charlemagne himself who knew where the true commercial interests of his empire lay, for the Jews, as had been proven in the empire of Islam, were the keys to success in international trade. Many charters testifying to the granting of protection and privileges to Jewish merchants are still extant.[16]

Charlemagne used the services of a Jew, Isaac by name, as an interpreter for the ambassador he sent to Harun-al-Rashid, caliph of Baghdad, in 797. As a result of this ambassadorial visit, the first *nasi*, or Jewish prince of Narbonne, a certain Rabbi Makhi, came from Baghdad to Septimania, where Charlemagne endowed him with great possessions.[17] There was another, equally important, reason for Charlemagne's determined protection of the Jews, for the historian of the Carolingian era, P Munz, writing long before any public disclosure of the Rex Deus traditions, asserted that Charlemagne claimed descent from the biblical kings of Israel. Munz concluded that Charlemagne deliberately engineered the situation in Septimania to arrange a marriage between his family and that of the *nasi*, who was also descended from the Davidic line. An alliance, that the emperor hoped, would demonstrate that the Carolingian dynasty had divine sanction as rulers.[18]

However, the most important responsibility of the new Nasi Makhir was to lead the Jews of Septimania and the Toulousain in the defence of the Spanish frontier and the Mediterranean coast, against raids by the Umayyad Moors of Spain and North Africa.[19] Thus, Charlemagne's motivation was many-faceted: it was commercial and directed towards trade; it encouraged Jewish scholarship as well as commerce; but, most importantly it had primarily a strong defensive element and also provided a unique opportunity for the union of two royal houses in marriage, with both claiming descent from the House of David. This complex range of aims and objectives succeeded beyond all expectations.

The descendants of the *nasi* were, with one exception, loyal supporters of the Carolingian dynasty throughout their long reign. The Jewish community in Narbonne grew steadily and prospered until the expulsion of the Jews from France under King Philippe le Bel in 1306, and records disclose that the Jews maintained considerable estates in the Narbonnais from the time of Pepin the Short until at least the middle of the eleventh century. Indeed, the noted Jewish chronicler Benjamin of Tudela wrote as late as the twelfth century:

> Narbonne is an ancient city of the Torah. From it the Torah goes out to all lands. Therein there are sages, magnates and princes (nas'im) at the head of whom is R Kalonymo... a descendant of the House of David as stated in his family tree. He holds hereditaments and [other] landed properties from the rulers of the country and no one may dispossess him by force.[20]

The extensive properties held by the Jews and their nasi at the time of their expulsion indicates that they occupied a sizeable portion of the countryside and city until the early years of the fourteenth century.[21]

Charlemagne's protection of the Jews, along with his statesmanship, military prowess and commercial acumen led to a growing reputation and an ever-expanding kingdom. To keep order within his sprawling dominions, he used the royal prerogative of *gratia* to create a warrior aristocracy,[22] rewarding his supporters and loyal aids by the granting of rank and lands. Within the empire, Charlemagne created over 600 counties[23] that enabled his orders to be implemented with considerable efficiency by his loyal counts. Who were the most trustworthy people he could appoint to these positions of power? Other members of the Rex Deus family group were the obvious choice, especially in the regions of greatest potential danger, the Marches or borderlands, which were ruled by a marquess and, under him, a number of counts. Thus, by the time of Charlemagne's death in 814, much of Europe – particularly France, Septimania, Provence, northern Italy and Saxony – were administered by nobility of the Rex Deus line.[24]

The Umayyad Dynasty in al-Andalus

The last surviving scion of the deposed Umayyad family, Prince Abd al-Rahaman I, landed in southern Spain in 755. In May 756, he defeated Governor Yusef outside the walls of Cordova and captured the capital, but forbade any looting by his troops. This merciful action persuaded the other cities to submit peacefully to his authority and Abd al-Rahaman I proclaimed himself emir of al-Andalus (756–88 CE). Thus came to power the one man above all others who can truly be called the great creator of Islamic Spain.

Abd al-Rahaman established close links between al-Andalus and his former homeland for both culture and commerce, and paid particular attention to enhancing agricultural production by means of accurate surveying and the installation of highly efficient irrigation canals. Sugar, cotton, rice and several varieties of fruit, vegetables and spices were imported from the Orient and all over the country, granaries were constructed to prevent famine occurring at times of shortage.[25] Industry was also actively encouraged, and among the most important occupations in al-Andalus were silk and wool manufacture; dyeing and leatherwork in the area around Cordova; armaments and steel from Toledo, while the Almeria became a centre for ceramics.[26] Commercial progress contributed greatly to the growing stability of the political situation.

Since the Battle of Poitiers in 732, there had been little overall political discipline in Spain, particularly in the north where the Pyrenees offered impregnable retreats to those dissatisfied with central government, for to local governors, or vali, it often seemed preferable to turn for help to the Franks rather than bend before the stern authority of the emir. Therefore, it is not surprising to learn that it took several decades before the restored Umayyad prince and his successors were fully accepted by the chiefs of the Arab and Syrian marauders. Nonetheless, under the rule of the Umayyad dynasty, the ninth century came to represent the peak of cultural achievement not only in Spain but in the entire European continent. The rise of Cordova was ensured by Abd al-Rahman II (822–52 CE), who devoted much time to cultural matters and began the construction of public buildings in Cordova that are still a source of pride in Spain today. During his reign, the Jewish population of Granada was estimated to be over 5,000, so it is no wonder that the Muslims called the city *Gharnatat al-Yahud*, the City of the Jews.[27]

It was Abd al-Rahaman III (912–61 CE) who succeeded at the age of 22 and finally unified the Islamic territories in Spain when he re-conquered Seville and Mérida and expelled the rival clan of Hasfun from al-Andalus. Exploiting the political weakness in the Christian lands, he concluded a treaty of protection with the kingdoms of León and Navarre who, in consequence, recognized Abd al-Rahaman III as the de facto ruler and arbiter in all Spain. Even the strong Christian kingdoms of Castille and Barcelona in the Spanish March paid him tribute. When, in January 929, he named himself caliph, Cordova became the third caliphate in Islam along with the caliphates of Baghdad and Cairo.[28]

The Caliphate of Cordova

The new caliph created a new and a strictly centralized internal administration, thus ensuring the country's rapid growth in prosperity based upon his grandfather's insistence on extensive irrigation and efficient agriculture. The arts flourished along with agriculture and Muslim sophistication paved the way for the new rulers to found trade guilds for skilled craftsmen who were prized and well rewarded.[29] The formulation of a just and effective tax system resulted in overflowing state coffers and allowed trade concessions for the Jews. All these factors, allied to sound municipal administration, enabled al-Andalus to become the most populous country in Europe at that time. Cordova, its capital, thrived as an economic and cultural centre to such an extent that it was compared favourably with Constantinople, the capital of the Byzantine Empire and may, indeed, have even exceeded that city as a centre of learning.[30]

The caliph's son, Crown Prince al-Hakkam (961–76 CE) shared in government from the age of 40, and, as caliph, continued to build upon his ancestor's achievements. A peace-loving and scholarly man, during his time as crown prince he surrounded himself with scientists and scholars and amassed many books, following the example of previous emirs who had also owned great libraries and attracted poets, philosophers and mathematicians to their courts.[31] In Cordova, Caliph al-Hakkam created a library of 400,000 books which were indexed in 44 catalogues, and he added his own commentaries to many of these volumes.[32] Thus Cordova became home to one of the greatest libraries in Europe, second only to the greatest in the world located in Baghdad at the heart of the Islamic Empire. This almost insatiable passion for learning, stimulated the production of between 70,000 and 80,000 bound volumes each year, which not only reflected local demand but also demonstrated the country's capacity for a phenomenal high-volume, top-quality production, many centuries before the invention of printing. Sciences, such as geography, agriculture and irrigation, astronomy, medicine and mathematics were actively encouraged, as was the serious study of philosophy based principally on classical Greek thought. With the expulsion of the persecuted Nestorian scholars from Europe as a result of Christian intolerance, the Arab world had become home to this vast collection of Greek learning in mathematics, philosophy and science, which now took root and flourished in Spain along with knowledge of classical medicine.[33]

It was not just the fruits of Greek civilization that came by this tortuous route into European consciousness, for along with them came more recent advances in medicine, art and architecture. Much of the classical knowledge of ancient Greece that we now treasure and take for granted would have withered away had it not been preserved and enhanced by Islamic scholars.[34] As caliph, al-Hakkam now commissioned many scholarly works on ethics, statecraft and history, taking a personal interest in popular literacy and education, establishing schools and centres of learning open to people of every social class. Thus his reign is rightly renowned as the apotheosis of science, scholarship and poetry in the history of Moorish Spain.[35]

Cordova eventually became the dominant centre of Islamic culture during the ninth century. The phases of construction of its extraordinary mosque, which became the second largest in all of Islam, reflect the cultural changes that took place between 785 and 980. Roman methods, still active, brought interesting new forms to oriental ideas: superimposed tiers of many-coloured arches and ribbed cupolas. This continuity with pre-Muslim tradition reflects the prosperity of this part of al-Andalus, famous for its weapons, leather goods and silks; an area whose growth and stability had never suffered serious attack or disturbance from Christian enemies – neither the Franks from across the Spanish Marches nor those Spaniards who had taken refuge in the northwest of Spain.[36]

The Jews, who were being treated as second-class citizens in the rest of Europe north of Spain and Septimania, enjoyed a rich cultural renaissance of their own[37] and the large Christian population was also allowed full religious liberty in Spain, as throughout the Islamic Empire. Most Spanish Christians were extremely proud to belong to a highly advanced and sophisticated culture that was light years ahead of the rest of Europe.[38] The legacy of Moorish Spain to the later development of European culture is considerable. Mozarabic Spanish Christian scholars and their texts later supplied much of the raw material for the emerging literature of the West.[39] Thus the variety of literary creation in Spain was both broader and richer than that which arose in the caliphate of Baghdad or North Africa.[40]

Under the rule of the Umayyad caliphs, Moorish Spain gained international renown for the poetry, literature and learning of both Cordova and Granada. The well-attended and richly endowed colleges in Andalusia were later to provide a model and a template for those founded in Oxford and Cambridge in England.[41] In an era when the vast majority of European Christian nobles, kings and emperors were barely literate, the Islamic Umayyad court at Cordova was the most splendid in Europe; one that provided a haven and an oasis of peace wherein philosophers, poets, artists, mathematicians and astronomers could pursue their studies.[42] This tradition continued long after the fall of the Umayyads, for later during the height of Abbasid power, Spain continued to enjoy an era of unexampled, independent prosperity.[43]

It was in the tolerant atmosphere of Muslim Spain that Jewish science found its most fertile soil with substantial and important contributions being made in many areas: medicine; geography; cosmology; developments of instruments for measurement, cartography and navigation, and, as importantly, with the translation of works from Greek into Arabic and from Arabic into Latin and other European languages. In Andalusia, as in the Muslim world at large, the Jews wrote their scientific, medical and philosophical treatises in Arabic, a language that they found best suited to this branch of human learning. It was as a result of this combination of the innate Islamic respect for learning and Jewish scholarship that the West first came into contact with classical Greek science and its Arabic commentators. In Toledo in al-Andalus, and in other centres in Septimania, Jewish scholars translated works in philosophy, mathematics, geometry, physics, astronomy, astrology, medicine, and magic, and thus provided the basis for the Latin science that evolved during the central and late Middle Ages.[44]

From the early tenth century, the previously unified Islamic Empire had already begun to fragment into smaller states, yet despite this apparent disunity, most remained highly sophisticated centres of wealth and learning that provided a fertile environment for both economic and cultural life.[45] As a result of their integration into what became, in effect, an Islamic free-trade zone, both Moorish Spain and the Islamic states in North Africa developed lucrative trade deals with the Levant.[46] This resulted in a sustained level of prosperity that lasted for nearly seven centuries; one that has left us an architectural and artistic heritage that is still a source of wonder to the modern world. Yet this magnificent and still highly visible flowering of art and architecture, important though it is, pales almost into insignificance when compared to the achievements in literature, poetry, medicine, mathematics and philosophy that accompanied it.

Spiritual Schools in Muslim Spain

It was not only secular learning that flourished under the benevolent rule of the Muslim caliphs in Spain. Religious and spiritual schools abounded in all three of the main religious communities; Muslim madrasas, Jewish yeshivas and Christian seminaries operated side by side in this tolerant country, each operating according to the religious requirements of their own community. The seminaries provided the priests necessary to minister to the large and flourishing Christian population. Jewish yeshivas provided the opportunity for the rigorous Bible study that was such an integral part of medieval Judaism. They also acted as centres of scholarship that refined and enhanced the various respected oral traditions of mysticism within the Hebraic tradition, such as the *maaseh bereshith*, based on the work of creation described in the first chapter of Genesis, and the *maaseh merkabah*, founded on accounts of Ezekiel's vision of the divine chariot; 'the Psalms of ascents' that is the mystical ascents to the higher heavens, or the ascent through the various degrees of Neoplatonic enlightenment or gnosis in another variation of the Merkabah tradition known as Hekaloth.[47] These now developed into a written form known as the kabbalah with its earliest version attributed to Aaron ben Samuel in Italy at the beginning of the tenth century.

The classical kabbalah is, allegedly, the oldest initiatory, mystical tradition that was received from Aaron and then passed down from master to pupil in an oral form of teaching that only reached written completion in the thirteenth century CE. The *Sefer ha-Zohar* or Book of Splendour expressed its principal aspects, mainly Jewish Gnosticism tinged with Sufi mysticism, recently synthesized Neoplatonism and magic.[48] It was written about 1280 and spread into Christian Europe from the rabbinical schools in Moorish

Spain and Septimania. Regular contact between Septimania and Spain were well established and yeshivas in Narbonne and Montpellier are now acknowledged to have played an important role in creating the first full written versions.[49] The *Sefer ha-Zohar* was attributed to the second-century sage and rabbi, Simeon bar Yohai, but took written form from the hand of Moses de León. Later, during the fourteenth and fifteenth centuries, the kabbalah spread into Christian Europe and a Christianized form of it became popular among scholars of a mystical inclination.

The Sufi mystery schools in Spain were the principal open and accessible sources of Muslim mystical teaching in a continent wherein the Christian Church actively discouraged spiritual exploration.[50] Sufism is a mystical tradition that derives its inspiration from the Qur'an and the teaching of the Prophet, and the Sufi orders were all founded by men who claimed spiritual and/or genealogical descent from Muhammed. However, unlike their counterparts within the Christian world who had to operate in secret for fear of persecution, the Sufis were able to operate openly within Islam and contributed significantly to its development. The poet and mythologist Robert Graves claims that Sufism in fact dates back to 2500 BCE and alleges that he found a 'Sufic signature' in accounts of the building of Solomon's Temple in Jerusalem.[51] The grandson of Judaism's greatest thinker, Moses Maimonides (1135–1204), also states that the Sufi tradition is Hebraic in origin when he wrote that Sufism is 'the pride of Israel bestowed upon the world'.[52]

Undoubtedly, the greatest medieval mystical writer was the Sufi teacher from Seville, Mohieddin ibn Arabi (1165–1240) who described the Great Prophet Muhammed as the manifestation of the 'Perfect Man'. Renowned as a mystic, philosopher and poet, ibn Arabi is known among the Sufis as Shaykh al-Akbar, or 'the greatest teacher'. In the West he became known as Doctor Maximus, an accurate translation of his Arabic title. He wrote profusely about the Prophet's mystical journey, ascent and travel through the heavens to Jerusalem, thereby reinforcing the pervasive influence of earlier forms of Jewish mysticism. His sublime poetry, which is even more popular today than it was in the medieval era, profoundly influenced such leading scholars as Friar Roger Bacon, Dante Alighieri, Cervantes, Averroes, St Francis of Assisi and Chaucer. From these brief examples, it is clear that Moorish Spain had a more profound influence on the development of European thought, scholarship and culture than any other single country in European history.

Classical Learning crosses from Spain to Christian Europe

Jewish scholars who could move with ease between Latin, Hebrew and Arabic, provided a vital link in the international dissemination of knowledge.[53] Knowledge of the Greek Classics crept back into European consciousness via the theological college founded by Bishop Fulbert of Chartres (960–1028). Fulbertus' pupils were probably the first in Christian western Europe to read the works of Plato, Aristotle, Pythagoras and Cicero as well as being familiar with mathematics, science and contemporary Arabic inventions such as the astrolabe.[54] Thus, the knowledge taught at Chartres came from that beacon of light in the Dark Ages, Moorish Spain, translated not from Greek, but from Arabic by Jewish scholars. How did this knowledge get from Spain to Chartres? The answer lies in the Rex Deus connection whereby nobles of the hidden family group passed translations of the classics sent by members in Spain to another of their group, Bishop Fulbert.[55]

Fulbert was called 'that venerable Socrates' by his disciples who now truly belonged to the international community of scholars.[56] The twelfth century marked the zenith of the Chartres School: Bernardus of Chartres, Gilbert de la Porée, Thierry of Chartres, and John of Salisbury, were its masters who were celebrated throughout France and attracted pupils from every province and even from abroad.[57] The school at Chartres marked the pivotal time that separated the Dark Ages from the early roots of the Renaissance, for it was from the time of Bernardus of Chartres (d. circa 1130) and Abelard of Paris (1079–1142) that one can date the first important breaching of the dam of ecclesiastically enforced ignorance. It was here that the philosophers of classical Greece were reinstated in the mainstream of European Christian philosophy.[58]

Under the leadership of Gerard of Cremona (1114–87), an influential school of translation developed in Toledo that attracted scholars from all over Europe. Its main area of interest was scientific and mathematical works which included the work of the Muslim Averoës of Cordova (1126–98). It was from this school that the distinguished Abbot of Cluny, Peter the Venerable, commissioned a translation of the Holy Qur'an into Latin in 1141. His motive was to create a scholarly basis for the refutation of Islam.[59]

Chapter 9

~

The West's Debt to Islam

JEWISH MERCHANTS ACCOMPANIED many of the caravans linking the extremities of the Islamic Empire and extended their trading links into Europe where, as in the lands of Islam, they brought the teachings of their yeshiva in Baghdad to many of their communities in the Diaspora.[1] Thus, Islamic tolerance encouraged the unification of Jewish community life throughout the world.[2] In the early years of trade with Europe, exotic goods were carried almost exclusively by these Jewish merchants and their Arab colleagues and, by the middle of the eleventh century, their efforts had created a degree of commercial unity within the Mediterranean area that allowed goods and people to move from one end to the other. However, in the late eleventh century, the virtual monopoly exercised by Islamic and Jewish businessmen was about to be challenged.[3]

Italian merchants, who were growing in power, seized the opportunities presented by the founding of the Kingdom of Jerusalem after the First Crusade. The cities of Genoa, Pisa and Amalfi established trade concessions with the crusader states while the Venetians concentrated their efforts upon breaking into the commercial zone created by the Byzantine Empire in the Aegean and the Black Sea.[4] They were not alone; trade with the countries of Islam was also carried on by merchants in several southern French ports, foremost among them Marseilles, and towns in the Spanish March such as Barcelona.[5] Between 1050 and 1250, western European and Christian merchants gradually broke the monopoly previously enjoyed by the Arabs, Jews and Byzantines.

What drove this surge of European entrepreneurial activity was the gaining of access to trade routes whose extremities lay in exotic countries on the eastern borders of the empire of Islam which no European had ever visited. A Florentine, Francesco Pegolotti, edited a book for merchants in about 1330, and in it listed nearly 300 'spices', most of which were imported from these eastern countries. The simple word 'spice' was one which covered a multitude of commodities: pharmaceutical ingredients, dyestuffs, cosmetic materials, and exotic fruits as well as the culinary spices such as cinnamon, cumin, dates, fenugreek, five types of ginger, indigo, madder, musk, opium, sandalwood, silk-worm eggs and turpentine.[6] Goods that were so highly desirable in Europe that the customers were prepared to pay a high price for them. The eventual linking of this Mediterranean commerce with the maritime trade of northern Europe, allied to the growth and development of financial techniques and infrastructures such as commercial partnerships, banking and credit facilities and accounting, ultimately led to the growth of European mercantile capitalism that later achieved world dominance.[7]

Intellectual Commerce

However, it was not trade in commercial goods that dominated contact between the Christian and Muslim worlds, for the most prolific and fruitful interaction between them was to be found in intellectual life. As I have mentioned earlier, the intellectual treasure trove that had been accumulated over the centuries by Islamic scholars began to be translated into Latin, the language of learning in western Christendom, and made available to European intellectuals from the eleventh century onwards. In the opinion of the English historian Richard Fletcher: 'This was a process whose significance in the intellectual history of the world would be hard to exaggerate.'[8] Indeed, Islamic scholarship became the firm foundation on which European culture was established.

I have described how al-Andalus became not merely the greatest cultural centre in Europe but in the entire Mediterranean basin.[9] There, as throughout the Islamic world, Jewish scientists wrote their treatises in Arabic, the language which they deemed best suited to this branch of learning. Early in the mid-tenth century, one leader of the Jewish community in Spain, Hisdai ibn Shaprut, who was also a high official in the court of the caliph at Cordova and an eminent physician, helped to transform the Arabic language into a scientific vehicle by composing a superb Arabic version of the *Materia Medica*, the great pharmaceutical compendium originally compiled in the first century CE by the Greek botanist, Dioscrides.[10] In Spain, Jews participated in the translation from Arabic to Latin of classical works of philosophy, serving thereby as a bridge between the culture of the ancient world and that of Europe in the Middle Ages.[11] Indeed, despite the bitter and burdensome trials they endured throughout the Diaspora, the spiritual and intellectual creativity of the Jewish people remained vibrant.[12]

The historian Louise Cochran described the scholar Adelard of Bath (*c*.1080–*c*.1150), as 'the first English scientist'.[13] Adelard travelled widely in Syria and the Norman Kingdom of Sicily for seven years in the early part of the twelfth century. In the course of these travels, he learned Arabic and acquired a considerable number of scholarly books. His corpus of written work comprises two translations from the Arabic, and several compositions of his own, all of which display his debt to Arab scholarship. He translated Euclid's *Elements* and thus introduced the European world to the most influential book on geometry ever written – it became the standard teaching text in the West for the next 800 years. By translating *Zijj*, the astronomical tables of al-Khwârizmî (d. 840) revised by Maslama al-Madjriti of Madrid (d. 1007) he brought the most up-to-date astronomical knowledge to the Western world. Composing a textbook on the abacus and another on the use of the astrolabe, Adelard made a significant intellectual contribution right at the start of an era of intense translation that resulted in the outpouring of a veritable cornucopia of knowledge to the immense benefit of European scholarship.

The vast majority of these translations were made in Spain and Italy and very few in Outremer, as the Holy Land was now called. In Italy, scholars mainly translated directly from Greek into Latin, and in this manner, James of Venice, who was a contemporary of Adelard, brought many of Aristotle's scientific works to the attention of Western scholars. In Spain, translations were mainly of Arabic works which included Arabic versions of classical Greek texts. The perceived disadvantage of working at one remove from the original text was more than compensated for by also translating a large number of works of commentary and amplification on these texts that had been compiled by Muslim scholars.[14]

With the establishment of the Kingdom of Sicily in the eleventh century, the Normans found themselves masters of a mixed population of Muslims and mainly Greek Christians. Rough and untutored though they were, the new rulers used courtly patronage to encourage an intermingling of cultures which yielded great achievements in scholarship. There were also beautiful accomplishments in the arts and architecture, for example, the Cathedral of Montreale near Palermo, built between 1174 and 1189, which is a sublime blend of the mixed cultural heritage of the island. Count Roger of Sicily (1130–54) commissioned al-Idrîsî, a Tunisian scholar, to produce a majestic work of geography called the *Book of Roger*. However, in 1223, the Holy Roman Emperor, Frederick II, deported most of the remaining Muslims to the southern Italian mainland where, little by little, they were assimilated into Christian culture.[15] The county of Champagne became famous as the home of the great Bible commentator, Rachi, while Provence and the Spanish March became the cradle of kabbalah, and the home of philosophical and ethical literature. All these achievements became precious assets of the literary and spiritual heritage of the Jewish people.[16]

Europe's First Universities

As I have mentioned, knowledge of the Greek Classics crept back into European consciousness from Spain via the theological college founded by Bishop Fulbert of Chartres in 990 CE.[17] That great scholar, Bernardus of Chartres said of the ancient Greek scholars: 'If we can see further than they could, it is not because of the strength of our own vision, it is because we are raised up by them and borne at a prodigious height. We are dwarves mounted on the shoulders of giants.'[18]

Chartres was not the only school of theology, there was another at Notre Dame de Paris and several more at other ecclesiastical centres in the vicinity. When the chancellor of Notre Dame tried to enforce his authority over the teachers and pupils within his diocese, they rebelled, for they wanted the right to appoint teachers and train students of the highest intellectual calibre, not just accept people in either capacity who had simply found favour with the Church. The rebels formed a *conjuratio*, a community of both the teachers and the taught, later called a *universitas*. They then sought papal approval for their new institution and, at or about 1200, they were granted certain privileges by King Philippe II and in 1208 gained the right to make their own regulations from Pope Innocent III. Paris University had been born.

The precursor of Oxford University was founded when a theologian from Paris, Roger Pullen, arrived there in 1133. By 1263, this establishment was a full university which claimed to be *schola secunda ecclesia*, second only to Paris. Cambridge University was founded soon afterwards and more followed in other European cities in the following years. The Church was, at long last, losing its stifling stranglehold on education. It was the well-known and respected colleges in al-Andalus that became the models on which Oxford and Cambridge were based.[19] These independent centres of learning in Christian countries, now studying the ever-increasing flow of scholarly works emerging from the world of Islam, gave European culture an impetus whose rapid development would, a few centuries later, equal and then outstrip its Islamic benefactor.

Jewish and Christian biblical scholars not only confronted one another in religious disputations but also met and learned from one another. Jewish help was sought by Christians to assist in deciphering difficult biblical passages and the phrase *hebraeus meus dicit* – a Jew told me – is frequently found in the writings of Andreas, a pupil of Adelard in the twelfth century.[20] The three related world religions of Judaism, Christianity and Islam rest upon divine revelations granted to humankind that are recorded in the sacred scriptures. This provided one area in which the rediscovery of classical Greek thought, especially the works of Aristotle, presented a serious challenge. His philosophical system claimed that the world was intelligible without revelation, and all that was required was the toolkit of reason: observation, measurement, logical inference, demonstrable causes and effects.

Two contemporaries, one Muslim and one Jewish, attempted to resolve these disquieting questions. Averroës (1126–98) made his response in commentaries on Aristotle as well as by a number of his own treatises, one of which bore the significant title of *On The Harmony of Religion and Philosophy*. Rabbi Moses Maimonides (1138–1204) who was born in Spain but lived in Egypt, composed the Jewish answers in his *Guide for the Perplexed*. The Christian answer necessarily came some time later, long after both Maimonides and Averroës were translated into Latin. The most notable and authoritative Christian response came from St Thomas Aquinas (c.1225–74) whose resolution of the conflicting claims of reason and revelation became the standard in the Catholic realms. In his own work, Aquinas cites Averroës more frequently than any other non-Christian thinker; indeed Averroës commentaries upon Aristotle were so highly regarded among theologians of the time that he became known simply as 'the Commentator'.[21]

The vast Islamic storehouse of intellectual excellence was far from exhausted, translations continued in every field of scholarly endeavour. Probably the most prolific of the Christian translators was Gerard of Cremona who spent nearly 50 years in Toledo, from circa 1140 until his death in 1187. While living there he translated nearly 90 works from Arabic into Latin. Over half dealt with mathematics, astronomy and related sciences; a third with medicine; and the rest with philosophy and logic. All these branches of knowledge became integral parts of the foundation for the so-called intellectual renaissance of the twelfth and thirteenth centuries.[22] In Spain, King Alfonso of Castille (1252–84) assembled a team of scholars who produced works in the vernacular, translated from Arabic: encyclopaedias of astronomy and astrology, an illustrated account of chess and other games and a guide to precious stones and their medicinal properties.

Education Gains Ground

If we assess the level of educational development a century or so after Adelard, we can begin to appreciate the full extent of the intellectual harvest that had been gathered. A wide range of Greek or Arab authors had now become available to scholars such as Robert Grosseteste, the Bishop of Lincoln (d.1253) and his pupil Roger Bacon (d.1292). It was an intellectual resource that would have astounded the scholars of Adelard's day. Learning had now moved away from the monasteries, with their deep, dogmatic conservative syllabus of study almost exclusively concerned with the Bible and the writings of the early Church fathers. Thirteenth-century scholars now studied and argued in new universities at Paris, Bologna and Oxford. Institutions free of Church domination, equipped with libraries, lecture halls and a vast new range of textbooks. The whole atmosphere of scholarship had changed so much that the thirteenth century became, recognizably, a part of the emerging modern world.[23]

Geometry was not the only mathematical subject that crossed from Islam into Christian Europe. Algebra, the development of instruments of measurement, cartography and navigation were also among the subjects translated by the Jewish scholars of Muslim Spain who thus played a role in creating the tools that would prove so useful in world exploration.[24] Part of this was based on the work of al-Bîrûnû, a highly skilled maker of scientific instruments who took sightings in 1018 near the modern city of Islamabad, on which he based calculations of the radius and circumference of the earth that were astonishingly accurate – only 15 and 200 kilometres in error, respectively, from the most modern estimates. The numerical system that we have used since the thirteenth century is Arabic in origin. The counting machine known as the abacus was brought to western Europe from Catalonia by the Frenchman Gerbert of Aurilliac in 960 CE. An effective system of accounting that was developed in the Empire of Islam in order to levy tolls on trade soon crossed the religious divide and became Europeanized. Even the English word 'customs', which translates into other European languages as *aduana*, *dogana*, or *douane* is derived from the Arabic word *dîwân* meaning account book

Islam's Medicine Chest

Western knowledge of the art of medicine, about which Usâma ibn Munqidh had been so scathing in twelfth-century Outremer, became totally transformed and reinvigorated by knowledge seeping into Europe from the empire of Islam. In the mid-eleventh century at the Benedictine monastery at Monte Casino in southern Italy, a monk called Constantine 'the African' because he came from Tunisia, started to translate medical works from Arabic into Latin because, in his own words, 'among Latin books I could find no author who gave certain or reliable information'.[25] Later, Gerard of Cremona translated Avicenna's *Cannon* and more than 25 other medical works. Averroës' medical masterpiece *Kulliyat* was added to the Latin corpus in the thirteenth century alongside several other works so that at the beginning of the fourteenth century a huge body of Greek and Arabic writings on medicine and related subjects was available in Europe. They dealt with a wide range of medical subjects and included catalogues of medicinal drugs and practical treatises on surgery or uroscopy. Schools of medicine had already been founded, such as that at Montpellier, where these texts were studied and practical skills learnt by the aspiring practitioners.

One example of the fruits of this explosion of medical learning can be seen in the life of Arnold of Vilanova. Arnold studied at Montpellier in the 1260s and remained attached to the medical school throughout his career and in 1309 he became the principal advisor for the papal statutes that regulated the syllabus of studies there. He was a prolific author who also translated medical books by Galen and Avicenna from Arabic into Latin. He wrote one work, a tract on military hygiene, for King James of Aragon, and also an important treatise on medical theory, the *Speculum Medicine* – The Mirror of Medicine.

At this time there was a vibrant growth in medical expertise in the territories that made up the Aragonese federation, centred mainly in the cities of Barcelona and Valencia. Medical training was in a state of constant improvement and in these centres of excellence there was an abundance of medical practitioners at every level from apothecaries to surgeons. They were developing a strong sense of collective identity, were imbued with justifiable professional pride, and played a valued role in their communities. All this progress was the outcome of the previous two centuries' translating activity, for the provision of health care in Christian Europe had improved dramatically as the fruits of Muslim research and scholarship became more widely available.[26]

Early Sociology?

Another early Islamic scientific study that has been tentatively linked with medicine, and has recently been investigated in depth for the first time in a ground-breaking study by Peter Biller entitled *The Measure of Multitude; Population in Medieval Thought*. This field of enquiry necessitated the development of disciplined thinking on the subject of population: its size, distribution, sex-ratio, marriage and procreation, disease levels and mortality. Biller demonstrates how medieval thought about population was again founded firmly on translations of classical Greek texts, especially those of Aristotle, and then developed further by comparing and contrasting the populations and cultures of Christendom with what they believed about the Islamic world or the worlds beyond it.

Useful Techniques

What we would now call technology was another benefit that passed from the world of Islam to Christian Europe. One age-old example of this was the raising of water for irrigation purposes by an animal-powered machine called a *saqiya*. In this, an animal is harnessed to a draw bar that turns a horizontal wheel which then turns a vertical one by gearing. The vertical wheel has pots fixed to its circumference which fill with water as it turns. Another was the abacus mentioned earlier. A third example is paper-making which spread from China to Baghdad before the end of the eighth century and then, over the following two centuries, throughout the Islamic Empire.[27] The Astrolabe was another simple invention that opened literally boundless opportunities to the Europeans and enabled the monk Nicolas of Lynne to make an exploration of the North Atlantic in the mid-fourteenth century.

The manufacture of high-quality coloured glass was passed by the Jews of Tyre to the Venetians who still benefit from this industry to this day.[28] Optical glass-making and the manufacture of lenses was another branch of technology that came to Europe from the Islamic Empire. Unlikely as it may seem, the most beautiful stained glass in Chartres Cathedral owes its manufacture to secret techniques that were brought from the East. These windows were created by master craftsmen using scientific knowledge that had been discovered by the Knights Templar in the Holy Land.[29] Indeed the earliest stained window-glass in the historical record was created by adepts in Persia at the beginning of the eleventh century. The French mystical writer, Louis Charpentier, claims that it was first produced at laboratories of such alchemists before the secrets were passed on to other initiates on a long journey that culminated in Europe.[30] However, it is not just the beautiful stained-glass windows that adorn Europe's great Gothic cathedrals that we owe to our Islamic brethren, it is also the basic architecture of the cathedrals themselves.

The Gothic Arch

The basic principle of Gothic architecture is the pointed arch that enabled the medieval masons to build to previously unprecedented heights in such a graceful style. Both the gifted English architectural historian, William Anderson, and the French scholar, Jean Boney, claim that the Gothic arch was introduced from Islamic culture.[31] My good friend Gordon Strachan is convinced that the origin of the pointed arch lies outside Europe and agrees with both William Anderson and Jean Boney that its origin is Islamic and, furthermore, that it came from the Holy Land. Gordon believes that the Gothic arch results from, 'a unique blending of indigenous building skills with the architectural genius of Islam'.[32]

The Templars, during their residence in Jerusalem, met members of the Sufi orders who were undergoing a revival in their fortunes at that time.[33] The Sufis were the main mystical order of Islam who were devout believers in a mystical form of inter-faith pluralism epitomized by the words of Jalaluddin Rumi: 'The religion of love is apart from all religions. The lovers of God have no religion but God alone.' Strachan claims that as a result of their contact with the Sufis, the Templars learnt the geometric method used to design the Islamic *mukhammas* or pointed arch. They put this to the test in Jerusalem building a three-bayed doorway with pointed arches on the Temple Mount that can still be seen today. Thus knowledge of sacred geometry gained an immense boost from contact between the initiatory orders of both faiths, and the end result was the development of the pointed arch into a totally new style of sacred building.

Jewish Scholarship

The benefits that accrued to Christian Europe as a result of this intense period of intellectual interchange and stimulation also rubbed off on the people who did the bulk of the translation work, namely the Jews. In the tolerant atmosphere of Muslim Spain they created a body of literature that was far richer than anything they had achieved in the Abassid caliphate of Baghdad or in North Africa.[34] However, while biblical studies flourished among the Jews in Christian Europe, their literary output there never reached the heights it achieved in the Andalusian period, but, nonetheless it had an important significance of its own.[35]

In Egypt, however, the contribution made by Rabbi Moses Maimonides, known as Rambam (1135–1204), is truly incalculable, encompassing every aspect of contemporary Jewish life, and his influence extended far beyond his lifetime and his country of residence. His writings were wide and varied, including scriptural commentaries, *Halakhah* (*Mishneh Torah*), medicine, epistles, philosophy and science. In his *Guide for the Perplexed* he created a complete philosophical system to interpret Jewish scripture. The book grappled with problems posed by both Christianity and Islam and the threat they posed to the spiritual and physical survival of the Jewish people.[36] The book was primarily intended for the Jewish intellectual who was firm in his faith but, having studied philosophy, was perplexed by biblical anthropomorphism. Aware of the dangers of teaching esoteric matters to the masses, the great thinker wrote in an enigmatic style, making contradictory statements, employing paradoxes and ultimately leaving the perceptive reader to uncover the author's true ideas.[37]

The contribution of the Jewish people to the development of European culture by the services they provided in translation, the dissemination of learning and their vast contribution to the art of medicine were, sadly, not greeted with gratitude by the Christian states in which they lived. However, slowly, the European world was changing, for explorers such as Marco Polo began to travel to Eastern lands and record their experiences for posterity. A growing awareness of the size and strange nature of the rest of the world was strengthened by the writings of Rubruck, de Joinville and others.

The period of 1250–1320 was an important development in the growth of the European mind, for while the mental horizons of the eleventh-century warriors who had listened to the *Chanson de Roland*, were narrow and strictly limited, by the early fourteenth century, however, Westerners were becoming aware that the world contained mountains and seas, animals and peoples, customs and beliefs that were unimaginably different from what was familiar to them at home. It cannot be wholly coincidental that the same period should have left us evidence of the first faint dawning of the notion that there might be a plurality of religions in the world as well. This was indeed a critically important development in the maturing of the mind of European Christendom, but one that would take a very long time to come to fruition.[38] For despite the belated interest in scholarship in some of the Christian countries, the on-going contrast in attitudes to learning and religious toleration between Christian and Islamic cultures had been made brutally obvious at the time of the Crusades. When enlightened Christians were sitting at the feet of Muslim scholars in Spain, others delighted in butchering 'infidels' after the capture of Jerusalem.

Part Four

◆

CHRISTIAN EUROPE AND THE
RESPONSE TO ISLAM

LIFE FOR THE MAJORITY OF people in mainland Christian Europe was short, brutal and barbaric when compared with the sophisticated, learned and tolerant regime in Islamic Spain. There, the religious tolera-tion that was an integral part of Islam, allied to a high degree of political stability, ensured prosperity for the masses and education for the many, irrespective of their religious faith and, above all, toleration for the People of the Book.

The often confusing stream of events that we call history, rarely con-forms to the needs of any thematic chronicler, therefore to understand the development of seemingly perpetual hostility that exists between the worlds of Christianity and Islam we need to go back in time. At first, the response of the Christians in the west of Europe to the rise of Islam was minimal until the warriors of North Africa invaded Spain. There, after a remarkably brief campaign, the answer was found in flight to the remain-ing Christian enclaves in the northeastern provinces of that country. Armed resistance to Muslim incursions into the land of the Franks, present-day France, were vigorously resisted and the Moorish advance was halted and then reversed at the Battle of Poitiers by Charles Martel. However, Charlemagne's policy of containment resulted in the creation of a series of buffer states that limited any further major advance of the forces of Islam into his territory. Thus, Septimania and the Spanish Marches came into being. The lands of the Spanish March included Barcelona which was contiguous with the northern Christian Kingdom of Navarre. The Muslim occupation of the Byzantine territories of Sicily and Malta lasted a little over a century and Islamic rule over these islands was effectively ended with the creation of the Norman Kingdom of Sicily and Southern Italy in 1071.

Chapter 10

~

Europe and the Roots of Holy War

THE WHOLE OF CHRISTENDOM was shocked and appalled when Jerusalem fell to the armies of Islam in 638, but in line with the basic principles of their faith, the Muslim conquerors were surprisingly tolerant of their Christian subjects. Indeed, many of the Christians now under the rule of the Islamic Empire preferred the life they led under their new political masters to that which they had endured for centuries under a succession of Byzantine emperors, who taxed them excessively and often persecuted them for their 'heretical' beliefs; heretical at least in the eyes of the rulers of Constantinople but, nonetheless, firmly held beliefs in Palestine, Syria and Egypt. Their new Muslim overlords now allowed them to believe whatever they wished and worship as they thought fit.[1]

The Limitations of Christendom

Christian Europe after the Council of Nicea in 325 CE was far from tolerant, for Christianity was an exclusive religion that Constantine the Great and his successors used as a unifying force to bind all their subjects to the imperial government.[2] With the fall of the Western Empire in the fifth century CE, wave upon wave of nomadic barbarians from across the Rhine and the Danube swept repeatedly across the Roman world, and the fabric of Western civilization disintegrated. By the final decades of the sixth century, a blanket of darkness enveloped the old heartlands of Rome. Pope Gregory the Great (590–604 CE) actually welcomed a virulent epidemic which was devastating Italy at that time with the words: 'When we consider the way in which other men have died... we may take comfort from the type of death which threatens us.'[3]

During the following centuries, little could be done to halt this slide towards destruction and decay, indeed, much hastened it, except in Charlemagne's time.[4] Long-distance trade had all but died, except that mostly carried on by Jews and Levantines in expensive and much prized luxuries such as jewellery, carved ivory, and incense for the Church. Thus, each small community was forced to become as self-supporting and self-reliant as possible.[5] As described in an earlier chapter, the Frankish state that developed under Charlemagne was extensive and powerful, yet compared to the Islamic Empire ruled by Harun al-Rashid, it was like a minnow placed beside a whale. Charlemagne's power depended upon the loyalty of a fundamentally unruly military aristocracy. These great families lorded it over their domains by military might rather than with any recognizable form of administrative government.

Literacy was limited to members of the clergy and, even among those who took holy orders it was vestigial, at least at the lower levels. Reading and writing were skills that were not prized in Europe, as they were in the Islamic world. The scientific and philosophical learning of ancient Greece had been swept away due to the Church's innate intolerance of anything tinged with pagan influence. The learning of classical antiquity had been replaced with a narrow and limited 'Christianized' intellectual culture based principally on the Bible and the works of the early Latin Fathers of the Church, such as St Augustine of Hippo. A deeply conservative and narrow culture thus developed, that looked inwards and backwards to the early years of the Church and no further.[6]

By the end of Charlemagne's reign, Muslim power dominated the Western end of the Mediterranean from Catalonia in Spain to

Tunis in North Africa. Moorish pirates preyed upon Christian shipping, the forces of Islam built castles in Italy and in Provence, and Rome itself had been sacked by the Muslims in 846.[7] The Islamic conquest of Sicily began in 827 and for more than a generation between 843 and 871, the Muslims maintained an important toehold on the mainland at Bari in Apulia, from which they launched regular raids on the Adriatic coast of Italy and Dalmatia. Ousted eventually from their base in Bari, they acquired another near Naples which they held until 915. Once the hold on Sicily was secure, the maritime regions of Calabria were repeatedly attacked.[8] A troublesome nest of Moorish pirates was also established near the end of the ninth century in the present-day region of Provence at La Garde-Freinet some 30 miles inland from St Tropez. The Saracens terrorized the surrounding area for nearly 80 years until their base at La Garde-Freinet was destroyed in 972.[9] Eventually, in the eleventh century, various bands of Norman mercenaries established themselves in southern Italy and then, gradually, between 1060 and 1091, they successfully wrested both Sicily and Malta from Muslim hands.[10]

In the era before the Crusades, famine was common in Europe in 48 years out of 100. By the eleventh century, invasion by waves of barbarians was no longer the main danger to Western Christian society, for that society had itself become barbarous. War and brutality were endemic; each petty lord fought with his rivals, lords fought against kings, kings fought one another and there was no central authority with sufficient power to control them, much less put an end to their murderous feuds. The kings and lords were simply illiterate thugs who lacked any semblance of honour, who betrayed each other without a qualm, who lied, cheated, raided, tortured and killed in a nightmare world fuelled by fear, greed and ambition.[11] Such literature as there was, the popular epics which were recited rather than read, gave enormous prestige to the military hero and, as a result, the pacifist acquired a disrepute from which he has never recovered.[12]

The Church, which claimed to follow the precepts of the man they called 'the Prince of Peace' namely the gentle Jesus, did at least try to mitigate or limit the extent of this barbarity. The bishops of Aquitaine, meeting to protect the immunity of the clergy at the Council of Charroux in 989, had the courage and commitment to suggest that the Church had a duty to guarantee that the poor might live in peace.[13] This, of course, they could not effectively do, yet, at a synod in Toulouse in Rousillon held in 1027, Oliba, the Bishop of Vichy, forbade all warfare during the hours of Sabbath.[14] This was later extended to include the feast days of the Church and, some time later, the Archbishop of Rouen proclaimed the 'Truce of God', which attempted to limit private wars to only three days a week.[15]

The idea of the 'Truce of God' was well established by the middle of the century, although it was most often honoured by its breach rather than its observance, so the Council of Narbonne held in 1054, sought to co-ordinate it with the idea of the 'Peace of God', which intended to protect the goods of the Church and those of the poor from the effects of war. The basic principle was established that no Christian should slay another Christian 'for he that slays a Christian sheds the blood of Christ'.[16] However, the innate bellicosity of the West and its taste for military glory could not be so easily quenched and so it was deemed more practical to attempt to make use of this barbaric energy by diverting it into warfare against the infidel.[17] Opportunities to do just that were not long in coming.

Fighting the Moors in Spain

In 1014, King Sancho III of Navarre, called the Great after uniting his kingdom with Castille, attempted to organize a league of Christian princes to fight the Moorish invaders. Indeed, war against the infidel in Spain was soon to acquire the status of a holy war and, in time, the popes in Rome began to play a significant role in its organization. Pope Alexander II (1061–73) promised an indulgence, remission of all sins, to all those who fought for the Christian cause in Spain.[18] Events within Muslim Spain conspired to facilitate this move to holy war and reconquest by the Christian armies. The eleventh century had become a time of upheaval in al-Andalus, for the powerful and unitary state centred on Cordova that was so imposing in its tenth-century prime, now experienced disputed claims to the succession, civil war and fragmentation. Its place was taken by a number of petty principalities, small 'city-states' based, for example, on places such as Seville or Valencia and their surrounding countryside, that became known as the minor-states, or *taifa* kingdoms.[19] With the renewed onslaught by the Christians they slowly began to fall one by one and the Castillians captured the important city of Toledo itself in 1085

Warfare and reconquest were not the sole focus of attention for Christianity in Spain. Pilgrimage to the sacred burial site of St James the Great in Compostela had been a major means of expressing religious devotion for centuries. The alleged tomb of the Apostle James was first discovered sometime between 813 and 818 CE but, ironically, the first account of pilgrimage to this site was recorded in 844 CE by the Muslim scholar Ibd Dihya. The prosperous city that grew up around the shrine was sustained by a constant flood of pilgrims who made their perilous way there from all parts of Europe and along the coast of the Christian kingdoms of northern Spain.[20] Pilgrimage was of vital importance to those living in the Dark Ages and the Medieval era that followed; life was hard, brutal and short. The ever-present fear of eternal damnation drove a desperate people to fulfil any demand the Church might make of them, especially one that carried with it the promise of the remission of sins and guaranteed entry into heaven. Thus pilgrimage, and later crusading, had an almost irresistible appeal. A geographical hierarchy of sacred sites of such pilgrimage developed, Compostela in Spain ranked next to Rome, the city where St Peter and St Paul were supposedly buried, and Rome, in its turn, ranked second only to Jerusalem and the holy places of Palestine where Jesus himself had lived. To make a pilgrimage to these places and gain eternal forgiveness for one's sins was everyone's deepest desire. [21]

In the middle of the eleventh century, the situation of Christians living in the Holy Land itself had seldom been so pleasant. The Muslim authorities were lenient, trade with Christian countries overseas was both prospering and increasing and never before had the Christians of Jerusalem seen so much wealth brought to them by the increasing flood of pilgrims from the West;[22] virtually throughout the eleventh century, at least until its last two decades, a seemingly unending stream of pilgrims poured eastward into the Holy Land, sometimes travelling in parties numbering thousands, composed of men and women of every age and class.[23] However, the success of the pilgrimage to Jerusalem depended on the maintenance of two conditions: that life in the Holy Land and the countries surrounding it should be orderly enough for the defenceless pilgrim to traverse in safety; and secondly, that the way should be kept open and cheap enough for the pilgrims to afford.[24]

The happy state of affairs that enabled such mass pilgrimage to take place, namely Muslim tolerance for the People of the Book, apparently came to a sudden end on 19 August 1071. Prior to that time, in 1055, the Seljuk Turks, who had been growing in power for many years, entered Baghdad at the invitation of the caliph, and thereafter, they soon became the real masters of the Islamic Empire which stretched from central Asia and southern Russia to the northern borders of Syria.[25] In 1071, the Turkish adventurer, Atiz ibn Abaq, captured Jerusalem without a struggle and then occupied the rest of Palestine down to the frontier fortress of Ascalon. In 1075 he took Damascus and the Damascene, and his successor, the Seljuk Prince Tutrush, became the sole ruler of a state stretching from Aleppo to the borders of Egypt in 1079.[26] The rising tide of Seljuk domination not only included the lands of the Islamic Empire, but also overran a vast swath of land in Asia Minor that had been ruled for centuries by the Emperor of Byzantium.

The Byzantine Empire

The Byzantines saw themselves as the heirs of the old Roman Empire and viewed their capital, Constantinople, as the New Rome. To these people, their ruler was the sole and legitimate successor to the emperors of ancient Rome. He was the instrument of God's chosen people, namely themselves, and the thirteenth

Apostle of God. Needless to say, this was not an opinion that was widely shared in the West for there their fellow-Christians regarded the Byzantine belief in the God-given status of their empire as a statement of unwonted arrogance, and, furthermore, the pope in Rome heaped ridicule on the claims of 'the king of the Greeks' to be the legitimate successor of Roman authority. To complicate this clash of authority between the pope and the emperor, by the eleventh century, serious theological differences had emerged between the Eastern and the Western Churches, and high among these was the vexed question as to the real nature and extent of papal authority.[27]

It was against this long-standing background of dispute and dissent that the Byzantine emperor had to act when faced with the conquest of much of his lands by the Seljuk Turks. Thus, Alexis I Commenus (1081–1118), the Emperor of Byzantium, did not appeal to the Christians of the West to help him restore the fortunes of his own empire, nor did he ask them simply to evict the Turks from Asia Minor, which was certainly high on his personal agenda. Instead, he appealed to the pope to help him rescue the Christians of the East and their churches from the tyranny of their Muslim conquerors. For Emperor Alexis complained that it was intolerable that the Christians of the Holy Land and the holy places within that country should now be crushed under the oppressive heel of the infidel Turks. Alexis then appealed for help to Pope Urban II (1088–99).[28]

Knowing the brutal reality of Western Europe at that time, there is a dreadful sense of inevitability about the whole idea of a holy war against the Turks to rescue the holy places of Christendom; it seemed bound to occur to someone and it certainly appealed to Pope Urban. His words evoked such a response in the hearts and minds of ordinary men and women throughout Western Europe, that the history of both Europe and the world was to be dramatically changed by them – but in a way very different from that hoped for by the emperor.[29]

Alexis despatched ambassadors to attend Urban's first great Church Council at Cremona in March 1095. They gave a graphic and exaggerated description of the plight of the Christians who were living in the East under Turkish domination. The pope, being somewhat cautious by nature, did not respond at once, for he needed time to develop a response that might solve the perceived problem of Turkish persecution and also give him some degree of power over Byzantine Christianity.

The Call for the First Crusade

Eventually Pope Urban summoned the bishops of France to join him at another Church Council at Clermont where, just before the council was due to end, Urban let it be known that he would make an important announcement at a session open to the general public on Tuesday 27 November. The pope, a great orator, used his skills to the full and his audience was spellbound. The pope claimed that the Christians in the East had recently appealed to him for help against the Turks who were advancing into Christian lands, maltreating innocent Christian men and women and desecrating their churches. This was surely enough cause for concern, but, to make matters worse, the Turks were also desecrating the holy places of Jerusalem and inflicting appalling indignities and brutalities on pilgrims to the Holy Land. The time had come for Christians in the West to rise up in righteous wrath and march to the rescue. Let the Christians of Europe stop making war on each other and wage a holy war against God's enemies instead. The pope claimed that God himself would lead them in battle and grant them a holy victory.

Urban promised that absolution and remission of all sins would be granted to all who 'took the Cross'[30] and died in the battle to free the Holy Land from the Turks. This intoxicating message produced an immediate response – loud cries of *Dieu le volt*, 'God wills it'. Urban had set a series of events in motion that was far greater than even he had any reason to expect. A massive tidal wave of enthusiasm spread from Clermont across France and spilled over its borders into every country in Western Europe, one that set all the Christian peoples alight with fanatical fervour.[31] Their actions were to leave a scar on the relationship between the Christian West and the world of Islam that would never fully heal – that result was the Crusades.[32]

All over Europe, various groups prepared to set out, as soon as the summer had come, with God to be their guide.[33] That year, Europe was blessed by a plentiful harvest of both grain and wine, for it seemed as though God himself had arranged matters to favour the coming crusade so that none should falter for lack of provisions on this holy enterprise. Hugh of Vermandois, the brother of King Philippe of France, set out first; he was followed by Bohemund of Taranto, the Count of Apulia. Godfroi de Bouillon, the Duke of Lower Lorraine, travelled through Hungary while Count Raymond of Toulouse and his Provençal army along with Adhemar Bishop of le Puy, crossed through Dalmatia. In October 1096, Robert Duke of Normandy set out for the Holy Land in company with Stephen of Blois and Robert Count of Flanders.[34] Far from being a unified and coherent expedition, the First Crusade was, therefore, composed of a series of small, independent groups of warriors interspersed with what can only be described as ill-disciplined, ravening mobs of enthusiastic peasants who, unlike the warrior class, were singularly ill-prepared for the trials ahead. All were united by one simple aim – to kill the enemies of Christ.

Massacres of the Jews

A priest called Gottschalk raised a small army of men in Lorraine and Bavaria, while in Bohemia another cleric, Volkmarr, did the same, and Count Emmich of Leisingen gathered another even larger army in the Rhineland. However, before any of these people departed for Asia Minor, one posed the question: 'Were there not enemies of Christ nearer home, who should be dealt with first?' Indeed, 'Why should they march over 2,000 miles through strange terrain to fight the Turks while some of the race who had crucified Christ were living in every great European city?'

While the Jews had long enjoyed some degree of protection from the more tolerant among the Christian rulers, they had never been popular in Europe.[35] Thus, the early summer of 1096 saw murderous outbreaks of anti-Semitic violence in many Christian kingdoms. It was Emmich of Leisingen who made the first move when on May 3rd, he and some of his men attacked the Jews of Spier, and killed dozens of them before forcing a young Jewess to take her own life rather than be raped. About two weeks later he marched his army to the city of Worms, where for some reason the Jews were more unpopular than in other places. Once his intentions became known, a mob of local peasants joined enthusiastically in his men's vicious attack on the Jewish quarter. The Bishop of Worms had opened his palace to give sanctuary to the Jews, nonetheless, Emmich and the mob forced their way into the Episcopal Palace and murdered 500 men, women and children.

It was then the turn of the Jews of Mainz who vainly tried to buy Emmich off with seven pounds of gold to save their lives. He graciously accepted the enormous bribe, but on the following day, gave orders to kill every Jew in the city. The killing continued for two days and few escaped.[36] Soon after Emmich's mass murder of the Jews of the Rhineland, news of these massacres reached Volkmarr's army in Prague so they immediately began to kill all the Jews they could find. Not to be left out of these acts of pious murder, Gottschalk and his men stopped at Ratisbon long enough to murder all the Jews there.[37]

During the summer of 1096, when the Jews of Germany and Central Europe were being brutally killed in the name of Christ, the various princes and nobles who had taken the cross were assembling their armies and supplies preparatory to their departure, for they knew that no military expedition had any chance of success without careful planning.[38] While the Rex Deus noble, Godfroi de Bouillon, the Duke of Lower Lorraine, was preparing to leave, he was given 1,000 pieces of silver by the Jews of Mainz and Cologne in order to speed him on his way, and also, it has been suggested, to induce him to leave them in peace. He then reassured them that he had no harmful intentions towards them, but, nonetheless, Godfroi gratefully accepted their generous offer to offset the heavy expenses of the campaign to come.[39]

As the restless, half-organized, savage bands of peasantry crossed Eastern Europe, being singularly ill-prepared for their journey, they robbed and pillaged as they went. This ravaging of the countryside of other Christian states did little to endear them to the local populations, so petty wars and skirmishes broke out en route. When they and the brutal, yet visionary chivalry of Western Christendom crossed the Bospherous under the watchful eye of Emperor Alexis and his fellow Byzantines, two very different cultures came into collision. Byzantium culture was very old, highly literate, sophisticated and immensely civilized; that of Western Europe, which was barely emerging from total barbarism, was warlike, ruthless and fanatically intolerant.[40] As the various armies arrived one by one, the Byzantine emperor kept them outside the city walls, entertained and presented gifts to their leaders and extracted oaths of allegiance from them.[41]

The oaths of allegiance taken by the various leaders of the First Crusade proved meaningless, for what oath could be taken that bound a Western Christian to the emperor of a heretical sect that did not bow the knee to the pope in Rome? Many of the nobles on the Crusade were landless younger sons of the nobility of Europe who sought to carve out an empire for themselves in the Holy Land of Palestine. While the main force of the crusader army set out towards Antioch, Baldwin of Boulogne, accompanied by about 100 horsemen and the historian Fulcher of Chartres, set out to find his fortune in the valley of the Euphrates.[42]

It is claimed that Baldwin's departure was as a result of an invitation from the Armenian Prince Thoros of Edessa who was seeking help from the crusaders to gain independence both from the Turks and from his original overlord, the Emperor of Byzantium. As Baldwin rode towards Edessa, the Armenian population rose up to greet him. Thoros adopted Baldwin as his son and heir and immediately co-opted him as joint ruler. Baldwin soon betrayed his new partner and, on March 7th, Thoros was deposed and three days later, Baldwin became the first crusader to obtain his own principality in the East. Baldwin's duplicity towards Thoros and the breach of his oath of allegiance to the Emperor Alexis did not pass unnoticed in Constantinople.[43]

Despite all claims to standards of knightly chivalry, the warrior nobles of Western Europe were, in the main, greedy, dishonourable and brutal thugs. Chivalry and honour were values they had yet to learn from their Muslim adversaries Their behaviour at the fall of Antioch clearly revealed the appalling reality of their Christian standards of chivalry for all the people of the East to see. The siege lasted nine months and the Emir of Antioch, Yaghi Siyan, defended the city with unprecedented bravery. When the city fell in June 1098, a truly barbarous massacre took place in which no-one was spared; Turkish women and children were butchered along with their men and a good many Greek and Armenian Christians along with them.[44] This was to set a pattern that was, sadly, to be oft repeated. Bohemund of Taranto became Count of Antioch despite further complaints from the Emperor Alexis that yet another crusader had broken his solemn oath of allegiance. After the successful defence of Antioch against a Turkish siege, Bohemund and Count Raymond of Toulouse set the date of November 1st for the crusaders departure for Jerusalem.

The 'Liberation' of the Holy City

The crusader's actions at the fall of Jerusalem have left a permanent and dark stain on any European pretensions to honour and chivalry. However, the actions of one man do stand out as a glowing example of what could have been achieved, for Raymond of Toulouse alone had behaved with honour and decency. In the battle for the Tower of David, the Muslim warrior Iftikhar who was fighting Raymond and his Provençal troops realized early in the afternoon that all was lost. Withdrawing into the Tower of David, he offered to hand it over to Raymond with a great treasure in return for his life and the lives of his men. Raymond accepted these terms and occupied the Tower, while Iftikhar and his men were safely escorted out of the city and permitted to join the Muslim garrison of Ascalon.[45] This was the sole instance of civilized behaviour shown by the crusaders when they took the Holy City, for once they were let loose inside the walls, they were overcome by an insatiable and terrible blood lust.

The Armies of Christ had no doubt that the Muslim defenders of the city were hateful to God, profaners of the holy places, servants of the anti-Christ and worshippers of the abomination of desolation mentioned in the Bible; so they killed every man, woman and child they could find with fiendish enjoyment. These brutal butchers were absolutely convinced that they were doing God's will. The following account was written by Daimbert, Archbishop of Pisa describing the fall of the Holy City:

> If you want to know what was done to the enemies we found in the city, know this: that in the portico of Solomon and in his Temple, our men rode in the blood of the Saracens up to the knees of our horses.[46]

The slaughter went on throughout the day and far into the following until, when there was no-one else left to kill, the victors processed through the corpse-littered streets to the Church of the Holy Sepulchre and there gave thanks to God for His manifold and great mercies.[47] The Jewish inhabitants of the Holy City fared no better than their Muslim counterparts when they fled in a body to their chief synagogue, for no mercy was shown to them even there. The synagogue was torched and they were all burnt alive within its walls.[48] When Raymond of Aguillers went to visit the Temple area, he was forced to pick his way through corpses and blood that reached up to his knees.[49] No-one can say with any degree of accuracy how many people were slaughtered, but Jerusalem was completely emptied of all of its Muslim and Jewish inhabitants. The massacre had an enormous impact on the world; many Christians were horrified and the Muslims, who might otherwise have accepted the crusaders as just another factor in the tangled politics of the time, developed a fanatical determination to drive the Franks out at all costs. According to Stephen Runciman, England's leading historian of the Crusades, it was this bloodthirsty proof of Christian brutal intolerance that rekindled the fanatical fires of Islam.[50]

Despite the concerted effort by the crusaders to capture the Holy City, no decision as to who would assume power over Jerusalem had been taken prior to the siege. Eight days after the massacre, a council of bishops and noble lords was charged with selecting a suitable king. They first decided to offer the throne to Raymond of Toulouse, but to the surprise of the assembled company, he refused the position on the grounds that there could only be one King of Jerusalem, and that one was Christ. After that the council asked Godfroi de Bouillon, who agreed to assume the leadership but not the title of king.[51] After some deliberation, Godfroi de Bouillon took the title of Advocatus Sancti Sepulchri, 'the dedicated defender of the Holy Sepulchre'.[52] He only reigned for one year but, on his deathbed, he named his brother, Baldwin of Boulogne, Count of Edessa, as his successor.

Chapter 11

~

The Holy Warriors

THE REX DEUS ARISTOCRACY in Western Europe played a significant role in the First Crusade in which Godfroi de Boullion, Baldwin of Boulogne, Raymond of Toulouse, Henri de St Clair of Roslin and many others had fought, and sometimes died, in the campaign to conquer the Holy Land. As all of these families claimed descent from the 24 *ma'madot*, the high-priestly families of the Temple in Jerusalem, it is reasonable to assume that in their eyes they were simply regaining their ancestral patrimony. Now they were about to take action that would strengthen their precarious hold on the Kingdom of Jerusalem.

The Rex Deus Conspirators

Bernard de Fontaine, later known as St Bernard of Clairvaux (1090–1153), joined the struggling Cistercian Order, along with 32 of his friends and relatives, in 1112.[1] He rose within the Church at an incredible speed and attained an almost unbelievable position of influence throughout the Christian world, becoming the principal personal advisor to the pope and counselling kings, emperors and the nobility. His membership of Rex Deus was an obvious asset in attaining this level of immense power and influence. Bernard then cooperated with other members of the hidden families in an enterprise that was to leave an indelible mark on European history. The conspirators included his cousin, Pierre de Serté, who later became the Latin patriarch of Jerusalem; his uncle André de Montbard; Hughes de Payen, of the Royal House of Lorraine; and one of the most important noblemen in Europe of that time, the Count of Champagne.

Hughes I of Champagne ruled a vast area to the east of Paris. He was the godson of King Philippe I of France to whom he owed allegiance; he also owed allegiance to the Holy Roman Emperor and the Duke of Burgundy. The Counts of Champagne were linked both by blood and marriage to the Rex Deus families of the St Clairs,[2] the Capetian kings of France, the Dukes of Burgundy, the Dukes of Normandy, and the Norman and Plantagenet Kings of England. Hughes' county seat, Troyes, was a rare centre of learning in an otherwise semi-barbaric continent; one that attracted scholars, knights and intellectuals of considerable stature as well as playing host to Christian Europe's leading Jewish yeshiva headed by Rabbi Solomon ben Isaac, the scholar known as Rachi. Rachi was a welcome guest at the court of Hughes de Champagne and attained such intellectual repute that as a biblical scholar he is still unequalled, and as a Jewish philosopher, he is considered second only to Maimonides. Thanks to the tolerance of Hughes de Champagne, Rachi was able to maintain a kabbalistic school of considerable stature in the city.[3]

In 1104, Hughes I de Champagne met in secret conclave with the leading noble members of the Rex Deus families of Brienne, De Joinville, Chaumont and Anjou. Then he left for the Holy Land and did not return to Champagne until 1108. In 1114 he made another brief and mysterious visit to Jerusalem and on his return made a donation of land to the Cistercian Order on which the monks built the Abbey of Clairvaux. Bernard de Fontaine was immediately appointed as its first abbot. Hughes de Champagne's visits to the Holy Land and his donation of land to the Cistercians were the prologue to concerted action by the Rex Deus families, not just in

Europe or even in the county of Champagne, but in the holy city of Jerusalem. These actions resulted in the foundation of an order of warrior-monks whose name resonates with mystery to this day – *The Poor Knights of Christ and the Temple of Solomon*, otherwise known as the Knights Templar.

The Foundation of the Knights Templar

A Cistercian abbey founded by Bernard in the principality of Seborga in northern Italy in 1113, has a document in its archives that records that in February 1117, Bernard came to the abbey with seven companions, released two Cistercian monks, Gondemar and Rossal, from their monastic vows and then gave a solemn blessing to the whole group before they departed for Jerusalem in 1118. The document states that Bernard nominated Hughes de Payen as the grand master of 'the Poor Militia of Christ' who was then consecrated in that rank by Abbot Edouard of Seborga.[4] However, a much later account written over 70 years after the events it describes, by Guillaume de Tyre places the foundation of the order of the Knights Templar in Jerusalem in 1118.[5] Granted quarters on the Temple Mount, supposedly on the site of Solomon's Temple, by King Baldwin II within a few weeks of the king's accession to the throne,[6] they first took the name of the 'Poor Fellow-Soldiers of Jesus Christ' which later became known as 'the Knighthood of the Temple of Solomon'.[7] The founding members were Hughes de Payen, who became its first grand master, André de Montbard, Geoffroi de St Omer, Payen de Montdidier, Achambaud de St-Amand, Geoffroi Bisol, Godfroi, Gondemar and Rossal.[8]

This supposedly randomly assembled group of knights were all closely associated with Count Hughes I of Champagne who had made several visits to the Holy Land prior to the foundation of the Templars. When he returned there in 1114, Ivo, Bishop of Chartres, rebuked him for abandoning his wife and vowing himself to the 'knighthood of Christ' in order to take up 'that gospel knighthood by which two thousand may fight securely against him who rushes to attack us with two hundred thousand.'[9] A rather bizarre mention of the order, four years before that generally accepted as the true date of its foundation.

In 1125, some years after the creation of the Knights Templar, Hughes de Champagne returned to the Holy Land and joined the order, thereby swearing unquestioning obedience to its first grand master, his own vassal, Hughes de Payen the cousin of Bernard of Clairvaux[10] and Hughes of Champagne.[11] De Payen was known as 'Hughes the Moor' because of his lineal descent from one of the emirs of Cordova. The man commonly regarded as the co-founder of the Templars, André de Montbard, was also an uncle of Bernard of Clairvaux,[12] a kinsman of the Duke of Burgundy and yet another vassal of Count Hughes of Champagne. The third member, Geoffroi de St Omer, was the son of a leading Flemish nobleman, Hughes de St Omer.[13] Payen de Montdidier and Achambaud de St-Amand were both closely related to the Royal House of Flanders, two of whose members, Godfroi de Boullion and his younger brother Baudouin of Boulogne, were later rulers of the Kingdom of Jerusalem – Godfroi as protector of the Holy Sepulchre and after his death, Baudouin as King Baldwin I.

The Knights Templar received official recognition from the patriarch of Jerusalem at the Council of Nablus in 1120.[14] The patriarch gave the order its first insignia, a red two-barred cross. The monk, Orderic Vitalis (1075–c.1141), recorded that in the 1120s, Count Fulk V of Anjou joined the 'knights of the Temple' for a period of time during his pilgrimage to Jerusalem. On his return to Europe he continued to pay them 30 pounds per annum of Anjou silver for their support. Orderic described the Templars as – *venerandi mitlites* – knights who should be held in great respect or admiration for he claimed that they devoted their lives to the physical and spiritual service of God, despised all worldly things and faced martyrdom daily.[15]

Mysterious Events in Jerusalem

The stated purpose of this new order of warrior-monks was the protection of pilgrims en route from the port of Jaffa to Jerusalem.

Yet Hughes de Payen was 48 years old at the time of the order's foundation and as most of his companions were of similar age, it is difficult to imagine how nine elderly knights were going to accomplish this mammoth task, particularly when we consider what they actually did during their first nine years of existence. Instead of policing the pilgrimage routes between Jaffa and Jerusalem, they spent their time excavating directly under their headquarters on the Temple Mount.[16] In the later part of the nineteenth century and the early years of the twentieth, Lieutenant Warren of the Royal Engineers re-excavated the 80ft vertical shaft that the Templars had dug and the system of radiating tunnels which joined it. He discovered a variety of Templar artefacts in the tunnels, including a spur, the remains of a lance, a small Templar cross and the major part of a Templar sword. These now repose in the care of the Templar archivist, Robert Brydon, in Edinburgh, along with a letter from Captain Parker who accompanied Warren on his explorations. Parker gave the finds to Brydon's grandfather for safekeeping in 1912.

Were these excavations the main objective that lay behind the founding of the order? What exactly were the Templars looking for? What did they find? How did they know where to dig? Just as importantly, how did they obtain quarters immediately above the site of their excavations? While it is impossible to document the answers to any of these questions, it is reasonable to speculate on the probable answers to some of them, based upon some foundations of fact.

One rather improbable clue may be a carving on a pillar in the north porch of Chartres Cathedral that depicts the Ark of the Covenant being transported upon a wheeled vehicle.[17] The Bible recounts that the Ark of the Covenant was buried deep beneath the Temple in Jerusalem long before the Babylonian invasion and a long-standing European legend claims that Hughes de Payen was chosen to retrieve it and bring it back to Europe.[18] Along with the Ark, it has been alleged, a vast quantity of ancient documents were uncovered that may have included copies of the Dead Sea Scrolls material found at Qumran. The translation of the Copper Scroll found at Qumran tends to confirm this theory, as it lists sites where Temple treasure and items of sacred import were hidden prior to the destruction of the Temple by the Roman army in 70 CE. Indeed, many of the sites listed in the Copper Scroll were excavated by John Allegro, the Dead Sea Scrolls scholar, and in several he found Templar artefacts but nothing whatsoever from the first century, which indicates that, without doubt, the Templars had got there before him.

One rational scenario that may explain these circumstances is that the knowledge of this secret hiding place beneath the Temple was passed down through the generations in the oral traditions of the Rex Deus families. As to the question of the careful positioning of their quarters immediately above the treasure they sought, King Baldwin II, another Rex Deus member, who granted the Templars their quarters, was obviously part of the conspiracy.

The Templars Return to Europe

King Baldwin II wrote to Bernard of Clairvaux requesting him to ask the pope to grant formal recognition to the order, for Bernard was not only a principal advisor to Pope Honorius II, but also his former teacher.[19] Hughes de Payen and his nine knights then set sail for Provence before travelling to Normandy for a meeting with the English King Stephen (1097–1154) who granted him and his party a *laissez-passer* to pass through England en route to Scotland where they stayed with the St Clairs of Roslin.

David, the king of the Scots, granted the order a donation of land at the village of Ballantrodoch that later became the head-quarters of the Templars in Scotland. Now renamed Temple, this land adjoins the St Clair estates, so that communication between the ancient Rex Deus family of the St Clairs and the new knightly order could be easily maintained. As a result of their return to Europe, the order was granted estates in Scotland, England, Champagne and Provence. There is still considerable dispute as to which of these was the first to be given as many such gifts were not confirmed by charter for some time. It is highly likely that the lands around Les Arcs-sur-Argens in Provence were first to be granted; Temple Cressing in England next; Balantradoch third; and Troyes fourth. These first donations of land had been long-planned and were followed by a cascade of gifts of estates, castles, towns, farms and villages throughout Christian Europe. However, many of these other gifts of property and money followed the pope's official recognition of the order and the award of its first 'rule'.

The Rule of the Templars

Pope Honorius II (1124–30) willingly gave his blessing to the warrior-monks and commanded the papal legate, Cardinal Matthew d'Albano, to call a council of the Church in France to legitimize the new order and grant the knights their first religious rule. This council opened at Troyes in the County of Champagne on 14 January 1128 under the direction of the cardinal, and attended by the archbishops of Rheims and Sens; the bishops of Orleans, Paris, Soissons, Auxerre, Meaux, Chalons, Laon and Samur; the abbots of Vezelay, Citeaux, Pontigny, Trois-Fontaines, Saint-Remy de Rheims, Dijon and Molesmes.[20] There is considerable doubt as to whether Bernard attended in person or not as he was in bad health, however, the entire council was certainly dominated by his thinking. Temporal power was represented by the new Count of Champagne, Thibaud IV, Count William II of Nevers, and another nobleman André de Baudemant. On 31 January 1128, the grand master, Hughes de Payen, and his fellow knights appeared before the council and were given their new 'rule' written for them by Bernard of Clairvaux.[21]

Ten years after this event, again at the behest of Bernard of Clairvaux, Pope Innocent II issued a papal bull entitled *Omne datum optimum* which made the Templars responsible, through their grand master, to the pope and the pope alone. This effectively freed the order from the authority of all bishops, archbishops, kings and emperors. Thus, less than 20 years after their foundation, the Knights Templar were completely freed from any control by prelates and princes and became thereby the most autonomous and independent religious order in the Christian world. It was soon to become the most powerful, both militarily and financially.

The donations of castles and other property came in so thick and fast in the years following the Council of Troyes that, in many cases, the order had to defer garrisoning their new lands due to a shortage of manpower, for their main focus was always the protection of the Kingdom of Jerusalem. The early recruits, all the knights and those capable of military service, were sent to the East as soon as possible following their grand master's example. Hughes, accompanied by 300 knights drawn from the noblest families in Europe, had returned to the Holy Land in 1129.[22] When one considers the time it took to arm and equip these men and then transport them across Europe, this massive influx of recruits and their rapid transportation to the Holy Land is just another example of the long-term planning that underpinned the foundation and rise to power of the Knights Templar.

Two years after the Council of Troyes, the Knights Templar began to acquire land in Portugal and had established close relations with the rulers; donations in the Spanish Marches came slowly but followed a similar pattern. The Templars were granted land in Aragon soon after 1130 and by the early 1140s they had acquired enough property and military personnel to maintain simultaneous military operations on two fronts, one in the Holy Land and the other in Spain where they acted as military advisors to the king of Aragon and fought in his campaigns against the Moors. Their numbers in these Spanish campaigns were never large, but they compensated for this apparent deficiency by their discipline, their ability to mobilize quickly and remain in the field as long as required.[23] Thus, both in Europe and the Kingdom of Jerusalem they became the first full-time professional standing army since the fall of the Western Roman Empire.

Bernard of Clairvaux wrote a tract *In Praise of the New Knighthood* between 1132 and 1136, which extolled the virtues of the new warrior order and listed the spiritual benefits that would accrue to those who supported its aims with acts of personal service, donations of land or money. Thus the influx of recruits and the ever-growing list of donations of land and property no longer originated solely from the families of Rex Deus. Noble recruits, gifts of land and money flowed into the arms of the Knights Templar and, needless to say, they were not the only beneficiaries; the Cistercian Order also underwent an extraordinary period of expansion, for in Bernard's lifetime they established over 300 new abbeys – the most rapid expansion on record of any monastic order before or since.

Furthermore, during the lifetime of Bernard of Clairvaux, to many people the Cistercians and the Knights Templar were simply regarded as two arms of the same body: one a contemplative monastic arm, the other the strong, swift, military arm. Eventually Templar estates, castles and churches were located within all countries between the Baltic and the Mediterranean and from the Atlantic coastline right across to the Holy Land. The income from these vast holdings was devoted to maintaining the order's army and fortifications in the Kingdom of Jerusalem. The order left no stone unturned to maximize its profits which were then used to increase the power and effectiveness of its military operations in the Holy Land.

The Knights Hospitaller

The earliest references to the Hospital of St John in Jerusalem date from the era of the Seljuk Turk's occupation of the Holy Land and are dated at or about 1071. Again, one of our sources for this information is the account by Guillaume of Tyre which was written nearly 100 years later. Pope Paschal II granted the hospital papal protection and privileges in 1113 and referred to Brother Gerard as 'the institutor of the hospital'.[24] Guillaume of Tyre claimed that merchants from the city of Amalfi asked the caliph of Egypt for a site within the city to house Italian pilgrims and that, as a result, they were granted quarters near the Church of Holy Sepulchre and built a Latin foundation there. Soon this was followed by the building of a hospital for sick pilgrims that was dedicated to St John the Almoner.[25]

Many modern historians, however, have questioned Guillaume of Tyre's account and now claim that the hospital was dedicated to St John the Baptist from its very inception.[26] Others claim that it was while under the mastership of Brother Gerard, who was elected about 1100, that this Hospitaller order changed its rule from Benedictine to Augustine and changed its patron from St John the Almoner to that of St John the Baptist.[27] They soon acquired a series of hospitals throughout Outremer, as the Kingdom of Jerusalem was now called, and gradually these spread into Europe along the pilgrimage routes.

Brother Gerard was succeeded as master of the Hospitallers in 1120 by Brother Raymond de Puy, an organizational genius. Under his command, the order's nursing work brought fame, and it began to receive grants of land from Godfroi de Boullion in Outremer and from nobles in France, Italy, Spain and England. Various popes gave the order privileges which made it almost as autonomous as the Templars, freeing it from the jurisdiction of the patriarch of Jerusalem and of archbishops and bishops throughout Christendom. Pope Innocent II placed the order beyond all forms of interdict or excommunication by any bishop.[28] Taken as a whole, the papal privileges granted prior to 1154 freed the order from all authority save that of the pope, so effectively it now enjoyed the same freedom as that of the Knights Templar.[29] They soon were to share a common purpose, namely the defence of the Holy Land. With the grant by King Fulk of Jerusalem of the Castle of Gibelin in 1136, we can see the undoubted beginnings of militarism within the order.[30] The English historian Desmond Seward claims that without the influence of Bernard of Clairvaux, it would never have been possible for the order to take up arms. Sadly, he does not clarify if this influence was simply by Bernard's support for the first of the military orders, the Knights Templar, which set an example other orders could follow, or whether Bernard took a more active and direct role in arming the Knights Hospitaller.[31]

From Care to Combat

Count Raymond of Tripoli confirmed the new fighting status of the Order of St John between 1142 and 1144 when he gave them a series of castles that guarded the frontier of his county against Muslim attacks. These castles included Castellum Bochee, Lacum, Felicium and Murabesh to say nothing of the greatest Hospitaller castle of them all, Krak des Chevaliers. The terms by which he granted these fortifications were generous; the Hospitallers would pay no feudal dues for these lands, which included several villages; they would retain half the booty gained by any military campaign in which he was present, or if he were not present, and neither were his constable or his marshall, the Hospitallers could keep all the booty for themselves.[32] Other similar donations on the frontier of the crusader states soon followed.

According to James de Vitry, the bishop of Acre, the Hospitallers took up arms following the example of the Knights Templar.[33] Be that as it may, with massive donations of castles and land within the crusader states, Spain, France, Italy and elsewhere within Europe, the Knights Hospitaller soon began to rival the Knights Templar in temporal power and military might. The internal organization and discipline within each of these orders generally mirrored that of the other. Military discipline was absolute; captured knights were not allowed to be ransomed and both orders were responsible through their respective grand masters to the pope and the pope alone. Without the warrior-monks of the Templars and Hospitallers it is well-nigh impossible to envisage how the crusader states would have been able to survive. Both fought in Spain as well as in the Holy Land and both were financed by the immense profits of their vast European estates.

Other Military Orders

As I wrote in *Rosslyn – Guardian of the Secrets of the Holy Grail*:

Imitation is the sincerest form of flattery and within a short space of time the Templars were emulated in many countries by knightly orders of warrior-monks who owed their allegiance to the king and not to the pope. One such order, the Teutonic Knights, were actually founded by the Knights Templar. Principal among the others who modelled themselves on the Templars were the Spanish Orders of the Knights of Calatrava and the Knights of Alcantara.[34] Both were founded shortly after the Knights Templar, and St Bernard of Clairvaux is now known to have played some shadowy role in their foundation.[35]

The Teutonic Knights were formed in 1198 when German noblemen who had come to the Kingdom of Jerusalem with an otherwise abortive German crusade, joined with the established minor order, that of the Hospital of St Mary of the Germans. The new order that was formed by this amalgamation became known as the Teutonic Knights of St Mary's Hospital of Jerusalem. Under its new master, Heinrich Walpot von Bassenheim, the order modelled itself on that of the Templars, but with a provision for Hospitaller work.[36] While their earliest military activities took place in the Holy Land, they soon spread their net to include the war in Spain against the Moors, in Greece against the Byzantines and the Turks and, eventually, in what became their main centre of operations, in the Baltic States.[37]

The Spanish orders of the Knights of Santiago, the Knights of Alcantara and the Knights of Calatrava were all products of a campaign against the Moors in Spain that effectively lasted for eight centuries. The Knights of Calatrava were founded in 1164 as an order fully affiliated to the Cistercians and, in the same year, they gained papal recognition as an order of warrior-monks. Shortly after the founding of the Knights of Calatrava, an order of warriors was formed to protect pilgrims en route to the shrine of Santiago of Compostela. In 1171, the papal legate, Cardinal Jacinto, granted them a rule, and Pope Alexander III gave them papal recognition in 1175 as the Order of Saint James of the Sword. The Order of Santiago had been born.[38]

What distinguished the Order of Santiago from the other military orders was that married men were accepted as full members right from the beginning. Prior to 1170, an armed brotherhood known as the Knights of San Julián de Pereiro began to transform itself into the Order of Alacantara. Thus, the concept of warrior-monks had developed from its small beginnings, supposedly protecting the pilgrimage routes to Jerusalem, into a complex web of military orders fighting the Christian cause from the Baltic to the Bospherous, freeing Spain from its Moorish conquerors and, above all, defending the Kingdom of Jerusalem and the other crusader states. This complex enterprise was sustained by a vast network of estates, commandaries, vineyards, castles, quarries and treasuries that spanned every climatic zone in Europe, all geared up to gain the profit that would fuel the Holy War against the infidel.

Chapter 12

~

He Who Kills a Christian, Sheds the Blood of Christ!

I N Septimania, under the protection of its Rex Deus nobility, the mixed population acted as an effective bulwark against Moorish invasion for many centuries after the death of Charlemagne. The growing and prosperous Jewish communities led by their *nasi*, or prince, lived in harmony with the majority of their Christian neighbours, however, as might be expected, they did attract the unwelcome attention of the papacy and Church hierarchy. In 768, only nine years after Pepin the Short took Narbonne, Pope Stephen III condemned the various royal gifts of land to the Jews of Septimania and wrote to Archbishop Aribert of Narbonne, expressing his extreme displeasure at these donations stating that he was distressed by them to 'the point of death'.[1]

Pope Gregory the Great also protested, but this time against Jews owning Christian slaves. Church councils in the sixth and seventh centuries also expressed unease at the growing Jewish ownership of properties around Narbonne.[2] Decrees passed by the second and third Councils of Gerona, in 1068 and 1078, clarify the true financial root of the Church's discontent by complaining that Jews in Septimania now possessed lands that had, in previous times, paid tithes to the Church.[3] The Jewish chronicler Benjamin of Tudela reported that, at the end of the twelfth century the *nasi* had significant land holdings[4] but that he had surrendered most of the political power he had possessed during the Carolingian era.[5]

Arab merchants maintained regular contact between Septimania and the Muslim world and many Arab and Jewish doctors reached the province both from the East and from across the Pyrenees. Indeed, Jewish doctors and scholars were held in such high regard that in Narbonne and Montpellier[6] they founded their own yeshiva, or religious school, where they compiled the first written versions of the kabbalah. The spiritual insight of the Jewish communities in Narbonne, Béziers and Carcassonne was the launching pad for the spread of kabbalistic studies in Europe.[7] The influence of Jewish and Muslim apocryphal writings was now becoming more widespread, reaching many of the Catholic clergy and sometimes even the common people. The town of Montpellier received its charter in 1141 and the influence of its Jewish doctors led to the establishment of its medical school later in the same century, with many of those doctors becoming teachers. A school of law was founded in 1160 and this intellectual tradition ultimately led to the founding of the University of Montpellier at the end of the thirteenth century.

Thus we can see that in Septimania, the Jews were not barred from public life as they were elsewhere in Europe, and in many towns they were appointed to the office of consul or magistrate.[8] This acceptance of the Jewish communities in Septimania was markedly different to their treatment in most parts of Christian Europe where, by the late twelfth century, the Jews were regarded as an alien minority, tolerated only when under the direct protection of the local lord or the king himself. In most of Europe the Jews were ritually, publicly humiliated and intermittently persecuted in the same way as heretical Christian groups.

Protected from invasion by the Pyrenees and buffered by the growing strength of the Spanish kingdoms of the Spanish March, the southwestern corner of France, the present-day departments of the Languedoc and Roussillon prospered quietly under the benevolent rule of their local Rex Deus aristocracy. Indeed, during the twelfth and thirteenth centuries, a truly dazzling civilization arose there; one illuminated by the principles of emerging democracy, love and, above all, religious toleration.[9] The local nobility encouraged trade, economic stability and a level of creative freedom that was truly exceptional for Europe at that time.[10] The feudal rule of the local counts was subject to a fair degree of democratic moderation by a well-established and wealthy bourgeoisie, who were assisted by groups of lawyers in the more prosperous towns and cities.[11] The influence of the Catholic Church had almost totally vanished in some areas and was in marked decline in the rest of the southwest.[12] As a result, the local nobility who had been tolerant of the large Jewish community in their midst, and who had seen the economic and intellectual benefits that flowed from their presence, now felt free to extend this toleration to a religious group known as the Cathars – Christians who claimed to follow the 'True Teachings of Jesus'. Within the Cathar faith, the congregation was known as 'the hearers' and the priests as '*les bonshommes*' or 'the good men'.[13] These 'good men' lived according to the ideals laid down by their Essene precursors, yet their hostile critics within the Christian Church called them 'perfecti', a corruption of the Latin term *hereticus perfectus*; they were also known as the Cathari, the pure ones.[14]

At the end of the eleventh century, Count Raymond of Toulouse had raised a considerable army to participate in the First Crusade and liberate his Rex Deus homeland from the infidel. However, by the mid-twelfth century, the local nobility were growing in confidence and in an atmosphere of declining Church power were becoming openly anti-clerical. Count Raymond IV, who died in 1222, was so favourably disposed towards the Cathar faith that he took a perfectus with him whenever he travelled. The Count of Foix welcomed Cathars into his lands, and his wife, once her family were raised, became a perfectus, a full initiate of the Cathar faith, herself.[15] Cathar perfecti tutored Raimond Roger Trençavel, the future Count of Carcassonne and Beziers, indeed, according to Giraud, the Catholic historian, the nobility of the Lauragais, the prosperous and populous area between Carcassonne and Toulouse, were

almost completely Cathar.[16] The Cathars encouraged the establishment of a class of skilled craftsmen within local society and supervised the operation of workshops specializing in the manufacture
of textiles, leatherwork and a skill that had crossed over from
Muslim Spain, paper-making.[17]

The Cathar Religion

Insofar as it can be established from the few records that survive,
the Cathar religion was a dualist form of Gnosticism whose roots
can be traced back to early Zoroastrian religion,[18] the school
of Pythagoras and the cult of Mithras, with this strange melange
of beliefs transformed by contact with early Christianity. Some historians also claim that it was a derivative of Manichaeanism, an
initiatory Christian cult of Persian origin based on the teachings of
the mystic, Mani (*c.*215–*c.*277 CE).[19] The perfecti were men and
women, easily identified by their distinctive robes, who lived in
egalitarian communities, irrespective of their previous social status.
They tended to the pastoral needs of the communities they served,
travelling the countryside in pairs, preaching, teaching and healing,[20] emulating the example of Jesus, the first Apostles and their
Essene companions.[21]

The Gospel of Thomas recounts that Jesus had said: 'He who
drinks from my mouth, I shall become he and he shall become me';
indicating that all true disciples would become capable of doing as
he did.[22] Spiritual union with God would be the ultimate result that
would flow from their humility and service. They believed that
sacred knowledge, or gnosis, came only from God and could be
accessed by following the true teaching of Jesus. This gnosis had
been passed to Jesus by John the Baptist, and by Jesus to John the
Divine and thence to the Cathars. They used a form of spiritual
baptism called 'the consolamentum' which was only granted to
believers after a three-year novitiate, or on their deathbed. This was
the outward sign of the attainment of enlightenment, and when
they received it, they attained the rank of perfectus.[23] They believed
in reincarnation and the transmigration of souls into animals.

Thus, as animals might contain the souls of the unperfected, the perfecti were vegetarians. Furthermore, as the creation of more humans could only delay the perfection and liberation of souls, perfecti abstained from all sexual relationships.[24] The hearers, or ordinary believers, were exempt from these restrictions.

Due to the rapid and considerable growth of the Cathar faith, four dioceses were established in the Languedoc by 1167: Agen, Albi, Carcassonne and Toulouse.[25] A fifth was later established at Razès.[26] In the light of my earlier description of the nobility of the Languedoc as members of the Rex Deus group of families, it will come as no surprise to learn that another Cathar diocese was founded in the county of Champagne, which later grew to include the Ile de France as a separate episcopal district. In northern Italy, the provinces of Lombardy and Tuscany had six more dioceses, and there were six more in the Balkans. Each diocese was ruled by a bishop and, under him, two assistants called the major and the minor son. With the death of the bishop, the major son inherited his position, the minor son moved up a rank and another minor son was elected.[27] Under the leadership of the bishop there was a deaconate and, under that, the communities of the perfecti.

One of the earliest references to the Cathars that can be found in Church documentation is a letter from Prior Ebwin of Steinfeld dated 1145 and addressed to Bernard of Clairvaux. The subject is a group he describes as 'the Cologne Heretics' who were led by an apostate monk named Henry. After some harassment by the Church authorities, Henry wisely moved to the more tolerant territory[28] of Toulouse, where he was followed by Bernard of Clairvaux. Bernard later wrote to the Count of Toulouse describing the conditions he found on his travels through the Count's domains. He stated:

> The Churches are without congregations, congregations are without priests, priests are without proper reverence, and finally, Christians are without Christ.[29]

He described Henry in Toulouse as 'revelling in all his fury among the flock of Christ'. Yet this leading churchman and advisor of popes spoke well of the Cathars whom he described as a people of simple and devout spirituality led by a gifted priesthood: 'No one's sermons are more spiritual.'[30] At about this time, the clergy in Liège wrote to the pope to inform him that a new heresy had arisen which seemed 'to have overflowed various regions of France, one so varied and so manifold that it seems impossible to characterize it under a single name'.[31] They went on to describe elements of the Cathar faith and claimed that it had attracted adherents throughout the Low Countries, Lombardy and the Languedoc.[32] The question they did not attempt to answer is: Where did this heresy come from?

While it is impossible to answer that question with precision, a consensus has arisen among historians that explains the most probable route by which the Cathar faith reached the southern parts of France. It has been claimed that this new faith arose when a priest, known as Bogomil, preached a dualistic form of belief in Bulgaria in about 930 CE.[33] After the Crusades, the empire of Byzantium strengthened the trade routes from Constantinople to both Venice and Genoa, thereby creating a viable means of communication between Eastern and Western Europe for the first time since the fall of the Roman Empire. Thus, paradoxically, the movement to Christianize the Holy Land also created the routes by which Eastern forms of heresy could infect Catholic Europe. The Cathar heresy was a pure form of initiatory Christianity whose only scripture, 'The Gospel of Love', otherwise known as The Secret Gospel of John,[34] taught the simple message that Jesus came to reveal and not to redeem. In this sense, the first identifiable parent of the Cathar faith can thus be found within the First Church in Jerusalem led by James the Righteous, the brother of Jesus.

Both the Catholic Church and the Cathar faith claimed to be based upon the teachings of Jesus the Nazorean, yet there were startling differences between the two creeds. The Cathars denied the validity of all the Church sacraments, especially that of the Eucharist with its cannibalistic overtones;[35] furthermore they refused to recognize the authority of the pope in Rome and disputed the concept of grace that was so central to Catholic dogma,[36] as well as dismissing out of hand the redemptive nature of Christ's sacrifice at Golgotha.[37]

The Response of the Church

As the Cathar religion grew in power and influence in the Languedoc, it began to rival, and in many districts, completely displace, the Church of Rome. This posed a threat to the Church that it could no longer tolerate. In response, the Church despatched a preaching ministry to the Languedoc headed by a fanatical Spanish Priest, Dominic Guzman.[38] His preaching fell upon deaf ears and the terrifying finale to his fruitless evangelical mission was a brutal warning.

> For years now I have brought you words of peace, I have preached, I have implored, I have wept. But, as the common people say in Spain, if a blessing will not work, then it must be the stick. Now we shall stir up princes and bishops against you, and they, alas, will call together nations and peoples, and many will perish by the sword. Towers will be destroyed, walls overturned and you will be reduced to slavery. Thus force will prevail where gentleness has failed.[39]

Those who heard his message were utterly incapable of understanding its harsh reality and simply could not visualize the brutal methods used by the Christian Church to repress any form of heresy. They were soon to be rudely awakened. In 1209, Pope Innocent III declared a religious war against the Cathars. He gave this dubious expedition the title of a crusade, which meant that any participant who served for 40 days was granted a papal indulgence giving absolution for all their past sins and any they might commit during the crusade.[40] They were entitled to seize the property of any heretic, be he prince or peasant; thus they were granted a papal licence to murder, steal, rape and pillage in the name of the gentle Jesus, the man the Church called 'the Prince of Peace'. Along with the crusading army came the clergy, who treated any suspected heretic with torture and the warm embrace of death at the stake. Yet, despite this being an official crusade, neither the Knights Templar nor the other crusading order of the Knights Hospitaller took any significant part in the action.[41]

In July of 1209, the crusaders advanced upon the prosperous city of Beziers. Viscount Raimond-Roger Trençavel, the Lord of both Beziers and Carcassonne, was certain that the city was indefensible and left in some haste for the superbly fortified city of Carcassonne. The considerable Jewish community of Beziers who knew of the persecution that their fellow Jews suffered in the north of France, fled with him. The community of Beziers took little notice of the appeals of their bishop, who sought an immediate surrender, and decided to defend the city.[42] The siege was short, and on the eve of the final assault the leaders of the besieging army sought the papal legate's guidance on how to treat their co-religionists in the battle to come. Instead of quoting the words of Jesus 'Love thy neighbour as thyself', or 'forgive thine enemies', the pope's representative ordered the Crusaders to: ' ... show mercy neither to order, nor to age, nor to sex ... Cathar or Catholic – kill them all ... God will know his own when they get to him.'[43]

The following day they slaughtered over 20,000 civilians without mercy, with 7,000 of those murdered within the cathedral where they had fled for sanctuary. Pierre des Vaux-Cernay claimed that the massacre was a punishment for the Cathar blasphemy against Mary Magdalene, on whose official feast day, July 22, the massacre of Beziers took place. He claimed:

> ... Beziers was taken on St Mary Magdalene's day. Oh, supreme justice of providence! ... the heretics claimed that St Mary Magdalene was the concubine of Jesus Christ... it was therefore with just cause that these disgusting dogs were taken and massacred during the feast of the one that they had insulted ...[44]

One immediate consequence was the unconditional surrender of Narbonne, whose leaders, both the viscount and the archbishop, not only offered material support to the crusaders but also promised to surrender any perfecti in the city and any property that the Jews of Beziers had owned within it.[45]

Following Beziers, the city of Carcassonne was besieged. After two weeks, when the wells within the city walls were running dry and access to the waters of the river was blocked by the crusading armies, the viscount was offered safe conduct by the crusaders in order to discuss the terms of surrender but, as promises made to a heretic were invalid, according to the Church, Viscount Trençavel was imprisoned[46] and the rights of inheritance of his son were set aside. He died in prison in November 1209 and according to most historians, his death was the result of foul play. When Carcassonne surrendered, the lives of its inhabitants were spared without religious discrimination, but they were forced to exit the city in their underclothes and leave their homes and possessions to the mercy of the crusading army.[47] One of the leaders of the crusade, Simon de Montfort, was awarded all the rights, feudal privileges and lands of the Trençavel family.[48]

Torture, Repression and Death

The first public burning of perfecti took place at Castres; after the siege and fall of Minerve, 140 perfecti, both men and women, were burnt alive and this became the inevitable fate of all perfecti who were captured.[49] Indeed, all who fought against the crusaders ran enormous risks. In 1210, the leader of the crusade, Simon de Montfort, inflicted a terrible punishment on the captured defenders of Bram by selecting a hundred of their number at random, gouging out their eyes and having their lips, ears and noses sliced off. One prisoner, who was only blinded in one eye, was ordered to lead his maimed companions to the castle of Cabaret[50] as a warning to the garrison there of the fate that awaited those who opposed the crusading army. Cabaret did not fall!

Having clearly established a typically Christian code of chivalry for the crusaders, de Montfort's army marched on to further conquests, and after the fall of Lavaur, the 80 knights who had valiantly defended the town were sentenced to be hung. The gallows collapsed under their combined weight and so, as an act of mercy, Simon de Montfort ordered that their throats be cut. Lady Guiraude, the chatelaine of the castle, was handed over to the crusaders and repeatedly raped, her bleeding body was then cast down a well and she was stoned to death as an adulteress.[51] After this victory, 400 Cathars were burnt on a huge fire; shortly afterwards 60 more were burnt at Lescasses.[52]

The king of Aragon joined the battle in support of the Cathar cause and was mortally wounded at the battle of Muret on 12 September 1213, where the slaughter exceeded that of Beziers.[53] To add to the terror of the crusade and the routine execution of the heretics, a deliberate scorched-earth policy was instituted and the crops were routinely burnt to starve the people into submission.[54] The brutal war lasted 30 years. Guillaume Tudelle recorded that 5,000 men, women and children were simply hacked to pieces after the fall of Marmande in 1226.[55] All these routine acts of barbarity were justified by the Church, who claimed that the crusaders were defending the true religion against heretics who, by definition, had no rights.

The Albigensian Crusade ended in 1244 with the surrender of the last Cathar stronghold of Montsegur after a siege of nearly a year. For once, the crusaders behaved with some semblance of chivalry, for the fighting men of the garrison and all non-heretics within the castle were spared but, when they marched down the mountain their path was lit by the flames arising from a vast funeral pyre where 225 perfecti were being burnt alive.[56]

The Holy Office

The Church did not rely on the crusade alone to stamp out the Cathar heresy. A new institution, the 'Holy Office of the Inquisition', was founded in 1233. The aim of this new institution was to create a climate of fear within which any form of heresy simply could not exist, but its most immediate objective was to extinguish the Cathar heresy once and for all.[57] Thus, the peace imposed by the Church was to prove even more terrifying than the horrors of the recent war.

Over the centuries that followed, the ignominious record of the Inquisition came to light and now even the devout Catholic historian Paul Johnson, condemns it vigorously and details its activities with horror.[58] The noted historian, H C Lea, described its actions as, 'an infinite series of atrocities',[59] and Lord Acton, another Catholic, condemned the Inquisition and the Church that spawned it with the words:

> Nothing short of religious assassination… the principle of the Inquisition was murderous for the popes were not only murderers in the grand style, but they made murder a legal basis of the Christian Church and a condition of salvation.[60]

The Inquisition simply ignored all written, state and customary laws that granted any semblance of protection to the accused and made a cruel mockery of papal justice for all time. The historian, H C Lea, was moved to write that:

> The judgement of impartial history must be that the Inquisition was the monstrous offspring of mistaken zeal, utilized by the selfish greed and lust of power to smother the higher aspirations of humanity and stimulate the baser appetites.[61]

Ecclesiam non novit sanguinem

Torture was routinely used from the beginning but did not receive formal papal sanction until 1252.[62] Yet, there was a tradition of some antiquity that declared that neither the clergy nor the Church was allowed to shed blood, and that was enshrined in the injunction, *ecclesiam non novit sanguinam*. To draw blood by lance, sword or dagger, was therefore deeply un-Christian and so the techniques of the Inquisition were designed to keep bloodshed to a minimum. So, in keeping with their monastic vows of obedience, the inquisitors ensured that the forms of torture they used neatly avoided shedding blood. These were devised to cause the maximum pain and suffering with the minimum of bloodshed and the mere sight of the instruments of torture was often enough to extract confessions of heresy. Of all the methods of torture used by the Inquisition, the supreme instrument was fire.[63]

At first the inquisitors themselves were prohibited from administering torture and simply acted as supervisors who instructed the civil executioner and made notes of anything the accused said under duress. In 1252, Pope Innocent IV formally authorized them to administer torture with the following proviso '...with the restriction that such compulsion should not involve injury to limb or danger of death'. Pointed and bladed implements were avoided in favour of the rack, thumbscrews and devices that caused blood to flow only as a secondary consequence. To tear flesh with pincers would undoubtedly shed blood, unless the pincers were heated to the point that hot metal cauterized the wound and staunched the bleeding. Under pre-existing civil law, certain categories of people were immune from torture, such as doctors, soldiers, knights and nobles however, the Inquisition did not feel bound by any of these restrictions in the war against heresy.

Methods of Torture

In the early years there were six main methods of torture: the ordeal by water, the ordeal of fire, the strappado, the wheel, the rack and the *stivaletto*. The ordeal by water caused the prisoner to be forced to swallow a quantity of water, either by means of a funnel or by soaking a piece of silk or linen and jamming it into the throat, which could result in blood vessels bursting. In an ordeal by fire, the prisoner was trussed immobile and placed before a hot fire with fat or grease applied to his feet so that they literally fried. The strappado, or pulley torture, was one of the principal forms of torture; the prisoner was stripped to his underwear, had his ankles shackled and his hands tied behind his back, then his wrists were tied to another rope that ran over a pulley on the ceiling above. The accused was then hoisted high above the floor, iron weights were attached to the feet and he was left hanging there from his tied wrists. He was then whipped and interrogated further. If he still remained uncooperative, he was hoisted higher still and then allowed to drop suddenly until just above floor level. Severe and multiple dislocations commonly resulted. At other times the victim was tied to a cartwheel and beaten with hammers, bars or clubs.

The rack was the most notorious form of torture used by the medieval Inquisition; a horizontal wooden frame with planks placed across it like the rungs of a ladder and, at each end, rollers to which the victim's ankles and wrists were attached. The inquisitor would question the victim while he was being positioned, then the rack was tightened by turning the rollers until the victim's body was stretched to breaking point. The *stivaletto* or *brodequins*, was a 'boot' type of torture, where two thick boards were attached to each leg with strong rope tied as tightly as possible. When questioning began, wooden or metal wedges were hammered between the boards and the victim's leg, until the pressure became intolerable and the ropes began to cut into the flesh or the inquisitor heard the sound of the splintering or crushing of bones. Permanent disablement was the inevitable result.[64]

When the accused inevitably confessed, his statement was recorded, read back to him, and he would be formally asked if it was true. If he replied yes, the transcript recorded that his confession had been 'free and spontaneous', and had not been induced by the influence of either 'force or fear'. Sentencing would follow, but a death sentence was only applied in about ten per cent of cases, for most inquisitors preferred to keep a 'saved' soul in a more or less intact body, which, through penances or on pilgrimage, would provide a living testimony to the mercy of the Church or, as one commentator observed: 'A convert who would betray his friends was more useful than a roasted corpse.'[65]

A heretic who abjured his faith after interrogation, could be imprisoned for life, suffer the loss of his property, or be condemned to wear a yellow cross sown on his clothes which effectively prevented him from making any form of social contact. Anyone who helped, employed, fed or spoke to someone who wore the yellow cross would be charged with heresy themselves or with harbouring heretics. Thus, to be sentenced to wear the yellow cross was, in fact, a sentence of slow death. Associating with a heretic during childhood was considered as proof of guilt and, therefore, inquisitors demanded details of a suspect's family and social life, and all those who were named as associates were interrogated in their turn. All suspects were deemed guilty of heresy simply because they were charged with it and the Inquisition became an instrument of terror that haunted the imagination of Europe for over 700 years.[66]

But even the Inquisition could not completely extinguish the Cathar faith. While many perfecti were burned and an innumerable number of believers were persecuted by the Inquisition in the 60-year period of repression that followed the war, some fled into exile and others learned the arts of dissembling and disguise. The Cathar religion as a visible entity vanished completely in the fourteenth century. Many Cathars joined the Templars in the final years of the Crusade, and after the fall of Montsegur;[67] many fled to Tuscany where they were assimilated into the tolerant local society. Others fled to the St Clair lands in Scotland where they founded a papermaking industry.

The brutal intolerance of the Christian Church to dissenters within its own ranks was mirrored by its belligerent attitude to people of other faiths, especially those who resided within Christian lands. This is in stark contrast to the inherent tolerance shown within Islam to the 'People of the Book'.

Christian anti-Semitism

I have described earlier in this chapter, the destruction of the Jewish communities in Septimania during the Albigensian Crusade. Far worse happened elsewhere for, as a direct result of Christian teaching, the Jews were not merely treated as second-class citizens but were almost universally reviled. Church doctrine determined the social inferiority and subordination of the Jews; rules denying them civic power applied not only to public office but to every social relationship, be it that of master and servant, physician and patient, and to any situation which might place a Jew in a position of authority over a Christian.

Since contact between Christians and Jews posed a perceived danger of undue influence, the Church recommended a policy of segregation. Hitler was not the first to force the Jews to wear readily distinguishable marks on their clothing, for in the Middle Ages an obligation of wearing distinguishable garments, or a special badge, was imposed on Jews.[68] Furthermore, in Christian lands the Jews had to contend with ignorant superstition fomented by rabid anti-Jewish preaching, and violent unprovoked attacks continued intermittently for centuries, with a total loss of life that was truly appalling.

Scarcely less savage were the decrees of expulsion imposed by a variety of Christian kings.[69] The decisions to expel the Jews from England in 1290[70] and from France in 1306[71] were the first steps in the dreadful process of purging Catholic Europe of the Jews.[72] In 1306, King Philippe le Bel hoped to achieve great financial gain from the expulsion of the Jews and the seizure of their property, for they were only allowed to take personal possessions with them and all else was forfeit to the Crown.[73] In Italy during the twelfth and thirteenth centuries, Jewish life was determined by a constantly fluctuating political climate, but with the Church consistently enacting anti-Jewish legislation.[74] This complex web of Christian anti-Semitism was to oppress European Jewry for centuries after the advent of humanitarian rationalism of the Enlightenment begun to slowly inculcate more positive attitudes among thinking people.[75]

Part Five

◇

ONGOING HOSTILITY BETWEEN ISLAM AND CHRISTIANITY

THE ORIGINS OF OUR CURRENT Western attitude towards Islam can most probably be traced back to the onset of the First Crusade, since when there has been an almost permanent state of hostility between the Christian West and the world of Islam. This era of distrust and hostility has been punctuated by times of bitter warfare that long outlasted the Crusades. With the rise of the Ottoman Empire, which was founded by Osman, an Ottoman Turk who overthrew the Abbasids in 1288, Europe faced a Muslim foe of considerable military strength whose territories included much of the Balkans and Greece. Nonetheless, hostile though relations were, this did nothing to limit trade and intellectual exchange between the two sides, a process from which Europe benefited enormously.

As Europe approached the Renaissance, it had already made considerable strides in education and learning based largely, up to that time, on the firm foundations laid by Islamic scholars. With the Renaissance and the new mood of intellectual inquiry that followed the Reformation, European intellectual attainments began to equal and then exceed that of Islam. This process was accentuated by a double blow that befell the world of Islam massively impeding further intellectual progress and from which it never recovered; firstly, the multiple invasions by Christian forces from the West, known as the Crusades and, secondly, an invasion from the East by the Mongol hordes under Genghis Khan, who sacked Baghdad and many other centres of Islamic culture and learning. Thus, by the seventeenth century, European progress in science, engineering and medicine had far outstripped those of the East. The new age of imperialism had dawned, and rather than waste valuable resources fighting the Ottoman Empire, the European nations began to explore and exploit the far-flung worlds of the Americas, Africa and the Far East. The Ottomans were left in peace.

Chapter 13

~

The Crusader States – The Principal Interface with Islam

I N THE CRUSADER STATES, the Frank's Muslim subjects generally accepted their new masters calmly, and eventually even admitted the justice of the Christian administration; understandably however, they could often become fractious if things were going badly for the occupying forces. The Jews, with good reason, longed for the days when the Arabs had ruled them, for their Islamic masters had always treated them with tolerance and kindness.[1] After the arrival of the crusaders, the number of Jews in the Holy Land and in Syria diminished substantially following the massacre at Jerusalem and from fear of persecution. The well-known traveller and chronicler of the Jewish people, Benjamin of Tudela, wrote in 1170 of his distress at how small their colonies had become when he visited the country.[2] It was only in and around Damascus that the Jews remained at all numerous.[3] For the Muslim peasantry there was little change despite the fact that the Kingdom of Jerusalem was superficially reorganized in a feudal manner.[4] However, the vast majority of Muslims, both outside and inside the occupied territories, never forgot the terrible massacre of their people by the crusaders in both Antioch and Jerusalem. Furthermore, throughout the entire history of the crusader kingdoms their life was marred by a steady influx of new crusaders and pilgrims from Europe, whose first question was 'Where are some Muslims that I may kill them?'[5]

The Latin rite of the Roman Church displaced the Byzantine practices that predominated among the local Christian communities before the First Crusade, but, in the short time between the founding of the military orders and the end of the twelfth century, the secular Church in the Holy Land was completely overshadowed by the military orders. These provided the king of Jerusalem with a reliable source of highly disciplined professional soldiers who not only cost the state nothing but were rich enough to build and maintain castles that few of his nobles could reasonably undertake. Without this on-going and dedicated aid, the crusader states would have perished far sooner than they did.[6]

Life in Outremer

With the passing of the years, the Franks of Outremer, as Palestine was now called, succumbed to a slow process of orientalization. Eventually, most of the knights abandoned Western fashions altogether and when they returned from battle they would remove their armour and wear a silk burnous in summer and sumptuous furs in winter.[7] To the newly-arrived Western pilgrims, life in Outremer sometimes seemed shocking because of its luxury and licence. It is possible that if the European forces had been more numerous then they might have kept up more of their Western ways, for throughout the entire period of their occupation, they remained a tiny minority, both racially and socially, in the lands they ruled.[8]

The standards of living of the Franks in Outremer were much higher than those they had experienced in Europe and they enjoyed far higher standards of medical care. The skill of Arab physicians was well in advance of that of doctors in the West, so in the crusader kingdoms, Christians consulted Arab or Jewish physicians in preference to those of their own culture. William of Tyre recorded that his contemporaries 'scorned the medicines and practices of our Latin physicians and believed only in the Jews, Samaritans, Syrians and Saracens.'[9]

Long-lasting hostility is, in itself, a relationship of sorts, one with its own rhythms and routines that necessitates interaction between the belligerent parties.[10] Slowly a degree of grudging diplomatic contact began to be established as the Franks entered into guarded relationships with their Islamic neighbours. They had to have dealings with the enemy as from time to time there were embassies to be exchanged, alliances to be negotiated against mutual enemies, truces to be arranged and, as a consequence of battle, prisoners to be ransomed.[11] One twelfth-century Muslim commentator, Usâma ibn Munqidh, left us an account of his views of the Christians whom he regarded as his enemies, but worthy ones. He referred to them as 'the Franks – may God confound them'.[12] He was contemptuous of their ignorance of medicine, and baffled by the social freedom permitted to Christian women. On the other hand, during periods of truce he was friendly with the Franks and found shared interests with many of them.[13] Despite the harsh reality of intermittent warfare, both sides grew to appreciate gestures of gallantry and chivalry, an attitude that the Christians learned from their Muslim opponents. In times of peace, nobles from each community often joined together for hunting expeditions and Christian and Muslim lords were sometimes honourably received at the court of the rival faith.[14]

Thus, between 1050 and 1300, Christian dominion first returned to Sicily under the Norman Kingdom, then came and went in Syria and Palestine, and eventually spread throughout most of Spain. This era was one of permanent hostility, which is subtly different from perpetual war, between the Christian and Islamic worlds around the Mediterranean. Does that mean that an impermeable wall of intolerance existed between the Christian and the Muslim?[15] There could never be lasting peace between the Franks and their Muslim neighbours, but there had to be considerable contact. Much of the revenues of the crusader states, for example, came from tolls levied on the trade between the Muslim interior and the coast and this, of necessity, demanded that Muslim merchants had to be allowed full access to Christian ports and be treated honourably.[16] It was indeed the new immigrants who had come to fight for the cause of Christianity whose crudity continually ruined any peaceful policy in Outremer. Furthermore, the policy of Holy Mother the Church seldom favoured any understanding with the infidel, for in the eyes of the hierarchy, no agreement made with an unbeliever could be binding.[17]

One problem plagued both sides in this state of perpetual hostility, and that was a lack of unity. The Christian forces were divided between several autonomous states and then complicated further by bitter personal rivalries and struggles for power. This situation was also writ large among the forces of Islam. Not only were the Muslim forces riven by local rivalries and tribal conflicts, but the majority of the empire was Sunni and the caliphate of Egypt was Shia. Thus the outbreaks of violence were generally localized because neither side could unite around a common purpose; temporary alliances between Christian and Muslim local lords against their co-religionists were not unknown. All this was soon to change.

Saladin

In 1138 Salah-al-Din Yusuf ibn Ayyub, or Saladin, was born. This was the leader who was eventually to unite the armies of Islam and lead them to victory over the crusaders. His father was the skilled general, Najm-al-Din Ayyub, and the young Saladin excelled in learning before he took up arms in the service of the Saracen leader, Nur el-Din. Under King Baldwin III (1130–62), Christian forces laid siege to the Arab city of Ascalon in 1153. After a prolonged siege, surrender terms were agreed and the Egyptian garrison, with the civilian population, was allowed to march out of the city unmolested; Baldwin III of Jerusalem strode in as its conqueror at the age of 23. As the English historian Anthony Bridge remarked with some surprise, 'unlike many of the Crusaders before him, he [Baldwin] kept his word.'[18] Such trustworthiness in keeping treaties was indeed rare among the Christian forces. Sadly, Baldwin III took sick and died on 10 February 1162. For the Christians he was irreplaceable, as he had the makings of a great king; his people mourned him bitterly and even the Muslim peasants of the country lined the road to pay their respects as his body was carried to Jerusalem. Someone urged Nur el-Din to grasp this opportunity to attack the Franks, but this chivalrous leader refused saying 'it would have been wrong to take advantage of a nation mourning the death of so great a prince.'[19]

The brutal and un-chivalrous attitude of the Christians manifested itself again at the fall of Bilbeis in Egypt in October 1168, when even some of the Franks themselves were shocked at the bloody and revolting massacre that followed. All of Egypt recoiled in horror and revulsion, for Muslims and Coptic Christians, women and children, old men and babies in arms were slaughtered with religious fervour. A few days later, when newly arrived crusaders from Europe captured the Coptic Christian port of Tanis, there was another holocaust. The mass of the Egyptians, who could easily have sided with the Franks, fell into the arms of Nur el-Din. Shortly afterwards the caliph died and Nur el-Din's general, Saladin, became ruler of Egypt.[20] By 1185, Saladin had united the disparate factions within the Muslim world through diplomacy, political realism and military prowess, and stood ready to act on his lifelong ambition – to wage jihad, or holy war, against the Christian forces of the Kingdom of Jerusalem and recapture the Holy City itself.

Saladin bided his time and used the period of a truce signed with the Christians in 1185 to unify his command of the forces of Islam. The truce between King Guy of Jerusalem and Saladin held firm, but they both reckoned without Reynald of Châtillon who is described as irresponsible and barbarous.[21] Under the truce, the great caravans which travelled between Damascus and Egypt had once more been passing without hindrance through Frankish lands. In May 1187 an enormous caravan was journeying from Cairo through Frankish territory accompanied by a small troop of Egyptian soldiers as protection against Bedouin raiders. In defiance of the truce, Reynald of Châtillon attacked it without warning as it moved into Moab, killing the small band of soldiers and taking the merchants and their families with all their possessions to his nearby castle at Kerak.[22] The booty was vast, much larger than he had ever seen before. Needless to say the news of this attack spread fast and soon reached the ears of Saladin. Mindful of the treaty, he sent a request to Reynald demanding the immediate release of the Muslim prisoners and full compensation for their losses. Reynald haughtily refused to even receive Saladin's envoys, who then travelled to Jerusalem and complained to King Guy. Guy listened sympathetically to the envoy's requests and promptly ordered Reynald to make due recompense. Reynald refused. Guy owed his throne to the support of Reynald and therefore could not, or would not, force his obedience.[23]

The Horns of Hattin

Saladin began to gather the largest army he had ever commanded across the frontier in the Hauran and this soon became known to the Franks. King Guy summoned his tenants-in-chief to bring their men to meet him at Acre. Both military orders, the Templars and Hospitallers, assembled all their available knights with the exception of the few necessary to garrison their castles. Thus, by the end of June 1187, 1,200 fully armed knights, a large number of light native cavalry, or Turcopoles, and 10,000 infantry were assembled outside the walls of Acre. The king held counsel with his barons when news came that Saladin and his army had crossed the Jordan. The majority of those present advised the king that their strategy should be purely defensive, for Saladin would not be able to keep his army in the field for long in that arid climate and would eventually be forced to retire.

However, Reynald of Châtillon and the hot-headed Gerard de Ridefort, grand master of the Templars, accused the others of cowardice. In consequence, the army then moved to Sephoria, another easily defensible base where the same argument broke out, but this time the king resolved to stay put. Later that night, again under pressure from the manipulative and inept Templar leader, he changed his mind, and thus the scene was set for disaster.[24]

Subsequently, at the Battle of the Horns of Hattin, Saladin defeated the largest Christian army ever assembled in Outremer and set in train the final decline of the crusader states. The fact that this debacle for the Christians was caused largely by the strategic incompetence of Gerard de Ridefort, the Templar grand master, as it was by Saladin's military genius, cannot mitigate the enormity of the defeat. After the battle, Saladin ordered the execution of all 230 surviving knights of the Templar and the Hospitaller orders saying: 'I wish to purify the land of these two monstrous orders, whose practices are of no use, who will never renounce their hostility and will render no service as slaves.'[25]

Ransom was forbidden to the warrior-monks by the rules of both orders, and Saladin knew this. Each of the knights was given the chance to convert to Islam, an offer that was predictably rejected, and was then handed over to the Sufis for beheading. Some have speculated as to why the Sufis undertook this task when their beliefs and those of the Templars had so much in common. The Sufis believed that all warriors who died for their faith went straight to paradise, so they obeyed orders in the certain knowledge that their victim's immediate entry to paradise was a more merciful fate than a lifetime of slavery. Reynald of Châtillon, who was captured at Hattin, was executed by Saladin himself for what we would now call war crimes.[26] Few shed any tears for him, for he was a violent and unscrupulous man, a violator of truces and an attacker of pilgrims making their way peacefully to Mecca. On his headless shoulders must lie the responsibility for the breach of the truce that led to the Battle of Hattin.

The author of the *Gesta Francorum*, who had himself fought the Saracens, claimed that 'you could not find a stronger or braver or more skilful soldier than they.'[27] The Christians, for all their faults, respected the moral worth and the military ability of their opponents. Saladin was the prime, but not the only, recipient of this type of admiration. He was a man of his word, who was pious, wise, clement and just. Harsh and terrible only to those like Reynald of Châtillon who flouted the laws of war. The Christian chronicler, John de Joinville, quoted Saladin's maxims with approval: 'Saladin said that you should never kill a man once you had shared your bread and salt with him.'[28]

Saladin's behaviour when he conquered the Holy City of

Jerusalem later the same year, stands in marked contrast to that bloody day that the Holy City was first captured by the Christian armies in 1099. Then there had been the usual bloodbath with the fanatical crusaders killing everyone in sight, Christian, Jew and Muslim, until the horses of the conquering knights waded up to their knees in blood. When the forces of Islam took the city, Saladin negotiated a peaceful surrender and its inhabitants were offered the chance to be ransomed and not massacred.[29] Indeed, many of those captured were ransomed by Saladin himself or by members of his family. Not one building was looted and no-one was injured.[30] Furthermore, as evidence of Saladin's innate Islamic tolerance for the People of the Book, Jews were encouraged to settle in Jerusalem once more.[31] Orthodox Christians and members of the Syrian Jacobite churches remained in the city, assured of their safety by their own earlier history under the benevolent rule of Islam.

The crusader states of Outremer were now reduced to a few cities and ports on the coast and the lands they defended. Jerusalem had fallen in 1187 and, on hearing the news, King Richard I of England took the Cross at Tours and vowed to liberate the Holy City once more. After conquering and subduing Cyprus en route to the Holy Land, Richard landed at Acre, a major fortified port in the truncated remnant of the Kingdom of Jerusalem, on 7 June.[32] It was in the Holy Land that Richard, who was probably the worst king that ever ruled England, established his reputation for all time as both a fearsome and chivalrous warrior. The battles between Richard the Lionheart and Saladin are truly the stuff of legend. For once the Christian forces had a leader whom they could respect as both brave and effective, and Richard earned the admiration of his opponent, Saladin. During one particular battle, Saladin watched Richard in grudging admiration, so moved by Richard's dauntless spirit that, when the English king's mount was killed under him, Saladin instructed one of his grooms to lead a pair of horses through the battle under a flag of truce and give them to the English king with his compliments.[33] It is also alleged that on another occasion when Richard lay ill, Saladin dispatched one of his own personal physicians to tend to his worthy adversary. True or not, this was widely believed by men on both sides of the conflict at the time, which gives some measure of the affection and respect inspired among fighting men by these two true giants of chivalry.

The customs of that time dictated that any leader of note should exploit his power for his own financial gain. However, Saladin was of such a devout character that he refused such opportunities and, uniquely for an Islamic sultan, he died in 1193, in almost total poverty and his brother even had to pay for his burial shroud.[34] Saladin had avenged the dreadful defeats inflicted on Islam by the crusaders, but in a manner that tempered courage with justice, humanity and generosity, and thus he won a resounding moral victory. He was renowned by both sides as a leader who had never been known to break his word to either friend or foe.[35]

After the capture of Jerusalem, the remaining crusader states in the Holy Land lingered on for over a century and, despite many attempts to revive the crusading spirit, any advances made by the forces of Christianity proved to be both temporary and illusory.

Another Crusade Against Christians

The Fourth Crusade in 1204 was a disaster that left a blot on the escutcheon of Christianity, which can never be removed. After a complex series of events, and inflamed more by greed than religious fervour, it was decided that the target would not be the Holy Land, but the Byzantine Empire, the home of Christians who spoke a different language, practised strange rituals and who refused to accept the authority of the pope in Rome.

This attack was demanded by the Venetians as payment for shipping the crusaders to the East. The pope, Innocent III, wrote to the leaders of the Crusade forbidding any such attack on a Christian state, but his letter arrived after the attack had begun. After two sieges of Constantinople, on Monday 12th April, the city fell to the crusaders. The next day a massacre began that beggars description; for 3 days, 20,000 armed and often drunken men, roved the city in bands, apparently leaderless and out of control, raping, murdering, and looting.

Constantinople was the home to artworks that had been brought there from all over the world for nearly 1,000 years. After the fall of the city, many of its crowning glories were looted by the Venetians, and even more destroyed by the French troops in an orgy of mindless violence. Priests robbed the churches; in the church of the Hagia Sophia, drunken and enraged soldiers tore down silk curtains, ripped the silver from the iconostasis, drank from the sacred vessels of the altar and installed a whore on the patriarch's throne, where she sang bawdy French songs. Others brought in horses and mules who defecated all over the floor. Outside in the streets no-one was spared; nuns were stripped naked and then violated; women and girls were subjected to similar obscenities and small children and babes-in-arms had their heads cracked like egg shells against the walls as the soldiers swung them by their heels. Nicetas, the Byzantine chronicler, wrote a lament for the city complaining bitterly that the Muslims would have been far more merciful than these so-called Christians. One crusader, Villehardouin, recorded that the invaders:

> ... all rejoiced and gave thanks to the Lord for the honour and victory He had granted them ... so that those who had been poor now lived in wealth and luxury. Thus they celebrated Palm Sunday and the Easter Day following with hearts full of joy for the benefits our Lord and Saviour had bestowed upon them.[36]

A French nobleman, Baldwin of Flanders, was elected emperor, and the noble estates in Greece and the other European territories of the Byzantine emperor were taken over by Venetian and French nobles who ruled them independently.

Despite his earlier reservations, when Pope Innocent III heard of the fall of Constantinople he celebrated, for this event established papal rule over the schismatic Church in the East. He wrote a letter of effusive congratulations to the new emperor, Baldwin, in which he expressed his unqualified approval of all that had happened. The Byzantine people had always despised the Franks who, in their eyes, were barbarians capable of any brutality. When they came to understand that the pope had given his blessing to the rape of their city and the massacre of its people their hatred for the West took on new dimensions. This was to have repercussions that would last for centuries.[37]

The Final Years of Outremer

Few of the Crusades that followed had any lasting impact on the advance of the forces of Islam in the Holy Land. Such Crusades that were mounted were ineffectual and Outremer was, as always, riven by personal rivalries, internecine strife and sometimes outright civil war. After the failure of the Crusade led by King Louis IX of France in 1244, a bitter civil war broke out over the ownership of the monastery dedicated to St Sabas that stood on a hill separating the Venetian and Genoese quarters of Acre. The Venetians allied themselves with the Pisans, the Templars, the southern French and the powerful Ibelin family; while the Genoese were supported by the Hospitallers and one or two of the most powerful nobles. There was bitter conflict in the streets of Acre, battles at sea between the rival Italian fleets, and violent struggles for control of the few Christian cities in Outremer.[38]

The various Italian merchant states who gained most of their income from trade with the Muslims, were constantly at each other's throats. They controlled virtually all of Outremer's commerce by their mastery of the seas, and they fought one another ruthlessly in their attempts to control the trade between Europe and the countries of the eastern Mediterranean, Christian or Muslim, regardless of the situation of their fellow Christians in Outremer. The military orders of the Templars, Hospitallers and Teutonic Knights were the only groups with anything like the same power as the Italian states, and they hated each other with as much venom as did the Italians. They too were rich, militarily stronger than any individual noble family, and completely ruthless when it came to defending their own selfish interests.[39] It is no small wonder that the Christian enclaves remaining in Outremer were doomed.

The Fall of Acre

Eventually, on 5 April 1291, the Muslim leader al-Ashraf appeared before the walls of Acre at the head of an army of a quarter of a million men. He found the city gates closed and its walls defended by knights and infantry from England, France and Italy, and virtually the entire complement of the Templars, Hospitallers and Teutonic Knights. The Christian forces had only one advantage, because of their command of the sea, food could be brought to them regularly from Cyprus.[40] However, the attack by al-Ashraf's forces led to the walls of the city being so weakened that they began to crumble and collapse. The grand masters of the Templars and Hospitallers led a furious counterattack, but although their knights fought with the immense courage for which they were rightly renowned, greatly outnumbered they could make no headway. The knights suffered heavy losses and, in the end they were driven back with William of Beaujeu, Grand Master of the Temple killed and John de Villiers, Grand Master of the Hospital, badly wounded.[41] Acre fell.

The remaining Frankish cities soon suffered the same fate as Acre; Tyre, which had twice defied Saladin, fell without a struggle; Sidon was defended for a time by a small group of Templars, but the odds against them were too great and they were forced to sail away and join other members of the order in the castle of Tortosa. Beirut fell next, and Haifa succumbed a few days later. The Templars were now not strong enough to garrison the three isolated castles they still possessed, so they abandoned Tortosa and Ahlit, and concentrated on defending the fortified island of Ruad. This they continued to hold until they were forced by the persecution of their order in France to abandon even that symbolic toehold off the coast of Outremer.[42] Thus the crusader cities were whittled away one by one, until the Christian forces lost their last viable foothold in that sacred but blood-soaked country.[43]

There had been plentiful criticism in Europe about the Crusades, but that had not been about fundamental principles of the crusading enterprise. It had concerned itself with the perceived moral state and disposition of the crusaders, or was limited to arguments about the ways and means of organizing particular crusading campaigns.[44] The moral tone of the crusaders was epitomized by their behaviour when they captured Jerusalem and other Muslim cities, by the thuggery of Reynald of Châtillon and the icy fanaticism of King Louis IX.[45] The moral superiority of their enemies was exemplified by the innately tolerant regime of Islam itself and the chivalrous behaviour of that great leader, Saladin.

Chapter 14

~

Europe and the Rise of the Ottoman Empire

EUROPE IN THE TWELFTH and thirteenth centuries was not only fighting the Muslims in the Holy Land but also on her southern flank in Spain. There the Moors were retreating step by step, as the *taifa* kingdoms fell one by one to the Christian forces, and, as a result, the threat posed by an Islamic state within Europe was gradually fading. In 1248, the Castilian conquerors of Seville initiated what we would now call 'ethnic cleansing' by expelling every Muslim from the city in an attempt to create an exclusively Christian territory. However, the new conquerors soon discovered that the city no longer functioned without the previous inhabitants and they grudgingly allowed the Muslims to return. These returnees became known by the Arabic term *al-mudajjar*, meaning those 'permitted to remain'.[1] The Reconquista came to a virtual halt in 1280, when the little kingdom of Murcia fell, leaving only the kingdoms of Granada and Malaga under Muslim control.[2]

The Demise of the Knights Templar

I have described in the previous chapter how in 1306, in an endeavour to buttress his ailing finances, King Philippe le Bel of France expelled the Jews and confiscated their property. He then expelled the Lombard bankers and devalued the coinage. His next target was the richest religious order in Europe, the Knights Templar. At dawn on Friday 13 October 1307, the king's agents throughout France opened sealed orders that had been distributed on 14 September.[3] They raided every Templar property within the kingdom and arrested the Templar grand master, Jacques de Molay, some 60 knights of the inner circle and all but 24 members of the order residing in France.[4] To justify these arrests, charges of heresy were levelled against the premier warrior order of Christianity described as, 'a bitter thing, a lamentable thing, a thing which is horrible to contemplate, terrible to hear of, a detestable crime, an execrable evil, an abominable work, a detestable disgrace, a thing almost inhuman, indeed set apart from all humanity.'[5] The knights were accused of causing Christ 'injuries more terrible than those he endured on the Cross',[6] a comment that implied that the Templars posed a greater danger to Christianity than the Saracens.

The king claimed that he was acting solely at the request of Guillaume de Paris,[7] the chief inquisitor of France, the pope's deputy and the king's confessor. However, it is blatantly obvious that the king was the prime mover in the whole affair and that the Inquisition was, in this instance at least, acting on the instructions of the state and not those of the pope. The inquisitors interrogated and tortured their knightly captives for nearly seven years and many died under their care; the archbishop of Sens, for example, supervised the burning of 54 Templar knights in 1310.[8] The denouement came on 18 March 1314 when the same archbishop of Sens, accompanied by three papal commissioners, sat on a stage erected outside the west front of Notre Dame de Paris. The bishop of Alba read out the confessions that had been extracted by torture from several of the knights and sentenced them to perpetual imprisonment.

At this point the Templar grand master, Jacques de Molay, redeemed himself by an act of calculated courage that has established his place in history for all time. This 70-year-old tortured wreck of a once great warrior, indicated that he wished to speak.

Under the mistaken impression that De Molay wished to confess, the assembled bishops graciously allowed him to address the crowd. The grand master then spoke:

> It is just that, in so terrible a day, and in the last moments of my life, I should discover all the iniquity of falsehood, and make the truth triumph.
>
> I declare, then, in the face of heaven and earth, and acknowledge, though to my eternal shame, that I have committed the greatest of crimes but... it has been the acknowledging of those which have been so foully charged on the order. I attest – and truth obliges me to attest – that it is innocent!
>
> I made the contrary declaration only to suspend the excessive pains of torture, and to mollify those who made me endure them.
>
> I know the punishments which have been inflicted on all the knights who had the courage to revoke a similar confession; but the dreadful spectacle which is presented to me is not able to make me confirm one lie by another. The life offered me on such infamous terms I abandon without regret.[9]

De Molay's words were greeted with roars of acclamation from the assembled crowd as Geoffroi de Charney stood beside the grand master as a sign of support and then spoke himself of the sanctity of the Templar order. He also revoked his confession.[10] The matter was resolved by clearing the square and immediately reporting the events to the king. He sentenced the two knights to a lingering death that same evening on the Isle des Javiaux. A slow fire was prepared to ensure that the Templar's agony would be prolonged and Jacques de Molay and Geoffroi de Charnay were slowly cooked to death. The Knights Hospitaller eventually inherited the vast majority of the Templar property in Europe.

The Templar order was never actually convicted of any of the charges laid against them, yet the order was still suppressed by the pope on 22 March 1312 by the papal bull, *vox in excelso*. The wording of this document is revealing:

...considering, moreover, the grave scandal which has arisen from these things against the Order, which it did not seem could be checked while this Order remained in being... even without blame being attached to the brothers... not by judicial sentence, but by way of provision, or apostolic ordinance, we abolish the aforesaid Order of the Temple... and we subject it to perpetual prohibition... Which if anyone acts against this, he will incur the sentence of excommunication *ipso facto*.[11]

Thus perished the Order of the Knights Templar, the organization whose protection of the pilgrimage routes throughout Europe had allowed long-distance overland trade to develop in a manner which, in conjunction with Templar banking practices, had encouraged economic activity, facilitated the accumulation of capital and, thereby, laid the foundations of the modern European economy. However, Templar tradition and spirituality lived on among the Rex Deus families and surfaced some centuries later in the form of Freemasonry. This now world-wide fraternity teaches its members by means of ritual and allegory, a spiritual pathway of tolerance and brotherhood based on the sure foundations of truth and justice.

The Expulsion of the Jews from Spain

Christian Spain eventually became united under the joint rule of Ferdinand V (1452–1516) and Isabella (d.1504) and their decision to banish the Jews from their kingdom was the culmination of systematic repression adopted in the 1470s. This new policy was made manifest by the establishment of the Spanish Inquisition between 1478 and 1480 during a period of religious elation that swept the country after the fall of Granada. The act of expulsion was written by the Inquisition, most probably by Tomàs Torquemada, signed by the joint sovereigns in March and proclaimed a month later. The edict ordered all Jews to leave Spain by the end of July. This mass forced exodus produced such a catalogue of suffering that even the Spanish and Italian chroniclers, who had no sympathy for the Jews, expressed their shock and horror. Many Jews fled to Portugal, but in vain, for four years later the king of Portugal, acting under pressure from Spain, issued his own edict of expulsion.[12]

The end result of these forcible expulsions of the Jews from Western Europe was a massive movement of people; a continual flow of Jews from Christian Europe to Muslim lands, which at times of severe persecution in parts of Europe, became a spate. The most massive exodus followed the expulsion of the Jews from Spain in 1492 when between 50,000 and 150,000 left, most of them for Morocco and the Ottoman Empire. This new Muslim empire had already received a large number of Jewish immigrants in the previous decades and made them all welcome, giving the new immigrants an opportunity to create a stable and prosperous life for themselves in a culture which had tolerance and respect for 'the People of the Book'.[13]

The Renaissance

Even in parts of Christian Europe there were occasional areas of toleration for the dispossessed Jewish migrants from Northern Europe, France, Spain and Portugal. The despots who ruled the northern city-states of Italy were tolerant of those who fled oppression elsewhere. It was under their tolerant rule that one of Europe's greatest flowerings of human genius, the Renaissance, took place; a massive explosion of creative talent that was unimpaired and forceful.[14] The banker and merchant, Cosimo de' Medici (1389–1464), the de facto ruler of the Florentine Republic, although he never held formal office, embarked upon a series of major projects that ultimately transformed Western civilization. In 1439 he sent agents all over the Mediterranean world in a quest for ancient manuscripts and, in 1444, he founded Christian Europe's first public library, the Library of San Marco in Florence, an institution that posed a direct challenge to the Church's increasingly feeble attempts to control access to education. Despite the earlier founding of the universities, the Church continued to delude itself that it was in control over all intellectual activity, hence the burning at the stake for heresy of the philosopher Giordano Bruno and the house arrest of Galileo for teachings contrary to Church dogma. Cosimo not only founded the library, but ordered the University of Florence to teach ancient Greek for the first time in seven centuries. Thus, thanks to the preservation of original manuscripts in Muslim libraries, pupils could now read the classics as they were written and no longer were forced to rely on translations.[15]

The study of the literature, philosophy and science of ancient Greece began to flourish and became the focus of the spirit of intellectual enquiry that triggered the Renaissance. Under the leadership of two Florentines, Petrarch (1304–74) and Boccaccio (1313–75), these studies were pursued with an understanding and appreciation never seen before in medieval Europe. Petrarch and Boccaccio searched for and rehabilitated classical works lying disregarded in the monastic libraries of Christian Europe and elsewhere[16] and after the Reconquista much of the learning of Hellenic times was transmitted to Florence from the Muslim Libraries of Granada and Toledo.[17]

The papacy did not view this outburst of creative activity and intellectual freedom with approval, and their power was brought to bear against the Rex Deus nobility in the north where Galezzeo Maria Sforza was assassinated in 1476 and Guliano de' Medici in 1478 as the result of a papal plot.[18] Despite these attempts to halt or even reverse the new spirit of intellectual inquiry and progress, Lorenzo de' Medici (1449–92), known as Lorenzo the Magnificent, consolidated his power in Florence and surrounded himself with scholars imbued with the mysticism of Egypt and the wisdom of Greece. Devotional literature, philosophy and science flourished, and artists of immense stature, such as Boticelli, Michelangelo, Veroccio and Ghirlandaio, all worked under his generous patronage.[19]

Northern Italy had previously been a vast jumble of more or less powerful city-states, each jealous and envious of their rivals' prestige, thus there was a pressing need for a truly equitable balance of power among the northern city-states. The man who did most to accomplish this Herculean task was Cosimo de' Medici, the clever political manipulator who converted the Florentine republic into a concealed tyranny. Cosimo made an alliance with Francesco Sforza, who later became Duke of Milan, and thus maintained the balance of power in northern Italy.[20] Francesco Sforza consolidated his hold on Milan after many years of fighting against the traditional enemy – Venice, which was now faced with an enemy who was a master of strategy.[21]

Sanctuary for the Jews in Italy

The Rex Deus nobles of northern Italy ruled lands which earlier had been a haven for religious dissidents such as the Cathars and the Templars, and now provided a safe refuge for the Jews fleeing persecution in other parts of Europe. The assets and financial acumen of the Jewish immigrants enhanced and accelerated the trend towards commercial success that resulted from the northern city-states' geographical advantages. Jewish immigrants now began to flock to northern Italy – yet at the same time there was already a well-established Jewish community in the Papal States which encompassed far more than just Rome. By the second half of the fourteenth century, Jews from Rome moved to the Po valley just as large numbers of Jews crossed the Alps into northern Italy fleeing from increased persecution in Germany. A third wave, smaller in number, arrived after being expelled from France in 1306 and 1396, and these settled mainly in Piedmont and Savoy.

The most prosperous period for Jews in northern Italy was the Renaissance, the time when their communities reached their zenith.[22] The settlement of Jewish banking families in the northern Italian city-states gave a great impetus to Jewish communities throughout the region. Ashkenazi Jews fleeing from persecution in northern Europe established themselves in northern Italy between 1350 and 1420.[23] The Pisa Bank, the largest Jewish bank in Renaissance Italy, was founded in Florence in 1438. Thus, the Medici family proved to be as tolerant of the financially astute Jewish community as their forefathers had been in Carolingian times. When the Jews were expelled from Spain and the Spanish territories of Naples and Sicily, they were encouraged to settle in Piedmont, Milan, Ravenna, Pisa, Genoa, Livorno and Florence.[24]

The Reformation

Christian Europe soon had internal religious problems that were to divert its attention away from its hostility to Islam. As the Renaissance exerted its beneficial effects, Christianity was being pressed to reform, but instead of reform it split into warring camps which soon displayed all the brutality and intolerance that had earlier characterized its holy wars. The Protestant Reformation set brother against brother, peoples against their rulers and the new Protestant states at war with their Catholic neighbours. Protestants in Catholic lands were treated as heretics, harried by the Inquisition and burned at the stake. Their Catholic counterparts fared no better in Protestant countries. However, it is fair to say that many of these wars between the two religions were fought for mundane reasons of temporal power as much as for religious identity. Many kings and princes in Northern Europe were only too glad to be free from papal interference.

Sadly, Jews fared no better living among Protestant communities than they had in Catholic ones, for Protestant rulers expelled them too or, at the very least, implemented many of the medieval restrictions against them. This complex web of Christian anti-Judaism did not cease with the Enlightenment some centuries later, but continued long after the advent of this new form of humanitarian rationalism began to inculcate a more positive attitude.[25]

The Ottoman Empire

The new Ottoman rulers of the world of Islam conquered the remnants of the Byzantine Empire during the fifteenth century, a task in which they were well supported by the Venetians and the Genoese with a nose for profit that was uncannily accurate. These new rulers, the Ottoman Turks, began by extending and strengthening their authority over the Balkans and over the shores of the

Black Sea.[26] At the capture of Constantinople on 29 May 1453, the Ottoman sultan made his solemn entry into the city, which he then delivered, to his soldiers fury, having first expressed the wish that the walls and the houses be left intact.[27] Thus was born a new empire which was now firmly established over virtually the same territories that the Byzantine Empire had covered at its peak.

However, Constantinople had to be repopulated by Greek immigrants from all the subjected regions and this, to a certain extent, determined the way relations between the Sultan and his Greek subjects were organized. Sultan Mehmed II (1402–81), submitted himself to Byzantine ceremonial when he invested Gennadios Scholarios with the title of Oecumenical Patriarch, and prided himself on his title Amiras Turkorromaion (Emir of the Turko-Romans). This, in his eyes, was intended to ram home the fact that he had replaced the Byzantine emperor at the head of a multi-ethnic empire, rather than simply ruling over a Turko-Greek empire. Thus, the privileges granted to the patriarchate of Constantinople increased his power over populations that were already well-established within the framework of Church organization. The Church emerged strengthened by this process and became the sole transmitter and preserver of both the Greek cultural legacy and Byzantine tradition, for it not only served as a focus of faith and ritual, but also provided the Greeks and the peoples of the Balkans and the Slav lands with the means of surviving in a dynamic way by preserving their cultural inheritance. A heritage which, many centuries later, was to provide the foundation on which their national identities could be built.[28]

From the middle of the sixteenth century the Ottoman Empire exercised considerable political and military power that enforced its authority from the Moroccan frontier to the Persian Gulf, from the Danube to the edge of the Sahara, and from the Black Sea to Arabia. A truly vast empire, one whose power was widely admired and respected; a seemingly unshakeable Colossus against which Europe only ever achieved defensive successes, but more often than not, had to circumvent. By uniting practically the whole Arab-Muslim world, the sultan became its temporal ruler and also, as the

'Commander of the Faithful', its spiritual leader, yet he still did not call himself Caliph. To the Christian world, he represented the power of Islam, yet he had no wish to crush the Christians, and certainly not those within his empire. Christian Europe, however, was bent upon conquering the world at the beginning of the sixteenth century, and the Ottoman Empire presented an insurmountable obstacle to those ambitions. It was present in all parts of the ancient world: the Mediterranean, eastern Europe and the Near East and, of course, the sultan was the incarnation of the Ottoman Empire; he wielded absolute power, was temporal ruler, leader of all Muslims and, in line with Islamic faith, culture and tradition, was the protector of the Jews and Christians.[29]

Tolerance for 'The People of the Book'

The citizens of the empire fell into two principal categories: Muslims, who enjoyed all the rights specified by Qur'anic law; and the non-Muslims, specifically Christians and Jews who were subordinate to their own religious leaders, patriarchs, metropolitans and grand rabbis.[30] In exchange for their freedom of religion and the protection granted them by the sultan, the Jews and Christians paid him a specific tax, and as the Ottoman's tolerance was well known in the Mediterranean world when waves of Jews were expelled from Spain in the sixteenth century, they found safe refuge in Constantinople and Salonika. In the Arab countries, the inhabitants – Muslim, Christian and Jewish – remained under the authority of their customary leaders and retained their traditional structures.[31]

For the Jews, the Ottoman conquest came as something of a salvation, as their situation both under the Byzantines in Asia Minor and Europe and Mameluke rulers in Egypt, had been extremely difficult. As a result, from early in the sixteenth century, the Jewish community in the Ottoman Empire became the largest in the world and enjoyed remarkable prosperity throughout that century. The empire was rapidly expanding and economic demand rose accordingly; the Jewish population could easily trade with Europe and soon began to enter the industries such as wool-weaving that were beginning to evolve.[32]

The Jews and Greek Christians were not the only beneficiaries of Islamic toleration, for many a Protestant in Transylvania and Hungary, rather than submit to the tender embrace of the Inquisition, opted to live under the tolerant banner of the Crescent. Indeed in any evaluation of Ottoman rule it would be hard to find any aspect that weighed more heavily in the balance for the Turks than their habit of religious toleration.[33]

Trade with the West

The Ottoman Empire was to last until the end of the First World War in 1918, but it was during the reigns of Selim I (1515–20) and Suleyman the Magnificent (1520–66) that it attained its greatest expansion in territory and reputation as a centre of cultural excellence.[34] Successive sultans strove to make their capital, now renamed Istanbul, a city unparalleled in its monuments and splendour, and these efforts resulted in a considerable growth of population. This population increase fuelled a growth in demand for products and goods which the East did not produce or which were of better quality in the West. It therefore became necessary to open the empire to foreign goods and Western nations profited from this and rushed to bring their produce to market.

Venice soon secured a strong position for herself, Genoa also profited from special trading concessions and the French had no problem securing the conditions of residence and trade which were known as *capitulations*. Another, rather odd, manifestation of this pseudo-alliance between the empire and the French, was the siege and capture of the city of Nice by the combined Ottoman and French fleets in 1543.[35]

Until the 1560s at the earliest, this newfound commercial activity did not suffer unduly from the Europeans' progressive exploitation of the sea-route around the Cape of Good Hope. Centuries-old patterns of trade cannot be turned in a few years or even a few decades, especially when so many people had a vested interest in their continuation. However, the influx of American silver coming to Europe via Spain, ultimately led to the devaluation of the asper, the basic Ottoman coin and this in turn led to the emergence of an economic crisis.[36]

Ottoman Culture

The conqueror of Constantinople, Sultan Mehmed II, was an extremely cultivated man who not only spoke several languages but also wrote poetry. He invited artists and writers to Istanbul, as Constantinople was now called, including Italians such as Gentile Bellini (1429–1507) who painted his portrait, and Greek and Italian writers such as Amitruzes of Trezibond, Cristobulus of Imbros and Ciraco of Ancona. Suleyman the Maginificent (1494–1566) was another highly cultured man who encouraged some of the greatest Turkish writers such as Fuzzuli (1480–1556); the first truly historical and critical Ottoman chronicles were compiled at this time and travel accounts and maps were drawn up by navigators like Piri Re'is and Sayd ali Re'is.

As was usual in Islamic countries, the study of science and medicine was pursued with vigour and, of course, the greatest of them all, namely religious science, was widely studied in the madrasas of the capital and the towns of the empire. Architecture flourished and was accompanied by a high standard of decorative arts which made striking use of glazed and decorated tiles, generally made in Nicea. Thus the reign of Suleyman the Magnificent became the golden age of the Ottoman Empire and he himself was an object of wonder for European travellers.[37] Suleyman 'the Magnificent', who the Turks called 'the Law-giver', reigned at the cultural and military zenith of the empire, for when the Hapsburgs occupied central Hungary in 1528, they were driven out by Suleyman, who besieged Vienna in a countermove in 1529.[38]

This was a truly unique epoch when culture and the arts blossomed, and the different religious communities enjoyed a large degree of cultural and judicial autonomy under the direct protection of the ruler. The Ottoman legal system developed a considerable degree of flexibility, especially when compared with traditional Islamic law which embraced different aspects of private and social life. Public law tended to work in favour of the organization and power of the state, and Suleyman himself gained special credit from his thorough codification and compilation of this system.[39]

A bastion of culture and military might, the Ottoman Empire was destined to last. However, when Suleyman retired to enjoy the pleasures of the harem towards the end of his life, he set a precedent which other sultans, who lacked both his culture and military prowess, sadly followed. These pleasure-seeking habits, aided and abetted by creeping corruption, were to bedevil the Ottoman Empire to one extent or another for the rest of its existence.

The Struggle for Freedom

During the seventeenth and eighteenth centuries, a European world hegemony arose based on economic dominance, institutions of government, military might, the mastery of communication, and all fuelled by dreams of empire. As the colonial powers treated their new subjects little better than the crusaders had used the Muslim people of the Holy Land, they were far from popular. European settlers in North America were not prepared to be treated like mere natives and, with the call 'no taxation without representation', rebelled against the British monarchy and defeated the British forces in the American War of Independence.

The profound influence exerted by Freemasons on the creation of the Constitution of the United States is a reflection of the inherently democratic traditions of Freemasonry. Supremely gifted men, possessed of great spiritual insight and a moral force have left a lasting imprint on the American nation in the form of the Constitution that is a ringing endorsement of the principles of freedom, democracy, and the rights of man – the lasting spiritual legacy of Freemasonry.[40] A large number of those who created and signed the American Constitution were Freemasons or Rosicrucians,[41] including such figures as George Washington, Benjamin Franklin, Thomas Jefferson, John Adams, and Charles Thompson. Freemasonry also contributed a great deal to the establishment of the principles of *liberté*, *égalité* and *fraternité* that inspired the French Revolution and, ultimately, the transformation of despotism into democracy.

Freemasonry also played a major role in the campaign for the reunification of Italy through its influence on the Carbonari, as both of the main leaders of this revolutionary movement, Garibaldi (1807–82) and Mazzini (1805–72), were active Freemasons. When their armies liberated Rome from the tyranny of the papacy, Pope Pius IX (1846–78), stripped of all temporal power, began his life-long exile in his self-imposed prison of the Vatican. The pope acknowledged that Freemasons were the authors of his downfall and fulminated against them in a series of encyclicals, papal bulls, and allocutions.

The aged pope was under no illusions as to the true origins of the organization that had stripped him of all earthly power. For him, Freemasonry derived directly from the heretical Order of the Knights Templar whom he described as being Gnostic from their inception and followers of the Johannite Heresy. Nor had he any illusions as to the true purpose of the Masonic fraternity, for, according to him, their aim was to destroy Holy Mother the Church. In his view, there was little difference between the true aim of the Rex Deus families of reforming the Church around the true teachings of Jesus, and the destruction of the Church that had propelled him to the dizzy heights of the papacy. Thus, the spiritual impact of Rex Deus had not only provided havens of refuge for Jews and heretics fleeing persecution, it had now helped liberate many European countries from tyranny and despotism.

The Decline of the Ottoman Empire

In the sixteenth century, the Ottoman Empire had been the most powerful state in the world but, by 1800 it only continued to exist because the European powers, whose attention had been diverted by their far-flung colonies, could not agree on precisely what to put in its place. Yet, oddly enough, both Britain and France were allied with this bastion of Islam in the Crimean War against Russia. From that point forward, Turkey, the principal seat of the empire, became known as 'the sick man of Europe'. In the aftermath of the First World War, the world of Islam was bullied, exploited and degraded by arrogant Westerners and experienced its deepest humiliation in the twentieth century. This fuelled resentments that are still with us,[42] which, in the light of the basic tolerance and respect for learning and progress that is inherent in Islamic culture, are otherwise impossible to explain.

Chapter 15

~

Divide and Rule – Twentieth-Century Imperialism

WHEN WE CONSIDER THE record of toleration for other faiths and cultures that is an integral part of Islam, especially in conjunction with the Jewish and Christian ethic of 'love thy neighbour as thyself', it is almost impossible to understand how the world today is riven by war, oppression and terrorism, all apparently waged under the banner of religion.

While Christian intolerance for other faiths is a matter of historical record, the Jews, as a people, did not make war for over 1,800 years. Why did they suddenly change after so many centuries of pacifism? Why did the world of Islam become so intolerant of the Jewish communities in their midst after a history of over 15 centuries of peaceful coexistence and acceptance? Why are Britain and America so hated in the Muslim world? Why did terrorists claiming to act on behalf of Islam, initiate the *intifada* in Israel, attack the twin towers in New York and plant bombs in Bali, Madrid and London? The roots of these complex issues have been dealt with in earlier chapters, but to understand their relevance today we need to learn how the Western powers have repeatedly abused, humiliated and betrayed the worldwide community of Islam.

Some Fruits of 'The War to End all Wars'

During the First World War, the Ottoman Empire made the tragic mistake of joining the losing side. Thus, when the war ended, German colonies and the territories of the Austro-Hungarian and Ottoman Empires were regarded as the spoils of war and divided among the victorious allies, the imperial powers of France and Britain. Thus, the Ottoman Empire was dismembered, its capital occupied and its sultan deposed. Its far-flung provinces were divided arbitrarily among the imperial powers with no consideration given to existing semi-autonomous regions, centuries-old patterns of governance, tribal loyalties or religious differences between Sunni and Shiite Muslims. The Kurds, for example, who had lived in one autonomous area under Ottoman rule, now found themselves brutally separated and living in five different and competing states. The Holy Land of Palestine had, as a result of British duplicity, been promised to two different peoples: the Arabs who had fought alongside the British army against their Ottoman rulers in the later part of the First World War; and the Jews who had been promised a 'National Homeland' in the Balfour Declaration of November 1917. The age-old imperial principle of 'divide and rule' came into play right across the Arab world. In Lebanon, the new French rulers favoured the sizeable Christian minority rather than the Muslim majority and, thereby, laid the foundations for the civil wars that have torn the country apart since independence.

New and completely artificial states were created, such as Iraq and Kuwait, by simply drawing lines on a map; new boundaries that grouped Kurds, Sunni and Shiite Muslims together in a manner which ignored systems of governance that had worked well for centuries, but which, nonetheless, conferred a considerable advantage to the British colonial masters. New rulers not only practised 'divide and rule' but also used the various peoples for bombing practice for the fledgling RAF, during the inevitable times of inter-community strife that ensued.

In Israel, new waves of Jewish settlement aroused deep fears and resentment among the Arab people who had lived there for centuries and who had been promised self-determination and self-rule by their new colonial masters. This gave rise to what is now a predominant factor in Islamic thinking today, a form of virulent anti-Semitism that was completely alien to the Muslim world prior to that time. However, these conflicts, and all those that followed, despite all claims to the contrary, are political in origin and not religious in nature, for the West has heaped duplicity, shame and humiliation on our Muslim brethren arrogantly and continuously for over 80 years.

The one success story was the creation of the modern state of Turkey by Kemal Attaturk (1881–1938). Working on the principle that you cannot modernize a nation by excluding 50 per cent of its population, this was one of the few Muslim countries that successfully achieved and sustained full emancipation for women while, at the same time, making a complete separation between religion and the state. Thus, modern Turkey is a democratic, secular state which is, nonetheless, predominantly and devoutly Muslim.

Elsewhere, matters developed in a different manner. In Arabia, for example, a political and military genius arose, Ibn Saud, a Bedouin leader who waged a war of unification which led to the creation of the state that bears his name, Saudi Arabia. A member of a strict fundamentalist sect of Islam, the Wahabis, he became not only the secular ruler, but also the guardian of the sacred cities of Mecca and Medina in 1926. Shortly after establishing his realm, which is administered in strict adherence to the sharia, the Qu'ranic law, oil was discovered in his territories. The Western powers rushed in to exploit this valuable resource and the early treaties establishing their commercial rights were negotiated by Harrison St John Philby, the father of Kim Philby who later achieved a degree of notoriety as a Russian spy. Oil changed the equation and gave the new king a significant economic power base which has increased over the years. Due to the massive oil revenues, which grew significantly after the exercise of OPEC (The Organization of Petrol Exporting Countries) power in the early 1970s, the state gained sufficient income to exist without taxing its people. The principle of 'there can be no taxation without representation' is now applied in reverse – there would be no representation of the people, because there was no need to tax them.

Thus, Saudi Arabia is far from a democratic state and, despite its close relations with the West, is repressive, denies women's rights and ruthlessly suppresses any form of political dissent. It is now ruled by the same family, which has swollen and includes some 6,000 members who are described by some fellow Muslims as lazy, ignorant and corrupt. Furthermore, it uses a considerable proportion of its oil revenues to fund, directly or through charitable foundations, the spread of Wahabi fundamentalism by financing madrasas or religious schools throughout the Muslim world. To adherents of the Wahabi sect, all other forms of Islam are heretical. Thus the West's need for oil indirectly aids and abets the rapid dissemination of a branch of Islam which, as we shall see, is vehemently anti-Western.

By the 1920s, Arab disempowerment by their colonial masters gave birth to a reaction based upon the religious unity of the Muslim world. A new organization sprang up, the Muslim Brotherhood, which claimed that the colonial powers and certain Muslim sympathizers had, by importing Western ideas and practices into Arab lands, betrayed their true Muslim heritage. This fundamentally nationalistic and religious movement worked on the ancient principle of 'my enemy's enemy is my friend', and they became closely allied to the Nazi party in Germany in the 1930s. German funding and expertise allied to Arab nationalism gave vent not only to anti-imperialist sentiments, but to violence, aimed at the Jewish settlers in Palestine and the occupying Western powers.

The Aftermath of the Second World War

Soon after the end of the Second World War, change began to sweep across the colonial remnants of the one-time Ottoman Empire. A new mood was afoot, the age of imperialism was drawing to its long-overdue close, and Arab countries began to gain their independence, but sadly under the artificial boundaries imposed decades earlier by Britain and France. The troubled land of

Palestine was partitioned by the United Nations, and the modern state of Israel was born in 1948. This was a traumatic event for the Arab world, for this new state was regarded as an imperial outpost of the West that had been imposed upon Muslims against their will.

The countries of the Arab League rejected the UN resolution that created the new state and no less than five well-armed Arab countries invaded Israel on the day of its birth, 15 May 1948. The Jewish settlers, with the memory of the Holocaust fresh in their minds, fought bravely for their very survival as individuals and as a people. With the exception of the Jordanian army which only achieved a stalemate position, the other four Arab armies were soundly and convincingly defeated. More humiliation and a further blow to Arab pride. The dissatisfaction of the Arab peoples with this performance resulted in the deposition or assassination of the heads of government of all five of the invading countries which soon became more or less repressive autocracies.

General Nasser (d. 1970) seized power as president of Egypt on 17 April 1954 after a military coup led by General Neguib. Nasser was a modernizer who wished to unite the Arab world, and allied himself with Soviet Russia who began to arm the Egyptians and the Arab States that followed Nasser's example. Due to the tensions of the Cold War, this led the USA to back Israel with massive economic aid, armaments and military advice. As this pleased the large and vocal Jewish lobby in America, the alliance became a fixture that no American president to date has had the courage to limit or curtail. Yet, paradoxically, when General Nasser allied himself with the USSR, the Muslim Brotherhood, who were appalled at his attempts to impose Western forms of modernization in Egypt, allied themselves, albeit temporarily, with the USA. Nasser's economic policy soon lay in ruins and Egypt was faced with an acute recession, a situation made far worse by the humiliating defeat it suffered at the hands of the Israeli army in the Six-Day War of 1967. In this conflict, Israel occupied Palestinian territories on the west bank of the Jordan, the city of Jerusalem, the Gaza Strip and Egyptian lands on the Sinai Peninsula.

Elsewhere in the Arab world, the Ba'ath party, modelled largely on the Nazi party in Germany, seized power in Syria and in Iraq. Now, for the first time in history, politically motivated Arabs were killing and torturing other Arabs irrespective of their shared faith in Islam. Some Arab States were supported by the Soviet Union, others by the Western powers; all were brutal, anti-democratic and repressive. Those states that did attempt some form of democratic reform, simply did not last. In Iran, for example, when it nationalized its oil industry in 1951 and then democratically elected Muhammed Mossadeq as Prime Minister, a British Labour government, which had nationalized the vast majority of its own industries, used gunboat diplomacy to bring down the elected government of the Iranian people in 1953. Power now rested solely with the shah of Persia.

The shah was a modernizer, an emancipator of women and distinctly pro-Western in his attitudes. However, he also maintained a highly efficient secret police force and repressed any dissent with brutal efficiency. He was one of the few who had the courage to exile religious leaders who criticized the state, among them the Ayatolla Khomeni. Yet, amid a tide of rising dissatisfaction with his rule, the shah was forced to abdicate (he reigned from 1941 to 1979 and died in 1980).

In 1979 the Ayatolla (d. 1989) returned in triumph and, after the American hostage crisis (October 1979), Iran became a virtual theocracy. The Ayatolla's Persian Shiite movement which was allied to the Muslim Brotherhood crushed all who opposed it. In fact there were more summary executions in the first 9 months of the Ayatolla's rule than in the previous 15 years of the shah's control. This was the first time in the entire history of Islam that clerics controlled the state. The Ayatolla had invented a new form of fundamentalist Islam, but this new form had sharp teeth and virulently anti-Western attitudes. For most of the Iranian people, a vicious form of religious tyranny had simply replaced a secular one.

The Ba'athist dictatorship in Iraq under the leadership of Saddam Hussein was comparable to Nazi Germany in Arab garb. Iraq's vast oil revenues provided a multitude of palaces for Saddam and his henchmen, funded an efficient and murderous secret police force and an ever-increasing army. Saddam slaughtered his people indiscriminately; political opponents; the Kurdish population in northern Iraq; men women and children; Marsh Arabs; Shiite Muslims; all were grist to the murderous mills of the Iraqi regime. When he went to war against his theocratic neighbour in Iran (September 1980–August 1988), another oil-rich and repressive state, God alone knows how many millions died in the senseless slaughter that lasted seven years. Yet, at the finish, who had gained? The borders between Iraq and Iran remained virtually unchanged. The only ones to profit from this pointless war were the armament manufacturers, mainly in the USA and Britain, who had armed Saddam's regime not merely for the profit, which was considerable, but to halt the rise of anti-Western sentiment in Iran. It does not reflect much credit on the US government to learn that its officials acted as sales personnel for the arms lobby that kept Saddam in power for decades. The West even provided this evil dictator with the raw materials for the poison gas he used so indiscriminately against the Kurdish population in northern Iraq.

When Saddam invaded the oil-rich state of Kuwait on his southern border in 1990, the USA assembled a coalition that included Britain, Saudi Arabia and other Arab countries, to restore the status quo. A brief and brutal war followed which resulted in the 'liberation' of Kuwait and its restoration to the despotic rule of its tribal leaders. The casualties among the armed forces of Iraq were beyond count, yet the dictator Saddam Hussein was left to persecute his people for another decade. His reign only ended with the Second Gulf War in 2003, initiated by President Bush and Prime Minister Tony Blair. This conflict, which was declared illegal by the secretary-general of the United Nations, was fought for highly dubious motives and promoted on specious grounds based upon so-called 'accurate' and up-to-date military intelligence which was viewed with considerable scepticism by the majority of the British public, but sadly accepted by a parliamentary majority in the House of Commons. This military intelligence supposedly proved that the Iraqi dictator possessed 'weapons of mass destruction' that posed an imminent threat to the world; it is now patently obvious that no such weapons existed. It has recently been admitted that the true reason for this war was regime change, an action that was in direct contravention of the Charter of the United Nations, a treaty to which both Britain and the USA were co-signatories.

The true cost of this war, or of the Afghan War which preceded it, will never be known. Eventually some economic price may be put on this conflict, but its true cost in human terms is almost incalculable. Military casualties among the British and American forces during the invasion were startlingly small. However, since the occupation began, American casualties in particular have steadily increased and are still rising. At the time of writing they have reached a total of 2,000 and, according to the best estimates compiled by the British Medical Association, civilian casualties among the Iraqi people exceed 100,000 innocent men, women and children, killed or maimed for life. Almost the entire infrastructure of this once thriving country has been destroyed; power and fresh water are only intermittently available; the Iraqi army was disbanded, as were the police; security is nonexistent and where there was no terrorist activity, there is now plenty, masked to some extent, by a full-scale rebellion against the occupying powers; played out against a backdrop of mass unemployment and social deprivation brought about by a conflict supposedly 'to liberate the Iraqi people from Saddam Hussein'.

For many Iraqis, the cure is infinitely worse than the disease. However, the Western allies arrogantly assume that they have the right to impose some form of Western democracy upon the Iraqi people. It took several years for the newly liberated American colonies in the eighteenth century to devise the Constitution, and that with the benefits of the Enlightenment and the guidance of founding fathers of the state steeped in the fraternal principles of Freemasonry. Yet, according to the American imposed timetable, the newly elected Iraqi representatives have to cook up a constitution in months, against a background of continuing civil war, and then sell that idea to a divided people. Few people are sanguine about the probable results that will flow from this inherently flawed process.

Muslim extremism, therefore, did not arise suddenly as a reaction to modern-day American economic or political imperialism; it was a predictable reaction against old-fashioned colonialism imposed by force after the First World War. American interference in recent years has simply made a bad situation infinitely worse. It is we in Western Europe who must shoulder much of the responsibility for the present state of affairs, in the full and certain knowledge that American interference in the internal politics of other countries since the Second World War has exacerbated these problems almost beyond belief. This situation has been aggravated by President Bush's declaration of a 'war against terrorism' which was interpreted by the vast majority of people as a war against Islam. A point reinforced by his use of the word 'crusade'.

The state of Israel has survived several wars, and its heady triumph in the Six-Day War was followed by near defeat in the opening days of the Yom Kippur War in 1973, which only turned to outright victory when Israeli forces fought their way to the east bank of the Suez Canal. An invasion of Lebanon followed in 1982, during which Ariel Sharon, later prime minister of Israel, was the general who stood idly by when the Lebanese Christian militia massacred innocent Palestinian civilians in the Shatilla refugee camp. Various attempts were made by the USA to broker a deal between Israel and its Arab enemies and a peace treaty between Egypt and Israel was signed by the Israeli prime minister, Monachim Begin (1977–83) and the president of Egypt, Anwar Sadat (1970–81). Sadat's reward was assassination by fundamentalist fanatics from among his own people.

Israel has, for many years now, engaged in outright war against the Palestinian inhabitants of the occupied territories in a manner that has caused outrage in the West. In Britain, a leading Jewish MP, Gerald Kaufman, wrote an open letter to Prime Minister Ariel Sharon in which he reminded the Israeli leader that the symbol of the Star of David was not the property of the state of Israel, it was the symbol of worldwide Jewry, one that Sharon had no right to besmirch with the blood of innocent Palestinian civilians. Needless to say, the slaughter and destruction continued unabated. We now have the obscene situation where the children of the inmates of the concentration camps of the Holocaust have become the guards in the giant concentration camp known as the occupied territories, surrounded by a huge concrete wall instead of the traditional barbed-wire fence. Despite the alleged pressure brought to bear by Prime Minister Tony Blair on President George W Bush of the United States, little constructive progress seems to be taking place, for the Palestinian people remain oppressed by the armies of Israel.

Palestinian reaction has been violent in the extreme and their response was to use a new weapon, the suicide bomber. Again the cure is worse than the disease. Fanatical young people have their clothes packed with explosive and are sent out to civilian areas within Israel to murder and maim other innocent men, women and children. Suicide is forbidden by the Holy Qur'an, as is the murder of innocent civilians, yet this obscene form of terrorism continues, not merely within Israel, but in New York, Madrid, London, Bali, Africa and Iraq. How can one demonstrate one's love of God by killing other innocent children of God? How did this vile form of warfare spread from Israel to the rest of the world?

Terrorism and guerrilla warfare have a long history. Guerrilla warfare was effective in the American War of Independence; proved its worth in the Peninsula campaign in the war against Napoleon and it was an essential aspect in Ireland's long and bloody war of independence. It was widely used in many campaigns during the Second World War and has raised its head countless times in many countries since then; countries such as South Africa, Bolivia, Nicaragua, Egypt with the assassination of Anwar Sadat and even in Saudi Arabia at the sacred site of Mecca during a time of pilgrimage. Terrorism has played its part in many conflicts and, it must never be forgotten, one man's terrorist is, as often as not, merely another man's freedom fighter. These facts have been widely recognized for many years. Terrorist attacks were an essential part of Israel's wars against the British mandate in Palestine – no one's hands are clean. When this tool is used by an aberrant and fanatical genius with access to almost limitless resources it becomes truly devastating, and this is precisely what has happened over the last few decades.

Osama Bin Laden is the son of a wealthy Saudi who first came to notice during the Afghan guerrilla war against the Russian occupying forces. As a volunteer member of the *mujaheddin*, he was trained, armed and encouraged by America's CIA and his home country of Saudi Arabia. He learnt his trade the hard way, as a fighter in a bitter war of terrorism and attrition. In 1990, he offered to help depose Saddam Hussein, an offer that was refused and he was officially expelled from Saudi Arabia in 1991 finding refuge in the Sudan and later in Afghanistan. A fanatical Wahabi, anti-American and anti-Western, superbly trained and with all the resources that his wealth and modern technology can supply, Osama Bin Laden had become a highly dangerous enemy of America in particular and Western values in general. His organization, al-Qaeda, a worldwide network of terrorism, launched attacks on American ships and military bases long before the spectacular and horrifying assault on the twin towers in New York. Since then there has been the brutal destruction of a nightclub in Bali with terrible loss of life, the massacre of innocent commuters in Madrid and, more recently, in London. It is also claimed, with some degree of plausibility, that since the overthrow of Saddam Hussein in Iraq, al-Qaeda has taken advantage of the state of near civil war in that country, to wage its war of terrorism against members of the Muslim population. Thus we live in a world scarred by terrorist attacks which occur without warning, which kill, maim and destroy the lives of innocent civilians, be they Christian, Jew or Muslim, and all this is committed in the name of Islam and the Holy Qu'ran.

Al-Qaeda does not represent Islam, although it does use and abuse genuine Islamic grievances to justify its actions – actions which run directly contrary to the teachings in the Holy Qu'ran. The long-running sore of the Israeli occupation of the Palestinian lands is used by these brutal killers not only to indoctrinate its operatives but also as a spurious excuse for a worldwide campaign of murder and mayhem.

Understanding the root causes of the present hostility between the West and Islam with its terrible consequences is only the essential first step in coming to terms with their appalling reality. The vital question to address is 'What can we do to alleviate and solve this problem?'

Chapter 16

~

A Common Heritage and Future

*Those who do not learn from history –
are condemned to repeat it!*

E VEN THE BRIEF STUDY OF history revealed in these pages
demonstrates that European culture owes an immense and
immeasurable debt to the world of Islam. Muslim scholars preserved and enhanced the learning of ancient Greece, laid the foundations for modern science, medicine, astronomy and navigation
and inspired some of our greatest cultural achievements. If it were
not for the inherent tolerance for the People of the Book that was
manifest within the Islamic world for over 15 centuries, it is highly
doubtful that the Jewish people could have survived as a racial and
religious entity, and we would have lost their contribution to art,
medicine, science, literature and music which is almost beyond
measure. We in the West owe a debt to the Muslim world that can
never be fully repaid. Despite our common religious and spiritual
roots, we have thanked them with centuries of mistrust, the brutality of the Crusades and an imperial takeover that was conducted
with callous indifference to the needs of the peoples we exploited.

While that was in the past, our collective arrogance at the present time has escalated almost beyond measure, for few in Europe
or the United States either know, or care about, the lessons we have
learned from our Islamic brethren. Collectively, we seem to regard

the Muslim world as a backwater, inhabited by people of strange habits and almost incomprehensible beliefs. The Arab lands only become important to the West when we view them as a collection of giant gas stations; mere providers of the raw material by which our economy is driven, hardly the basis for any realistic understanding between peoples of different cultures and faiths.

European nations all went through periods of despotism, dictatorship and internecine strife, but with the rising tide of education and the inspiration of Freemasonry impelling our democratic dreams we rose above that, sometimes peacefully and sometimes in violent rebellion. It is really only in the last century or so that the move towards democracy really took hold, a process that is still going on in parts of Eastern Europe today. We need to recognize that the internal political problems of Muslim countries, whatever the nature of their regimes, must be left to their own people to solve. History has proved beyond all doubt that the world of Islam is founded on spiritual principles that have an innate capacity for fostering tolerance, understanding and promoting brotherhood between all races and creeds. Furthermore, they have the same right to develop in line with the needs and aspirations of their people as the European nations had before them. Britain, France, America and Russia were all co-signatories of the founding charter of the United Nations organization and one of its principal terms states that no country has the right to intervene in the internal political affairs of another, a rule that has been repeatedly broken by the United States of America and a number of European countries.

Our elected representatives in the West are our elected servants and not our masters. They should not have the freedom to initiate wars of aggression without the consent of the people they serve. Nor should they be permitted to prop up repressive regimes purely for commercial advantage. Trade is always to be encouraged, the subsidy of tyranny should be forbidden. The American Constitution starts off with the words 'We the People'. Were 'we the people' consulted about the wars in Afghanistan or Iraq? Was our permission sought before Saddam Hussein was armed? I doubt it. The British government went to war against Iraq despite anti-war demonstrations in London and other major cities in which more than one million people took part, and that war has made the situation infinitely worse, not better. It has not solved problems, it has created them.

The state of nearly constant repression of the Palestinian people by the Israelis needs to be ended by a just and equitable peace settlement that gives Israel the security it deserves and creates an economically and politically viable Palestinian State – a concept that is admitted in principle but that seems as far way as ever. As for al-Qaeda, bereft of its main sources of propaganda, namely the Western powers' support of Israel and interference in Iraq and Afghanistan, it would wither away in time, for it has become an acute embarrassment within Islam and a greater danger to the Muslim people than the Western powers.

To work even within this simple framework requires courage; the United States government once brokered a peace treaty between Israel and Egypt, it is time for it to act again, this time effectively, bringing the Israelis and the Palestinians to the negotiating table without preconditions. United Nations forces, preferably drawn from Arab countries, should be left to restore order in Iraq and the Western allies should withdraw as quickly as possible. Western aid for that troubled country should be generous in reparation for the enormous damage that has been done.

Can the world of Islam solve its own problems? It has done so in the past and, thanks to the basic principles of its faith, it has done so with tolerance and respect for other faiths and cultures, a lesson that the West has still to fully appreciate. Sustained by their firm and unshakeable faith, and imbued with the desire for freedom, who or what can stop them? The religion of Islam has inspired so much in the past and it will triumph again in the fields where it has more experience than others – tolerance, creativity and respect. Grant them the same respect that they have shown to us when they, unconditionally, shared the fruits of their culture with us.

Source Notes

Introduction

1 Goodwin, Geoffrey, *Islamic Spain*, pp. 8–9
2 Eusabius, *Ecclesiastical History*, Book III, ch.xi; Armstrong, Karen, *A History of Jerusalem*, p. 153
3 Hattstein, Marcus and Delius, Peter (eds) *Islam Art and Architecture*, p. 12
4 Hattstein, Marcus and Delius, Peter (eds) *Islam Art and Architecture*, p. 14
5 Hattstein, Marcus and Delius, Peter (eds) *Islam Art and Architecture*, p. 16
6 Armstrong, Karen, *Muhammad*, pp. 23–4
7 Armstrong, Karen, *Muhammad*, p. 22
8 Wallace-Murphy and Hopkins, *Rosslyn: Guardian of the Secrets of the Holy Grail*, p. 83
9 Akbar, S W Ahmed, *Discovering Islam*, p. 4
10 Goodwin, Geoffrey, *Islamic Spain* p. 5
11 Ravenscroft and Wallace-Murphy, *The Mark of the Beast*, p. 132
12 Armstrong, Karen, *Muhammad*, p. 29

Part I introduction

1 Wilson, Colin, *The Occult*, p. 35
2 Wilson, Colin, *The Occult*, p. 35
3 Cited by Colin Wilson in *The Occult*, p. 38

Chapter 1

1 Wilson, Colin, *From Atlantis to the Sphinx*, p. 81
2 Bauval Robert and Gilbert Adrian, *The Orion Mystery*, p. 58

3 Edwards I E S, *The Pyramids of Egypt*, p. 150
4 Bauval Robert and Gilbert Adrian, *The Orion Mystery*, p. 63
5 Bauval Robert and Gilbert Adrian, *The Orion Mystery*, p. 63
6 Edwards I E S, *The Pyramids of Egypt*, p. 151
7 Faulkner, R O, *The Ancient Egyptian Pyramid Texts*, p. v
8 West, John Anthony, *Serpent in the Sky*, p. 1
9 Rohl, David, *Legend: the Genesis of Civilization*, p. 310
10 Rice, M, *Egypt's Making: The Origins of Ancient Egypt 5000–2000 BC*, p. 33
11 Kantor, H J, 'The Relative Chronology of Egypt and its Foreign Correlations Before the Late Bronze Age', in *Chronologies in Old World Archaeology*, p. 6
12 Derry, D E, 'The Dynastic Race in Egypt', (1956) *Journal of Egyptian Archaeology*, issue 42, 1956, pp. 80–5
13 Bauval and Hancock, *Keeper of Genesis*, p. 203
14 Rohl, David, *Legend: the Genesis of Civilization*, p. 265
15 Bauval and Hancock, *Keeper of Genesis*, p. 228
16 Reymond, E A E, *Mythical Origins of the Egyptian Temple*, p. 273
17 VandenBroeck, André, *Al-Kemi*,
18 Wilson, Colin, *From Atlantis to the Sphinx*, p. 32
19 de Lubicz, René Schwaller, *Sacred Science*, p. 120
20 Pauwels and Bergier, *The Dawn of Magic*, p. 247
21 Wilson, Colin *From Atlantis to the Sphinx*, p. 14
22 Genesis, ch. 20, v. 12
23 Rachi, *Pentatuque selon Rachi, La Genèse*, p. 251
24 Genesis, ch. 11, v. 27
25 Genesis, ch. 11, v. 29
26 Genesis, ch. 17, v. 5 and v. 15
27 Genesis, ch. 17, v. 4
28 *Sepher Hajashar*, ch. 26
29 Genesis, ch. 21, v. 21
30 Genesis, ch. 12, v. 15
31 'Have you seen the old man and woman who brought a foundling from the street and now claim him as their son?' *The Babylonian Talmud*
32 The Koran, (The Prophets) Sura 21, v. 72
33 Genesis, ch. 14, v. 19
34 The term is used repeatedly by both Abraham and Melchizadek in Genesis, ch. 14
35 Genesis ch. 17, v. 10
36 *Encyclopaedia Brittannica*, London 1956, Vol. 5, p. 721
37 Freud, S, *Moses and Monotheism*
38 Sellin, E, *Moses and His Significance for Israelite-Jewish History*

39 Genesis, ch. 22, v. 2

40 Genesis, ch. 22, v. 18

41 Exodus, ch. 2, vs. 1–10

42 Freud, S, *Moses and Monotheism*

43 Sabbah, M and R, *Les Secrets de L'Exode*

44 Sabbah, M and R, *Les Secrets de L'Exode*

45 Sabbah, M and R, *Les Secrets de L'Exode*, p. 6; Freud, *Moses and Monotheism*, pp. 96 and 123 (French edition)

46 The Journal *Imago*, 1, 1912, pp. 346–7

47 Feather, R, *The Copper Scroll Decoded*, p. 34 also confirmed by Joseph Popper-Linkeus in *Der Sohn des Konigs von Egypten. Phantasieen eines Realisten*, Carl Resiner, 1899

48 Cotterell, M, *The Tutenkhamun Prophecies*, p. 335

49 Osman, Ahmed, *Moses Pharaoh of Egypt*

50 Freud, S, *Moses and Monotheism*

51 Cited by Feather, R, *The Copper Scroll Decoded*, p. 36

52 Deuteronomy, ch. 5, vs. 6–9

53 Petrie, F, *The Religion of Ancient Egypt*

54 Sabbah, M and R, *Les Secrets de L'Exode*, p. 99

55 Faulkner, R O, *The Ancient Egyptian Book of the Dead*, p. 29

56 Exodus, ch. 20, vs. 13, 15, 16

57 Psalms, 104, v. 24

58 Gedes and Grosset, *Ancient Egypt Myth and History*, p. 268

59 Sabbah, M and R, *Les Secrets de l'Exode*

60 D'Olivet, A F, (1768–1825), *La Langue Hébraïque restituée*

61 Sabbah, M and R, *Les Secrets de l'Exode*

62 Sabbah, M and R, *Les Secrets de l'Exode*

Chapter 2

1 I Kings, ch. 12, v. 11 and II Chronicles, ch. 10, v. 11

2 Cited in *The Historical Atlas of the Jewish People*, p. 22

3 II Kings, ch. 24, v. 14

4 Johnson, Paul, *A History of the Jews*, p. 82

5 Epstein, I, *Judaism*, p. 83

6 Fox, Robin Lane, *The Unauthorised Version: Truth and Fiction in the Bible*, p. 53

7 Cohn-Sherbok, Dan, *A Concise Encyclopedia of Judaism*, pp. 43–4

8 Cohn-Sherbok, Dan, *A Concise Encyclopedia of Judaism*, pp. 61 and 62

9 Fox, Robin Lane, *The Unauthorised Version: Truth and Fiction in the Bible*, p. 72

10 Armstrong, Karen, *A History of God*, p. 79

11 Cantor, Norman, *The Sacred Chain*, p. 29

12 Cantor, Norman, *The Sacred Chain*, p. 29

13 Vermes, *Jesus the Jew*, p. 79

14 Armstrong, Karen, *A History of Jerusalem*, p. 116

15 Eisenman, Robert, *James the Brother of Jesus*, p. 200

16 Eisenman, Robert, *James the Brother of Jesus*, p. 133

17 Ezekiel, ch. 18, vs. 17–21

18 Zohar 59b on "Noah"

19 Armstrong, Karen, *A History of Jerusalem*, p. 96

20 Armstrong, Karen, *A History of God*, p. 75

21 Cantor, Norman, *The Sacred Chain – a history of the Jews*, p. 7

22 Cantor, Norman, *The Sacred Chain – a history of the Jews*, p. 11

23 Freud, S, *Moses and Monotheism*

24 Johnson, P, *A History of the Jews*, p. 42

25 Allegro, J M, *The Dead Sea Scrolls and the Christian Myth*, p. 65

26 Allegro, J M, *The Dead Sea Scrolls and the Christian Myth*, p. 40

27 Psalms, 99, v. 7

28 Allegro, J M, *The Dead Sea Scrolls and the Christian Myth*, p. 173

29 Ecclesiasticus, ch. 24, v. 4

30 Proverbs, ch. 9, v. 1

31 Keller, W, *The Bible as History*, Hodder and Stoughton, London, 1956

32 Cantor, Norman, *The Sacred Chain – a History of the Jews*, Fontana, London, 1996

33 Fox, Robin Lane, *The Unauthorised Version: Truth and Fiction in the Bible*, pp. 225–33

34 Allegro, J, *The Dead Sea Scrolls and the Christian Myth*, p. 61

35 Semitic Gods, pp. 132–3

36 Armstrong, Karen, *A History of Jerusalem*, p. 30

37 Baring, A and Cashford, J, *The Myth of the Goddess*, p. 454

38 *Jerusalem Bible*, p. 419, Eyre and Spottiswoode, London, 1968 (NB The Jerusalem Bible has been translated directly from Hebrew and not via Greek) See also Zeitlin, I M (1986) – *Ancient Judaism*, Polity Press, Cambridge, UK, p. 173 and Hancock, G, *The Sign and the Seal*, 1992, pp. 419–20

39 II Kings, ch. 23, v. 12

40 Armstrong, Karen, *A History of Jerusalem*, p. 59

41 Armstrong, Karen, *A History of God*, p. 19

42 Ussishkin, D, 'King Solomon's Palaces', *Biblical Archaeologist*, 35, 1973

43 I Kings, ch. 6, v. 19

44 I Kings, ch. 6, v. 26

45 II Chronicles, ch. 4, v. 2

46 Armstrong, Karen, *A History of Jerusalem*, p. 34

47 II Chronicles, ch. 3, vs. 15–17
48 I Kings, ch. 11, v. 7
49 Armstrong, Karen, *A History of Jerusalem*, p. 27
50 I Kings, ch. 8
51 I Chronicles, ch. 23, v. 24
52 Sanmell, S, *Judaism and Christian Beginnings*, p. 22
53 Epstein, I, *Judaism*, p. 85

Chapter 3

1 Johnson, Paul, *A History of Christianity*, p. 10
2 Strabo, *Geographica*, Book 16, ch. 2, p. 46
3 Richardson, Peter, *Herod, King of the Jews and Friend of the Romans*, pp. 184–5
4 Josephus, *War*, Book I, ch. 4, 22 and *Antiquities*, Book XVI, ch. 1, 47
5 Josephus, *War*, Book I, ch. 4, 24 and *Antiquities*, Book XVI, ch. 1, 47
6 Josephus, *Antiquities*, Book XV, ch. 2, 59–65
7 Macrobius, *Saturnalia*, Book 2, ch. 4, 1
8 Matthew, ch. 1, v. 22 ff.
9 Ravenscroft and Wallace-Murphy, *The Mark of the Beast*, p. 113
10 Josephus, *Antiquities*, Book XVII, ch. 10, 9; *Wars*, Book II, ch. 5, 1
11 Jospehus, *Antiquities*, Book XVII, ch. 10, 10; *Wars*, Book II, ch. 5, 2
12 Eisenman, Robert, *James the Brother of Jesus*, p. xxi
13 Josephus, *War*, Book I, ch. 1
14 Josephus, *Antiquities*, Book XVIII, ch. 1, 2–6
15 Armstrong Karen, *A History of Jerusalem*, p. 121
16 Johnson, Paul, *A History of Christianity*, p. 17
17 Josephus, *Antiquities*, Book XVIII, ch. 1, 5
18 Josephus, *Antiquities*, Book XVIII, ch. 1, 5
19 Epstein, I, *Judaism*, p. 106
20 Epstein, I, *Judaism*, p. 112
21 Johnson, Paul, *A History of Christianity*, pp. 15–16
22 Eisenman, Robert, *The Dead Sea Scrolls and the First Christians*, p. 227
23 Epstein, I, *Judaism*, p. 97
24 Josephus, *Antiquities*, Book XVIII, ch. 6
25 Epstein, I, *Judaism*, p. 103
26 Epstein, I, *Judaism*, p. 105
27 *Jerusalem Talmud*, Sanhedrin, X, 5
28 Schonfield, Hugh, *The Essene Odyssey*, p. 39
29 Malachi, ch. 3, vs. 1–4
30 Malachi, ch. 4, vs. 5–6
31 John, ch. 1, v. 21

32 Johnson, Paul, *A History of Christianity*, p. 19
33 Johnson, Paul, *A History of Christianity*, pp. 19–20
34 Josphus, *Antiquities*, Book XVIII, ch. 5, 2
35 Crossan, John Dominic, *Jesus a Revolutionary Biography*, p. 34
36 Taylor, Joan E, *The Immerser, John the Baptist in Second Temple Judaism*, p. 278
37 Wilson, A N, *Jesus*, p. xvi
38 Armstrong, Karen, *A History of Jerusalem*, p. 145
39 Acts, ch. 2, v. 46
40 The Gospel of Thomas, 108
41 Morton Smith, *The Secret Gospel*
42 Matthew, ch. 1, vs. 5–6
43 Matthew, ch. 29, v. 19
44 Matthew, ch. 21, vs. 1–11; Mark, ch. 11, vs. 1–11; Luke, ch. 19, vs. 28–44; John, ch. 12, vs. 12–19
45 Luke, ch. 19, v. 38
46 Matthew, ch. 21, v. 12; Mark, ch. 11, v. 15; Luke, ch. 19, v. 45
47 Philo of Alexandria, *De Legatione ad Gaium*, p. 301; Epstein, I, *Judaism*, p. 106; Wilson, A N, *Paul the Mind of the Apostle*, p. 56
48 Epstein, I, *Judaism*, p. 107
49 Tacitus, *Annals*, Book XV, ch. 44

Chapter 4

1   Burton, Mack, *Who Wrote the New Testament?*, p. 4
2   Schonfield, Hugh, *Those Incredible Christians*, p. 48
3   Matthew, ch. 13, v. 55
4   Eusabius, *Ecclesiastical History*, Book II, 234–5; Epiphanius, *Against Heresies*, section 78, ch. 14, p. 1
5   In a series on St Paul on BBC Radio 4 broadcast
6   Wilson, A N, *Jesus*, p. 101
7   Hassnain, Fida, *A Search for the Historical Jesus*, p. 84
8   John, ch. 2, vs. 1–5
9   Hassnain, Fida, *A Search for the Historical Jesus*, p. 84
10 Rex Deus, *The True Mystery of Rennes-le-Chateau and the Dynasty of Jesus*, ch. 7, *Custodians of Truth*, ch. 6 and *Cracking the Symbol Code*, ch. 4
11 Published by Bear and Co.
12 From the Gospel of Thomas v. 12, as translated in The Nag-Hammadi Library, James Robinson ed.
13 Pseudo-Clementine *Recognitions*, Book 1, p. 43
14 Epiphanius, *Against Heresies*, section 78, ch. 7, v. 7

15 Acts, ch. 12, v. 17
16 Eisenman, Robert, *James the Brother of Jesus*, p. xx
17 Welburn, Andrew, *The Beginnings of Christianity*, p. 55
18 Galatians, ch. 2, v. 9
19 Eisenman, Robert, *James the Brother of Jesus*, p. xix
20 Epiphanius, *Against Heresies*, section A29, ch. 4, v. 1
21 Eisenman, Robert, *James the Brother of Jesus*, p. 79
22 Eisenman, Robert, *The Dead Sea Scrolls and the First Christians*, p. 340
23 Johnson, Paul, *A History of Christianity*, p. 35
24 second-century Ebionite document known as the *Kerygmata Petrou*
25 Acts, ch. 7, v. 59
26 Paul's Epistle to the Romans, ch. 16, vs. 10–11
27 Wilson, A N, *Paul, the Mind of the Apostle*, p. 54
28 Josephus, *Antiquities*, Book XIV, ch. 8, 3
29 Eisenman, Robert, *The Dead Sea Scrolls and the First Christians*, p. 230
30 Philippians, ch. 4, v. 18
31 Philippians, ch. 4, v. 21
32 The Gospel of Mark, ch. 12, v. 17
33 Galatians, ch. 1, v. 17
34 Acts, ch. 24, v. 14
35 Acts, ch. 11
36 Eisenman, Robert, *The Dead Sea Scrolls and the First Christians*, p. 146
37 The Community Rule, viii, 2off.
38 Galatians, ch. 2, vs. 11–13
39 Galatians, ch. 2, vs. 15–16
40 Johnson, Paul, *A History of Christianity*, p. 41
41 II Corinthians 3:1
42 Johnson, Paul, *A History of Christianity*, p. 41
43 Acts, ch. 16, v. 1
44 Acts, ch. 24, v. 24
45 Paul's First Epistle to the Corinthians, ch. 9, vs. 1–2
46 Paul's First epistle to Timothy, ch. 2, v. 7
47 Wallace-Murphy and Hopkins, *Rosslyn: Guardian of the Secrets of the Holy Grail*, p. 67
48 Cited by Laurence Gardner in *The Bloodline of the Holy Grail*, p. 154
49 Galatians, ch. 5, vs. 1–4
50 I Corinthians, ch. 9, vs. 24–6
51 Acts, ch. 21, v. 33
52 Robert Eisenman devotes an entire chapter to Paul's attack on James citing a variety of sources – Chapter 16, *James the Brother of Jesus*. See also the Pseudo-Clementine *Recognitions*.

53 Acts, ch. 23, vs. 20–21

54 Acts, ch. 23, vs. 23–4

55 Acts, ch. 24, vs. 1–27

56 Acts, ch. 8, v. 9 and ff.

57 B. San. 81b–82b

58 Armstrong, Karen, *A History of Jerusalem*, p. 151

59 Jerome, *Lives of Illustrious Men*, ch. 2

60 Eisenman, Robert, *The Dead Sea Scrolls and the First Christians*, p. 262

61 Armstrong, Karen, *A History of Jerusalem*, p. 151

62 Ranke-Heninemann, Ute, *Putting Away Childish Things*, p. 173

63 Josephus, *War*, Book II, ch. 17, 4

64 Josephus, *War*, Book II, ch. 20, 1

Chapter 5

1 Faulkner, Neil, *Apocalypse – the Great Jewish Revolt against Rome*, p. 276

2 Eisenman, Robert, *James the Brother of Jesus*, p. xxi

3 Armstrong, Karen, *A History of Jerusalem*, p. 156

4 Sifre on Leviticus, ch. 19, v. 8

5 Armstrong, Karen, *A History of Jerusalem*, pp. 168–9

6 Eusabius, *Ecclesiastical History*, Book IV, ch. v

7 Eusabius, *Ecclesiastical History*, Book III, ch. xi ; also Armstrong, Karen, *A History of Jerusalem*, p. 153

8 Hassnain, Fida, *A Search for the Historical Jesus*, pp. 55–60

9 Hopkins, Simmans and Wallace-Murphy, *Rex Deus*, p. 79

10 *Guidebook to Les Saintes Maries de la Mer*, p. 3

11 Welburn, Andrew, *The Beginnings of Christianity*, p. 87

12 Armstrong, Karen, *A History of Jerusalem*, p. 155

13 Powell, Mark Allen, *The Jesus Debate*, p. 41

14 Eisenman, Robert, *James the Brother of Jesus*, p. 54

15 Schonfield, Hugh, *Those Incredible Christians*, p. 56

16 Mack, Burton L, *The Lost Gospel*, p. 2

17 Johnson, Paul, *A History of Christianity*, pp. 67, 76 and 82

18 Moore, L David, *The Christian Conspiracy*, p. 61

19 Johnson, Paul, *A History of Christianity*, p. 67

20 Christie-Murray, David, *A History of Heresy*, p. 1; Johnson, Paul, *A History of Christianity*, p. 76

21 Moore, L David, *The Christian Conspiracy*, p. 62

22 Johnson, Paul, *A History of Christianity*, p. 88

23 Moore, L David, *The Christian Conspiracy*, p. 63

24 Fox, Robin Lane, *Pagans and Christians*, p. 656

25 Johnson, Paul, *A History of Christianity*, p. 88
26 Gardner, Laurence, *Bloodline of the Holy Grail*, p. 159
27 Wallace-Murphy, Hopkins and Simmans, *Rex Deus*, p. 97
28 Moore, R I, *The Formation of a Persecuting Society*, p. 12
29 Johnson, Paul, *A History of Christianity*, pp. 116–117
30 Cardinal Ratzinger speaking in 1990, cited in Baigent and Leigh's *The Dead Sea Scrolls Deception*, p. 191
31 Moore, R I, *The Formation of a Persecuting Society*, p. 12
32 Johnson, Paul, *A History of Christianity*, p. 87
33 Ravenscroft and Wallace-Murphy, *The Mark of the Beast*, p. 124
34 Ravenscroft and Wallace-Murphy, *The Mark of the Beast*, p. 79
35 Wallace-Murphy, Tim, *The Templar Legacy and the Masonic Inheritance within Rosslyn Chapel*, p. 12
36 Johnson, Paul, *A History of Christianity*, pp. 135–8
37 Bede, *A History of the English Church and People*, p. 66
38 *Trias Thermaturga*, p. 156b
39 HRH Prince Michael of Albany , *The Forgotten Monarchy of Scotland*, p. 30
40 Elder, Iasabel Hill, *Celt, Druid and Culdee*, pp. 131–2 and 134
41 Dunford, Barry, *The Holy Land of Scotland*

Part III introduction and Chapter 6

1 De Lange, Nicholas, *Atlas of the Jewish World*, p. 38
2 Armstrong, Karen, *A History of God*, pp. 156–7
3 The Preliminary Discourse by George Sale used as an introduction to his translation of the Koran
4 Armstrong, Karen, *A History of God*, p. 159
5 *Larouse Encyclopaedia of Ancient and Medieval History*, p. 260
6 Hattstein, Marcus and Delius, Peter (eds) *Islam Art and Architecture*, p. 12
7 Armstrong, Karen, *A History of God*, p. 159
8 Beinhart, Chaim, *Atlas of Medieval Jewish History*, p. 19
9 Beinhart, Chaim, *Atlas of Medieval Jewish History*, p. 19
10 Wallace-Murphy and Hopkins, *Custodians of Truth*
11 Armstrong, Karen, *A History of God*, p. 159
12 Hattstein, Marcus and Delius, Peter (eds) *Islam Art and Architecture*, p. 12
13 Armstrong, Karen, *A History of God*, p. 155
14 Armstrong, Karen, *A History of God*, pp. 158–9
15 Armstrong, Karen, *A History of God*, pp. 160–1
16 The Holy Koran, Sura 96, v. 1 (Muhammed Asad trans. who added the words in square brackets for clarity in English)
17 Ibn Ishak, Sira 153, in *A Life of Muhammed*, (Guillaume trans)

18 Armstrong, Karen, *A History of God*, p. 162
19 Hattstein, Marcus and Delius, Peter (eds) *Islam Art and Architecture*, p. 14
20 Wallace-Murphy and Hopkins, *Custodians of Truth*
21 Armstrong, Karen, *A History of God*, p. 163
22 Jalal ad-Din Suyuti, *al-itiqan fi'ulum al aq'ran* from Rodinson's Mohammed, (Anne Carter trans.) p. 74
23 Bukhari Hadith cited in Ling, Martin, *Muhammed, His Life Based On the Earliest Sources*, pp. 44–5
24 The Holy Qur'an, Sura 42, v. 7
25 Hattstein, Marcus and Delius, Peter (eds) *Islam Art and Architecture*, p. 23
26 Ibn Ishaq Sira 228, Cited by Guillaume (trans) *A Life of Muhammed*, p. 246
27 Armstrong, Karen, *A History of God*, p. 171
28 Hattstein, Marcus and Delius, Peter (eds) *Islam Art and Architecture*, p. 14
29 Cited by Karen Armstrong in *A History of God*, p. 176
30 *Larouse Encyclopaedia of Ancient and Medieval History*, p. 261
31 Armstrong, Karen, *A History of God*, p. 180
32 Armstrong, Karen *A History of God*, pp. 177–8
33 Hattstein, Marcus and Delius, Peter (eds) *Islam Art and Architecture*, p. 27

Chapter 7

1 Barnavi, Eli (ed), *A Historical Atlas of the Jewish People*, p. 80
2 Barnavi, Eli (ed), *A Historical Atlas of the Jewish People*, p. 80
3 Beinhart, Chaim, *Atlas of Medieval Jewry*, p. 21
4 Barnavi, Eli (ed), *A Historical Atlas of the Jewish People*, p. 81
5 Barnavi, Eli (ed), *A Historical Atlas of the Jewish People*, p. 82
6 Barnavi, Eli (ed), *A Historical Atlas of the Jewish People*, p. 86
7 De Lange, Nicholas, *Atlas of the Jewish World*, p. 39
8 Fossier, Robert (ed), *The Cambridge Illustrated History of the Middle Ages*, p. 204
9 Fossier, Robert (ed), *The Cambridge Illustrated History of the Middle Ages*, p. 246
10 Fossier, Robert (ed), *The Cambridge Illustrated History of the Middle Ages*, p. 195
11 Fossier, Robert (ed), *The Cambridge Illustrated History of the Middle Ages*, p. 203
12 Hattstein, Marcus and Delius, Peter (eds), *Islam Art and Architecture*, p. 60
13 Fossier, Robert (ed), *The Cambridge Illustrated History of the Middle Ages*, p. 194
14 *Larouse Enclyclopedia of Medieval History*, p. 269

15 Hattstein, Marcus and Delius, Peter (eds), *Islam Art and Architecture*, p. 91

16 *Larouse Encyclopedia of Medieval History*, p. 269

17 Hattstein, Marcus and Delius, Peter (eds), *Islam Art and Architecture*, p. 92

18 Hattstein, Marcus and Delius, Peter (eds), *Islam Art and Architecture*, p. 90

19 *Larouse Encyclopedia of Medieval History*, p. 271

20 *Larouse Encyclopedia of Medieval History*, p. 271

21 Fossier, Robert (ed), *The Cambridge Illustrated History of the Middle Ages*, p. 247

22 *Larouse Encyclopedia of Medieval History*, p. 270

23 *Larouse Encyclopedia of Medieval History*, p. 271

Chapter 8

1 Fossier, Robert (ed), *The Cambridge Illustrated History of the Middle Ages*, p. 199

2 Hattstein, Marcus and Delius, Peter (eds), *Islam Art and Architecture*, p. 208

3 Holmes, George (ed), *The Oxford Illustrated History of Medieval Europe*, p. 4

4 Holmes, George (ed), *The Oxford Illustrated History of Medieval Europe*, p. 4

5 Hattstein, Marcus and Delius, Peter (eds), *Islam Art and Architecture*, p. 208

6 Fossier, Robert (ed), *The Cambridge Illustrated History of the Middle Ages*, p. 200

7 Barnavi, Eli, *A Historical Atlas of the Jewish People*, p. 81

8 Hattstein, Marcus and Delius, Peter (eds), *Islam Art and Architecture*, p. 208

9 Ravenscroft and Wallace-Murphy, *The Mark of the Beast*, p. 24

10 Hattstein, Marcus and Delius, Peter (eds), *Islam Art and Architecture*, p. 209

11 Hattstein, Marcus and Delius, Peter (eds), *Islam Art and Architecture*, p. 208

12 Hattstein, Marcus and Delius, Peter (eds), *Islam Art and Architecture*, p. 209

13 Roth, Cecil, *A Short History of the Jewish People*, pp. 165–6

14 Zuckerman, A J, *A Jewish Princedom in Feudal France 768–900*, p. 37

15 Zuckerman, A J, *A Jewish Princedom in Feudal France 768–900*, p. 49

16 Roth, Cecil, *A Short History of the Jewish People*, p. 165

17 Zuckerman, A J, *A Jewish Princedom in Feudal France 768–900*, p. 60

18 Zuckerman, A J, *A Jewish Princedom in Feudal France 768–900*, p. 34

19 Zuckerman, A J, *A Jewish Princedom in Feudal France 768–900*, p. 112

20 Adler, M N, *The Itinerary of Benjamin of Tudela 459–467*

21 Saige, G, *Les Juifs du Languedoc*, pp. 272–93; Regne, *Juifs de Narbonne*, pp. 127–32

22 Fossier, Robert (ed), *The Middle Ages*, p. 484

Source Notes

23 Fossier, Robert (ed), *The Middle Ages*, pp. 426–7

24 Wallace-Murphy and Hopkins, *Custodians of Truth*, p. 107

25 Hattstein, Marcus and Delius, Peter (eds), *Islam Art and Architecture*, p. 210

26 Hattstein, Marcus and Delius, Peter (eds), *Islam Art and Architecture*, p. 211

27 Beinhart, Chaim, *Atlas of Medieval Jewry*, p. 36

28 Hattstein, Marcus and Delius, Peter (eds), *Islam Art and Architecture*, p. 214

29 Goodwin, Geoffrey, *Islamic Spain*, p. 10

30 Goodwin, Geoffrey, *Islamic Spain*, p. 5

31 Goodwin, Geoffrey, *Islamic Spain*, p. 12

32 Goodwin, Geoffrey, *Islamic Spain*, pp. 42–3

33 Holmes, George, (ed), *The Oxford Illustrated History of Medieval Europe*, p. 61

34 Ravenscroft and Wallace-Murphy, *The Mark of the Beast*, p. 125

35 Hattstein, Marcus and Delius, Peter (eds), *Islam Art and Architecture*, p. 216

36 Toynbee, Arnold (ed), *Larouse Encyclopaedia of Ancient and Medieval History*, p. 272

37 Armstrong, Karen, *Muhammad*, pp. 23–4

38 Armstrong, Karen, *Muhammad*, p. 22

39 Holmes, George (ed), *The Oxford Illustrated History of Medieval Europe*, p. 15

40 Barnavi, Eli, *A Historical Atlas of the Jewish People*, p. 100

41 Akbar, S W Ahmed, *Discovering Islam*, p. 4

42 Goodwin, Geoffrey, *Islamic Spain*, p. 43

43 Guillaume, Alfred, *Islam*, p. 84

44 Barnavi, Eli, *A Historical Atlas of the Jewish People*, p. 96

45 Holmes, George (ed), *The Oxford Illustrated History of Medieval Europe*, pp. 57 and 59

46 Holmes, George (ed), *The Oxford Illustrated History of Medieval Europe*, p. 32

47 Eisenman, Robert, *James the Brother of Jesus*, p. 200

48 Wallace-Murphy, Tim, *The Templar Legacy and the Masonic Inheritance within Rosslyn Chapel*, p. 16

49 Wallace-Murphy and Hopkins, *Custodians of Truth*, p. 156

50 Wallace-Murphy and Hopkins, *Rosslyn: Guardian of the Secrets of the Holy Grail*, p. 83

51 Robert Graves in his Introduction to the first English Edition of *The Sufis* by Idries Shah

52 Maimonides, Obedyah, *The Treatise of the Pool*, p. ix

53 Holmes, George, (ed) *The Oxford Illustrated History of Medieval Europe*, p. 208

54 Ward, Colin, *Chartres the Making of a Miracle*, p. 8

55 Wallace-Murphy and Hopkins, *Custodians of Truth*, p. 113–14

56 Ward, Colin, *Chartres, the Making of a Miracle*, p. 8

57 Clerval, *Les Écoles de Chartres au Moyen Age*, 1895

58 Ravenscroft and Wallace-Murphy, *The Mark of the Beast*, pp. 73–4

59 Holmes, George (ed), *The Oxford Illustrated History of Medieval Europe*, pp. 207–8

Chapter 9

1 Barnavi, Eli (ed), *A Historical Atlas of the Jewish People*, p. 82

2 Barnavi, Eli (ed), *A Historical Atlas of the Jewish People*, p. 86

3 Fletcher, Richard, *The Cross and the Crescent*, p. 100

4 Fletcher, Richard, *The Cross and the Crescent*, p. 101

5 Fletcher, Richard, *The Cross and the Crescent*, p. 105

6 Fletcher, Richard, *The Cross and the Crescent*, pp. 106–7

7 Fletcher, Richard, *The Cross and the Crescent*, pp. 107–8

8 Fletcher, Richard, *The Cross and the Crescent*, p. 117

9 Barnavi, Eli (ed), *A Historical Atlas of the Jewish People*, p. 96

10 Barnavi, Eli (ed), *A Historical Atlas of the Jewish People*, p. 96

11 Beinart, Chiam, *Atlas of Medieval Jewish History*, p. 52

12 Beinart, Chiam, *Atlas of Medieval Jewish History*, p. 52

13 The subtitle of Louise Cochran's *Adelard of Bath* (London 1994)

14 Fletcher, Richard, *The Cross and the Crescent*, pp. 116–19

15 Fletcher, Richard, *The Cross and the Crescent*, p. 111

16 Beinart, Chiam, *Atlas of Medieval Jewish History*, p. 52

17 Ward, Colin, *Chartres the Making of a Miracle*, p. 8

18 Cited by John of Salisbury in his *Métalogique* III, 4. Patrol. Lat. Vol CXCIX, col 900

19 Akbar, S W Ahmed, *Discovering Islam*, p. 4

20 Beinart, Chiam, *Atlas of Medieval Jewish History*, p. 52

21 Fletcher, Richard, *The Cross and the Crescent*, pp. 121–2

22 Fletcher, Richard, *The Cross and the Crescent*, pp. 120–1

23 Fletcher, Richard, *The Cross and the Crescent*, pp. 121–2

24 Barnavi, Eli (ed), *A Historical Atlas of the Jewish People*, p. 96

25 Fletcher, Richard, *The Cross and the Crescent*, p. 123

26 Fletcher, Richard, *The Cross and the Crescent*, pp. 124–5

27 Fletcher, Richard, *The Cross and the Crescent*, pp. 54–7

28 Beinart, Chiam, *Atlas of Medieval Jewish History*, p. 46

29 Charpentier, Louis, *The Mysteries of Chartres*, p. 139

30 Charpentier, Louis, *The Mysteries of Chartres*, p. 141

31 Anderson, William, *The Rise of the Gothic*, p. 39; Boney, Jean, *French Gothic Architecture of the 12th and 13th Centuries*, p. 17

32 Strachan, Gordon, *Chartres*, p. 4
33 Shah, I *The Sufis*, pp. 166–193
34 Barnavi, Eli (ed), *A Historical Atlas of the Jewish People*, p. 100
35 Barnavi, Eli (ed), *A Historical Atlas of the Jewish People*, p. 101
36 Beinart, Chiam, *Atlas of Medieval Jewish History*, p. 55
37 Barnavi, Eli (ed), *A Historical Atlas of the Jewish People*, p. 102
38 Fletcher, Richard, *The Cross and the Crescent*, p. 99

Chapter 10

 1 Bridge, Anthony, *The Crusades*, p. 26
 2 Runciman, Stephen, *A History of the Crusades*, vol I, p. 6
 3 Bridge, Anthony, *The Crusades*, p. 15
 4 Bridge, Anthony, *The Crusades*, p. 16
 5 Bridge, Anthony, *The Crusades*, p. 17
 6 Fletcher, Richard, *The Cross and the Crescent*, p 50
 7 Runciman, Stephen, *A History of the Crusades*, vol I, p. 88
 8 Fletcher, Richard, *The Cross and the Crescent*, pp. 42–4
 9 Fletcher, Richard, *The Cross and the Crescent*, p. 44
10 Fletcher, Richard, *The Cross and the Crescent*, p. 82
11 Bridge, Anthony, *The Crusades*, p. 18
12 Runciman, Stephen, *A History of the Crusades*, vol I, p. 84
13 Mansi, Concilia, vol xix, pp. 89–90
14 Mansi, Concilia, vol xix, pp. 483–88
15 Bridge, Anthony, *The Crusades*, p. 18
16 Mansi, Concilia, vol. xix, p. 827
17 Runciman, Stephen, *A History of the Crusades*, vol I, p. 87
18 Runciman, Stephen, *A History of the Crusades*, vol I, 90–1
19 Fletcher, Richard, *The Cross and the Crescent*, p. 72
20 Wallace-Murphy and Hopkins, *Rosslyn Guardian of the Secrets of the Holy Grail*, p. 142
21 Bridge, Anthony, *The Crusades*, p. 26
22 Runciman, Stephen, *A History of the Crusades*, vol I, p. 37
23 Runciman, Stephen, *A History of the Crusades*, vol I, p. 49
24 Runciman, Stephen, *A History of the Crusades*, vol I, p. 50
25 Bridge, Anthony, *The Crusades*, p. 26
26 Runciman, Stephen, *A History of the Crusades*, vol I, pp. 75–6
27 *Chronicles of the Crusades*, p. 20
28 Bridge, Anthony, *The Crusades*, p. 44
29 Bridge, Anthony, *The Crusades*, pp. 39–41
30 Fulcher of Chartres, Book 1, ch.iii, pp. 130–138; Robert the Monk, 1, i–ii, pp. 727–9

31 Bridge, Anthony, *The Crusades*, pp. 45–5

32 Bridge, Anthony, *The Crusades*, p. 27

33 Fulcher of Chartres, Book 1, ch.iii, pp. 130–8; Robert the Monk, 1, i–ii, pp. 727–9

34 *The Chronicles of the Crusades*, pp. 64–5

35 Bridge, Anthony, *The Crusades*, p. 33

36 *The Chronicles of the Crusades*, p. 69

37 Bridge, Anthony, *The Crusades*, pp. 54–5

38 Bridge, Anthony, *The Crusades*, p. 60

39 Bridge, Anthony, *The Crusades*, p. 54

40 Bridge, Anthony, *The Crusades*, p. 71

41 *Chronicles of the Crusades*, p. 60

42 Fulcher of Chartres, Book 1, ch. xiv, p. 208

43 Runciman, Stephen, *A History of the Crusades*, vol 1, pp. 205–7

44 Bridge, Anthony, *The Crusades*, p. 95

45 Gesta Francorum, Book x, ch. 38, pp. 202–4

46 Letter from Daimbert of Pisa and other leaders to the pope.

47 Bridge, Anthony, *The Crusades*, p. 111

48 Ibn al Qalânisî, *Continuation of the Chronicle of Damascus: the Damascus Chronicle of the Crusades*, (H.A.R. Gibb trans) London, 1932

49 Gesta Francorum Book xx, pp. 204–206

50 Runciman, Stephen, *A History of the Crusades*, vol I, p. 287

51 Bridge, Anthony, *The Crusades*, p. 115

52 Raymond of Aguillers, xx, p. 301

Chapter 11

1 Article entitled *Une Vie par réforme l'église* by Michel Kluber published in the journal *Bernard de Clairvaux*, les editions de l'Argonante.

2 St Clair, L-A de, *Histoire Généalogique de la Famille de St Clair*

3 Wallace-Murphy, Tim, *The Templar Legacy and the Masonic Inheritance within Rosslyn Chapel*, p. 18

4 Hopkins, Simmans and Wallace-Murphy, *Rex Deus*, p. 114

5 William of Tyre, Book xii, ch. 7

6 Robinson, John J, *Dungeon, Fire and Sword*, p. 31

7 Addison, Charles G, *The Knights Templar*, p. 5

8 Knight, C and Lomas, R, *The Second Messiah*, p. 73

9 Nicholson, Helen, *The Knights Templar*, p. 22

10 Robinson, John, *Dungeon, Fire and Sword*, p. 36

11 Gardner, Laurence, *The Bloodline of the Holy Grail*, p. 256

12 Hopkins, Simmans and Wallace-Murphy, *Rex Deus*, p. 112

13 Hopkins, Simmans and Wallace-Murphy, *Rex Deus*, p. 112

14 Nicholson, *The Knights Templar*, p. 22

15 Anon., *Secret Societies of the Middle Ages*, p. 190; Nicholson, *The Knights Templar*, p. 26

16 Hancock, Graham, *The Sign and the Seal*, pp. 94 and 99; see also Ravenscroft and Wallace-Murphy, *The Mark of the Beast*, p. 52

17 Hancock, Graham *The Sign and the Seal*, pp. 49–51

18 Ravenscroft and Wallace-Murphy, *The Mark of the Beast*, p. 52

19 Robinson, John J, *Dungeon, Fire and Sword*, p. 37

20 Bordonove, Georges, *La vie quotidienne des Templiers*, p. 29

21 Anon., *Secret Societies of the Middle Ages*, p. 199

22 Anon., *Secret Societies of the Middle Ages*, p. 199

23 Nicholson, *The Knights Templar*, p. 96

24 Papal Bull *Pie postulation voluntatis*, 1113

25 *Willemi Tyrensis Archiepiscopi Chronicon: Guillaume de Tyr, Chronique.* (Huygens R.B.C. ed) 2 vols, Corpus Christianorum Continuatio Medievalis 68–68a, (Turnholt 1986) 2, pp. 814–17

26 Nicolson, Helen, *The Knights Hospitaller*, p. 3

27 Seward, Desmond, *Monks of War*, p. 15

28 Papal Bull *Ad hoc nos disponente*

29 Nicholson, Helen, *The Knights Hospitaller*, p. 7

30 Nicholson, Helen, *The Knights Hospitaller*, p. 11

31 Seward, Desmond, *The Monks of War*, p. 19

32 Nicholson, Helen, *The Knights Hospitaller*, p. 11

33 De Vitry, *Historia Orientalis*

34 Wallace-Murphy, Tim, *The Templar Legacy and the Masonic Inheritance within Rosslyn Chapel*

35 Wallace-Murphy and Hopkins, *Rosslyn: Guardian of the Secrets of the Holy Grail*, p. 102

36 Seward Desmond, *The Monks of War*, p. 63

37 Seward Desmond, *The Monks of War*, pp. 64–5

38 Lomax, D W, *La Orden de Santiago 1170–1275*, CSIC, Madrid, 1965

Chapter 12

1 Regne, J, *Études sur la condition des Juifs de Narbonne*, pp. 90–1

2 Regne, J, *Études sur la condition des Juifs de Narbonne*, pp. 27–9

3 Regne, J, *Études sur la condition des Juifs de Narbonne*, pp. 90–1

4 Adler, M N, *The Itinerary of Benjamin Tudela*, p. 459

5 Zuckerman, A J, *A Jewish Princedom in Feudal France*, p. 96

6 Costen, Michael, *The Cathars and the Albigensian Crusade*, p. 38

7   Beinhart, Chaim, *Atlas of Medieval Jewry*, p. 53; Stoyanov, Yuri, *The Hidden Tradition in Europe*, p. 160

8   Oldenbourg, Zoé, *Massacre at Montségur*, pp. 24–5

9   Aué Michèle, *The Cathars*, p. 3

10 Stoyanov, Yuri, *The Hidden Tradition in Europe*, p. 159

11 Costen, Michael, *The Cathars and the Albigensian Crusade*, pp. 32–4

12 Costen, Michael, *The Cathars and the Albigensian Crusade*, pp. 37–9

13 Costen, Michael, *The Cathars and the Albigensian Crusade*, p. 59

14 De Vries, Simon, *Cathars, Country Customs and Castles*, p. 2

15 Stoyanov, Yuri, *The Hidden Tradition in Europe*, p. 160

16 Aué Michèle, *The Cathars*, p.13; Guirdham, Arthur, *The Great Heresy*, p. 15

17 Guirdham, Arthur, *The Great Heresy*, p. 16

18 Aué Michèle, *The Cathars*, p. 3

19 Stoyanov, Yuri, *The Hidden Tradition in Europe*, p. 158

20 Guirdham, Arthur, *The Great Heresy*, pp. 35–6

21 Guirdham, Arthur, *The Great Heresy*, p. 38

22 The Gospel of Thomas in the Nag Hammadi Library.

23 Costen, Michael, *The Cathars and the Albigensian Crusade*, pp. 66–7

24 Guirdham, Arthur, *The Great Heresy* pp. 42–5

25 Stoyanov, Yuri, *The Hidden Tradition in Europe*, p. 164

26 Guirdham, Arthur, *The Great Heresy*, p. 18

27 Guirdham, Arthur, *The Great Heresy*, p. 18

28 Stoyanov, Yuri, *The Hidden Tradition in Europe*, p. 156

29 Bernard of Clairvaux's letter cited in Wakefield and Evans, *Heresies of the Middle Ages* pp. 122–4

30 Stoyanov, Yuri, *The Hidden Tradition in Europe*, p. 156

31 Stoyanov, Yuri, *The Hidden Tradition in Europe*, p. 156

32 Stoyanov, Yuri, *The Hidden Tradition in Europe*, p. 156

33 Costen, Michael, *The Cathars and the Albigensian Crusade*, p. 58

34 De Vries, Simon, *Cathars, Country Customs and Castles*, p. 2

35 Costen, Michael, *The Cathars and the Albigensian Crusade*, p. 65

36 Costen, Michael, *The Cathars and the Albigensian Crusade*, p. 66

37 Serrus, Georges, *The Land of the Cathars*, p. 35

38 Costen, Michael, *The Cathars and the Albigensian Crusade* pp. 112–14

39 Serrus, Georges, *The Land of the Cathars*, p. 15

40 Aué Michèle, *The Cathars*, p. 15

41 Stoyanov, Yuri, *The Hidden Tradition in Europe*, p. 173

42 Costen, Michael, *The Cathars and the Albigensian Crusade*, p. 123

43 Caesarius of Heisterbach, vol II pp. 296–8

44 Guébin et Moisoineuve, *Histoire Albigeoise de Pierre des Vaux Chernay*

45 Costen, Michael, *The Cathars and the Albigensian Crusade*, p. 125
46 Serrus, Georges, *The Land of the Cathars*, p. 20
47 Costen, Michael, *The Cathars and the Albigensian Crusade*, p. 128
48 Aué Michèle, *The Cathars*, p. 11
49 Stoyanov, Yuri, *The Hidden Tradition in Europe*, p. 174
50 Guirdham, Arthur, *The Great Heresy*, p. 63
51 Costen, Michael, *The Cathars and the Albigensian Crusade*, p. 132
52 Aué Michèle, *The Cathars*, p. 12
53 Serrus, Georges, *The Land of the Cathars*, p. 26
54 Costen, Michael, *The Cathars and the Albigensian Crusade*, p. 151
55 Guirdham, Arthur, *The Great Heresy*, p. 69
56 Costen, Michael, *The Cathars and the Albigensian Crusade*, p. 160
57 Stoyanov, Yuri, *The Hidden Tradition in Europe*, p. 178
58 Johnson, Paul, *A History of Christianity*, pp. 253–5
59 Lea, H C, *The Inquisition in the Middle Ages*, NY, 1955
60 De Rosa, Peter, *Vicars of Christ*, p. 249
61 Lea, H C, *The Inquisition in the Middle Ages*, NY, 1955
62 Papal Bull of Innocent IV 1252 *Ad extirpanda*
63 Baigent and Leigh, *The Inquisition*, pp. 27–8
64 Burman, Edward, *The Inquisition: The Hammer of Heresy*, pp. 62–5
65 Baigent and Leigh, *The Inquisition*, pp. 34–6
66 Costen, Michael, *The Cathars and the Albigensian Crusade*, pp. 169–74
67 Guirdham, Arthur, *The Great Heresy*, p. 89
68 Bernavi, Eli, ed, *A Historical Atlas of the Jewish People*, p. 104
69 Lange, Nicholas, *Atlas of the Jewish World*, p. 35
70 Beinhart, Chaim, *Atlas of Medieval Jewish History*, p. 57
71 Beinhart, Chaim, *Atlas of Medieval Jewish History*, p. 59
72 Bernavi, Eli, ed, *A Historical Atlas of the Jewish People*, p. 104
73 Beinhart, Chaim, *Atlas of Medieval Jewish History*, p. 59
74 Beinhart, Chaim, *Atlas of Medieval Jewish History*, p. 48
75 Fletcher, Richard, *The Cross and the Crescent*, p. 99

Chapter 13

1 Ibn Jubayr, (Wright ed) *Voyage*, Leyden, 1852, pp. 304–5
2 Benjamin of Tudela, *Voyages*, (Adler ed), Hebrew text, pp. 26–47
3 Benjamin of Tudela *Voyages*, (Adler ed), Hebrew text, p. 47–8
4 Runciman, Stephen, *A History of the Crusades*, vol II, p. 297
5 Bridge, Anthony, *The Crusades*, p. 135
6 Runciman, Stephen, *A History of the Crusades*, vol II, p. 312
7 Bridge, Anthony, *The Crusades*, p. 127

8 Bridge, Anthony, *The Crusades*, p. 125

9 Bridge, Anthony, *The Crusades*, p. 131

10 Fletcher, Richard, *The Cross and the Crescent*, p. 86

11 Fletcher, Richard, *The Cross and the Crescent*, p. 87

12 Cited by Francesco Gabrielli, *Arab Historians of the Crusades*, p. 73

13 Fletcher, Richard, *The Cross and the Crescent*, p. 91

14 Runciman, Stephen, *A History of the Crusades*, vol II, p. 319

15 Fletcher, Richard, *The Cross and the Crescent*, p. 85

16 Runciman, Stephen, *A History of the Crusades*, vol II, p. 318

17 Runciman, Stephen, *A History of the Crusades*, vol II, p. 320

18 Bridge, Anthony, *The Crusades*, p. 170

19 Bridge, Anthony, *The Crusades*, pp. 174–5

20 Bridge, Anthony, *The Crusades*, pp. 179–80

21 Bridge, Anthony, *The Crusades*, p. 167

22 *The Chronicles of the Crusades*, p. 152

23 Estoire d'Eracles R.H.C. Occ. vol II, p. 34

24 Runciman, Stephen, *A History of the Crusades*, vol II, pp. 454–6

25 Regan, Geoffrey, *Lionhearts: Saladin and Richard I*, p. 91

26 Fletcher, Richard, *The Cross and the Crescent*, p. 88

27 *Gesta Francorum et aliorum Hierosolimitanorum*, trans. Hill, Rosalind, (Edinburgh 1962) p. 21

28 De Joinville, *Life of St Louis*, p. 245

29 Bridge, Anthony, *The Crusades*, pp. 202–3

30 Runciman, Stephen, *A History of the Crusades*, vol II, p. 466

31 Runciman, Stephen, *A History of the Crusades*, vol II, p. 467

32 Regan, Geoffrey, *Lionhearts: Saladin and Richard I*, pp. 155–6

33 Bridge, Anthony, *The Crusades*, p. 226

34 Regan, Geofrey, *Lionhearts: Saladin and Richard I*, p. 218

35 Bridge, Anthony, *The Crusades*, pp. 202–3

36 Bridge, Anthony, *The Crusades*, pp. 237–8

37 Bridge, Anthony, *The Crusades*, pp. 238–9

38 Bridge, Anthony, *The Crusades*, p. 279

39 Bridge, Anthony, *The Crusades*, p. 279

40 Bridge, Anthony, *The Crusades*, p. 293

41 Bridge, Anthony, *The Crusades*, pp. 294–5

42 Bridge, Anthony, *The Crusades*, p. 296

43 Wallace-Murphy and Hopkins, *Custodians of Truth*, ch. 14

44 Fletcher, Richard, *The Cross and the Crescent*, p. 85

45 Fletcher, Richard, *The Cross and the Crescent*, p. 92

Chapter 14

1 Fletcher, Richard, *The Cross and the Crescent*, p. 112
2 Fossier, Robert, ed., *The Cambridge Illustrated History of the Middle Ages*, vol III, pp. 65–6
3 Barber, Malcolm, *The Trial of the Templars*, p. 45
4 Baigent, Leigh and Lincoln, *The Holy Blood and the Holy Grail*, p. 46
5 Lizerand, *Le Dossier de l'Affaire des Templiers*, p. 16
6 Barber, Malcolm, *The Trial of the Templars*, p. 45
7 Barber, Malcolm, *The Trial of the Templars*, p. 47
8 Partner, Peter, *The Knights Templar and their Myth*, p. 82
9 Hopkins, Simmans and Wallace-Murphy, *Rex Deus*, p. 172
10 Partner, Peter, *The Knights Templar and their Myth*, p. 83
11 Papal Bull of Clement V, *Vox in excelso*
12 Barnavi, Eli, *A Historical Atlas of the Jewish People*, p. 120
13 Lange, Nicholas, *Atlas of the Jewish World* p. 41
14 Fisher, H A L, *A History of Europe*, p. 388
15 Baigent, Leigh and Lincoln, *The Holy Blood and the Holy Grail*, p. 109
16 Orton, Previte, *Outlines of Medieval History*, p. 469
17 Goodwin, Geoffrey, *Islamic Spain*, p. vii
18 Fossier, Robert, *The Middle Ages*, vol. III, p. 504
19 Wright, Esmond, *Medieval and Renaissance World*, p. 218
20 Orton, Previte, *Outlines of Medieval History*, p. 467
21 Fisher, H A L, *A History of Europe*, p. 393
22 Barnavi, Eli, *A Historical Atlas of the Jewish People*, p. 126
23 Barnavi, Eli, *A Historical Atlas of the Jewish People*, p. 126
24 Barnavi, Eli, *A Historical Atlas of the Jewish People*, p. 127
25 Lange, Nicholas, *Atlas of the Jewish World*, p. 37
26 Fossier, Robert, ed., *The Cambridge Illustrated History of the Middle Ages*, vol. III, p. 306
27 Fossier, Robert, ed., *The Cambridge Illustrated History of the Middle Ages*, vol. III, p. 321
28 Fossier, Robert, ed., *The Cambridge Illustrated History of the Middle Ages*, vol. III, p. 325
29 Fossier, Robert, ed., *The Cambridge Illustrated History of the Middle Ages*, vol. III, p. 337
30 Fossier, Robert, ed., *The Cambridge Illustrated History of the Middle Ages*, vol. III, p. 339
31 Fossier, Robert, ed., *The Cambridge Illustrated History of the Middle Ages*, vol. III, p. 340
32 Barnavi, Eli, *A Historical Atlas of the Jewish People*, p. 130
33 Fisher, H A L, *A History of Europe*, p. 727

34 Fossier, Robert, ed., *The Cambridge Illustrated History of the Middle Ages*, vol. III, p. 326

35 Fossier, Robert, ed., *The Cambridge Illustrated History of the Middle Ages*, vol. III, pp. 340–1

36 Fossier, Robert, ed., *The Cambridge Illustrated History of the Middle Ages*, vol. III, p. 343

37 Fossier, Robert, ed., *The Cambridge Illustrated History of the Middle Ages*, vol. III, p. 343

38 Hattstein, Marcus, *Islam Art and Architecture*, p. 538

39 Hattstein, Marcus, *Islam Art and Architecture*, p. 539

40 Wallace-Murphy, Tim and Hopkins, Marilyn, *Templars in America*, p. 205

41 Wallace-Murphy, Tim and Hopkins, Marilyn, *Templars in America*, pp. 207–8

42 Fletcher, Richard, *The Cross and the Crescent*, pp. 159–60

Selected Bibliography

Addison, Charles G, *The History of the Knights Templars*, Black Books, 1995

Adler, M N, *The Itinerary of Benjamin of Tudela*, Joseph Dimon Pangloss Press, 1993

Akbar, S W Ahmed, *Discovering Islam*, Routledge, London, 2002

Allegro, J M, *The Dead Sea Scrolls*, Penguin, 1964

—— *The Dead Sea Scrolls and the Christian Myth*, Abacus, London, 1981

Anderson, William, *The Rise of the Gothic*, Hutchinson, London 1985

Anon. *Secret Societies of the Middle Ages*, R A Kessinger Publishing Co., 2003

Armstrong, Karen, *A History of God*, Mandarin, London, 1994

—— *A History of Jerusalem*, HarperCollins, 1996

—— *Muhammad*, HarperCollins, San Francisco, 1993

Aué, Michèle, *Cathar Country*, MSM, 1995

Baigent, Leigh and Lincoln, *The Holy Blood and the Grail*, Jonathan Cape, 1982

Baigent, Michael and Leigh, Richard, *The Dead Sea Scrolls Deception*, Corgi, 1992

—— *The Inquisition*, Penguin, 1999

Barber, Malcolm, *The Cathars*, Pearson Education Ltd, 2000
—— *The Trial of the Templars*, CUP, 1994
Baring, A and Cashford, J, *The Myth of the Goddess*, Penguin, 1993
Barnavi, Eli, *A Historical Atlas of the Jewish People*, Hutchinson, 1992
Bauval, R and Hancock, G, *Keeper of Genesis*, William Heineman, London, 1996
Bauval, R and Gilbert, Adrian, *The Orion Mystery*, William Heinmann, 1994
Bede, *A History of the English Church and People*, Penguin, 1978
Beinhart, Haim, *Atlas of Medieval Jewish History*, Robert Lafont, 1970
Betro, M C, *Hieroglyphes, Les Mysteres de l'ecriture*, Flammarion, 1995
Birks, Norman and Gilbert, R A, *The Treasure of Montségur*, The Aquarian Press, 1990
Bordonove, Georges, *La vie quotidienne des Templiers*, Hachette, Paris, 1990
Bridge, Anthony, *The Crusades*, Granada, London 1980
Breasted, J H, *Development of Religion and Thought in Ancient Egypt*, University of Pennsylvania Press, Philadelphia, 1972
Burman, Edward, *The Inquisition: The Hammer of Heresy*, Aquarian Press, 1984
—— *The Templars, Knights of God*, Destiny Books, Rochester VT, 1990
Burton, Mack, *Who Wrote the New Testament?*, HarperCollins, San Francisco, 1989
Bussel, F W, *Religious Thought and Heresy in the Middle Ages*, Robert Scott, London, 1918

Cannon, Dolores, *Jesus and the Essenes*, Gateway Books, 1992
Cantor, N, *The Sacred Chain – a History of the Jews*, Fontana, London, 1996
Charpentier, Louis, *Les Mystères Templiers*, Lafont, 1993
—— *The Mysteries of Chartres Cathedral*, RILKO, 1993
Christie-Murray, David, *A History of Heresy*, OUP 1989
Cohn-Sherbok, Dan, *A Concise Encyclopedia of Judaism*, Oneworld, Oxford, 1998

Costen, Michael, *The Cathars and the Albigensian Crusade*, Manchester University Press, 1997

Cotterell, M, *The Tutenkhamun Prophecies*, Headline, London, 1999

Crossan, John Dominic, *Jesus – a Revolutionary Biography*, Harper Collins, 1994

De Clari, Robert, *The Conquest of Constantinople*, (E H Neal, trans.), University of Toronto, 1997

De Lange, Nicholas, *Atlas of the Jewish World*, Guild Publishing, London 1984

De Lubicz, Rene Schwaller, *Sacred Science*, Inner Traditions International, 1988

De Vries, Simon, *Cathars, Country, Customs and Castles*, Comtal Press, 1993

D'Olivet, A F, *La Langue Hebraique Restitue*, L'Age d'Homme, Paris, 1990

Dowley, Tim, Ed., *The History of Christianity*, Lion Publishing, Herts, 1977

Edwards, *The Pyramids of Egypt*, Penguin, London, 1986

Eisenman, Robert, *The Dead Sea Scrolls and the First Christians*, Element, 1996

—— *James the Brother of Jesus*, Faber and Faber, 1997

—— *Maccabbees, Zadokites, Christians and Qumran*, E J Brill, 1983

Eisenman, Robert and Wise, Michael, *The Dead Sea Scrolls Uncovered*, Element, 1992

Elder, Isabel Hill, *Celt, Druid and Culdee*, Covenant Publishing Co. Ltd, 1994

Eusabius, *Ecclesiastical History*

Epstein, Isadore, *Judaism*, Penguin 1964

Faulkner, Neil, *Apocalypse – the Great Jewish Revolt against Rome*, AD 66–73, Tempus Publishing Ltd, 2002

Faulkner, Robert, *The Ancient Egyptian Book of the Dead*, British Museum Press, London, 1972

—— *The Ancient Egyptian Pyramid Texts*, Aris and Philips, Warminster, 1993

Feather, R, *The Copper Scroll Decoded*, Thorsons, London, 1999

Fisher, H. A. L, *A History of Europe*, Edward Arnold and Co, 1936

Fletcher, Richard, *The Cross and the Crescent*, Allen Lane, Penguin, London, 2003

Fossier, Robert (ed) *The Middle Ages*, 3 Vols, CUP 1989

Fox, Robin Lane, *Pagans and Christians*, Penguin, 1988

—— *The Unauthorised Version: Truth and Fiction in the Bible*, Penguin, 1991

Freud, S, *Moses and Monotheism*, London 1939

Gardner, Laurence, *Bloodline of the Holy Grail*, Element Books, 1995

Gibbon, Edward, *The Decline and Fall of the Roman Empire*, 8 Vols, The Folio Society

Glover, T R, *The Conflict of Religions in the Early Roman Empire*, Methuen and Co., London, 1909

Goodwin, Geoffrey, *Islamic Spain*, Chronicle Books, 2000

Goyon, G, *Le Secret des Batisseurs des Grandes Pyramides: Kheops*, Pygmalion, Paris, 1991

Guébin and Moisoineuve, *Histoire Albigeoise de Pierre des Vaux-de-Chernay*, Paris, 1951

Guillaume, Alfred, *Islam*, Penguin, London 1956

Guirdham, Arthur, *The Great Heresy*, C W Daniel, Saffron Walden, 1993

Halam, Elizabeth (ed.), *The Chronicles of the Crusades*, Bramley Books, 1997

Hamill, John and Gilbert, *World Freemasonry*, Aquarian Press, 1991

Hamilton, B, *The Albigensian Crusade*, The Historical Association, London, 1974

Hancock, Graham, *The Sign and the Seal*, Mandarin Paperbacks, 1993

Hassnain, Prof. Fida, *A Search for the Historical Jesus*, Gateway Books, 1994

Hattstein, Marcus and Delius, Peter (eds) *Islam Art and Architecture*, Könemann, Cologne, 2000

Hay, Fr. *The Genealogie of the St Clairs of Roslin*, Maidement, Edinburgh, 1835

Holmes, George (ed.), *The Oxford Illustrated History of Medieval Europe*, OUP

Isserlin, B S J, *The Israelites*, Thames and Hudson, London, 1998

Selected Bibliography

James, Bruno S, *St Bernard of Clairvaux*, Hodder and Stoughton, London 1957

Jedin, Hubert (ed.), *The History of the Church*, Vol 1, Burns and Oats, 1989

Johnson, Paul, *A History of Christianity*, Weidenfeld and Nicolson, London 1978

—— *A History of the Jews*, Orion Books, London 1993

Josephus, *The Antiquities of the Jews and The Wars of the Jews*, Nimmo, 1869

Kersten, H. and Gruber, E R, *The Jesus Conspiracy*, Element, 1994

Knight, Chris and Lomas, Robert, *The Second Messiah*, Century, 1997

Lacroix, P, *Military and Religious Life in the Middle Ages*, Chapman and Hall, 1874

Lea, H. C, *The Inquisition in the Middle Ages*, NY 1955

Leroy, Thierry, *Hughues de Payns, Chevalier Champenois, Fondateur de L'Ordre des Templiers*, Editions de la Maison du Boulanger, France, 2001

Lizerand, *Le Dossier de l'Affaire des Templiers*, 1923

Lost Books of the Bible, The, Gramercy Books, New Jersey, 1979

Mack, Burton L, *The Lost Gospel*, Element, 1993

Maimonides, Obedyah, *The Treatise of the Pool*, Octagon Press, 1981

Malmes, *History of the Kings*, George Bell and Sons, London 1908

Maspero, Gaston, *Recueil des Travaux Relatifs a la Philologie et l'Archaeologie Egyptiennes et Assyriennes*, III, Travaux, Paris, 1878

McManners, John (ed.), *The Oxford History of Christianity*, OUP 1993

McNeal, E H, *The Conquest of Constantinople*, Robert de Clari, University of Toronto Press, 1997

Moore, L David, *The Christian Conspiracy*, Pendulum Press, 1983

Moore, R I, *The Formation Of A Persecuting Society*, Basil Blackwell and Co., Oxford 1990

Murray, David Christie, *The History of Heresy*, OUP 1976

Nicholson, Helen, *The Knights Hospitaller*, Boydell Press, 2002

—— *The Knights Templar*, Sutton Publishing, 2004

Oldenbourg, Zoé, *Massacre at Montségur*, Phoenix, 1999

Orton, Previte, *Outlines of Medieval History*, CUP 1916

O'Shea, Stephen, *The Perfect Heresy*, Profile Books Ltd, 2000

Osman, Ahmed, *Moses, Pharaoh of Egypt*, Paladin, 1991

—— *Moses Stranger in the Valley of the Kings*, Freethought Press, 2001

—— *Out of Egypt*, Century, London 1998

Partner, Peter, *The Knights Templar and their Myth*, Destiny Books, 1990

Pauwels, Louis and Bergier, Jaques, *The Dawn of Magic*, Gibbs and Phillips, 1963

Petrie, F, *The Religion of Ancient Egypt*, Constable, London, 1908

Philips, Graham, *The Moses Legacy*, Sidgwick and Jackson, London 2002

Powell, Mark Allen, *The Jesus Debate*, Lion Publishing, 1998

Rachi, *Pentatuque selon Rachi, La Genese*, Samule et Odette Levy, 1993

—— *Pentatuque selon Rachi l'Exode*, Samuel et Odette Levy 1993

Ranke-Heninemann, Ute, *Putting Away Childish Things*, HarperCollins, 1995

Ravenscroft, Trevor, *The Cup of Destiny*, Samuel Weiser, 1982

Ravenscroft Trevor and Wallace-Murphy, Tim, *The Mark of The Beast*, Sphere Books, London, 1990

Regan, Geoffrey, *Lionhearts: Saladin and Richard I*, Constable, London, 1998

Regne, J, *Études sur la Condition des Juifs de Narbonne*, Lafitte Reprints, Marseilles, 1981

Reznikov, Raymonde, *Cathars et Templiers*, Editions Loubatières, 1993

Rice, M, *Egypt's Making: The Origins of Ancient Egypt 5000–2000 BC*, London, 1990

Richardson, Peter, *Herod, King of the Jews and Friend of the Romans*, University of South Carolina Press, 1996

Robinson, James M, (ed.), *The Nag-Hammadi Library*, HarperCollins, 1990

Robinson, John J, *Born in Blood*, Arrow Books 1993

—— *Dungeon, Fire and Sword*, Brock Hampton Press, 1999

Rohl, David M, *A Test of Time*, Century, London, 1995

Roth, Cecil, *A Short History of the Jewish People*, East West Library, London, 1953

Runciman, Stephen, *A History of the Crusades*, 3 vols, Pelican, 1971

Sabbah, M and R, *Les Secrets de L'Exode*, Godefroy, Paris, 2000

Saige, G, *Les Juifs du Languedoc*, Greg International, Farnborough, 1991

Sanmell, S, *Judaism and Christian Beginnings*, OUP, New York, 1978

Schonfield, Hugh, *The Essene Odyssey*, Element, 1985

—— *The Passover Plot*, Element, 1985

—— *The Pentecost Revolution*, Element, 1985

Sellin E, *Mose und seine Bedenturg fur die israelitisch-judische Religiosgeschichte*, A Deichertsche, 1922

Sepher Hajasha, Prague 1840

Serrus, Georges, *The Land of the Cathars*, Editions Loubatières, Portet-sur-Garonne, 1990

Seward, Desmond, *Monks of War*, The Folio Society, 1999

Shah, Idries, *The Sufis*, Jonathan Cape and Co., 1969

Smith, Morton, *The Secret Gospel*, Aquarian Press, 1985

St Clair, L-A de, *Histoire Genealogique de la Famille de St Clair*, Paris, 1905

Stoyanov, Yuri, *The Hidden Tradition in Europe*, Arkana, 1994

Strachan, Gordon, *Chartres*, Floris Books, 2003

Taylor, Joan E, *The Immerser: John the Baptist in Second Temple Judaism*, Wm B Eerdmans Publishing Co, 1997

Thurston, Herbert (trans) *Memorandum of P. D'Arcis*, part of an article 'The Holy Shroud and the verdict of History' published in the journal *The Month* CI 91903) – The original document is in the collection of the Bibliotheque Nationale in Paris among the Collection de Champagne, vol 154 Folio 138

Trevor-Roper, Hugh, *The Rise of Christian Europe*, Thames and Hudson, 1965

Upton-Ward, J M, *The Rule of The Templars*, Boydell Press, 1992

VandenBroeck, Andre, *Al-Kemi*, Lindisfarne Press, 1987

Vermes, Geza, *Jesus the Jew*, Augsburg Fortress Publishing, 1981

Wakefield and Evans, *Heresies of the Middle Ages*, Columbia University Press, 1991

Wallace-Murphy, Tim, *The Templar Legacy and the Masonic Inheritance Within Rosslyn Chapel*, The Friends of Rosslyn, 1994

Wallace-Murphy, Tim and Hopkins, Marilyn, *Rosslyn: Guardian of the Secrets of the Holy Grail*, Element Books, 1999

Wallace-Murphy, T, Hopkins, M, Simmans, G, *Rex Deus*, Element Books, 2000

Ward, Colin, *Chartres the Making of a Miracle*, Folio Society, 1986

Weighall, A E P, *Travels in the Upper Egyptian Desert*, London 1909

—— *The Life and Times of Akenhaten*, London, 1910 and 1923

Welburn, Andrew, *The Beginnings of Chrsitianity*, Floris, 1991

West, John Anthony, *Serpent in the Sky*, HarperCollins, London, 1979

Wilson, A N, *Jesus*, HarperCollins, 1993

—— *Paul, the Mind of the Apostle*, Pimlico, 1998

Wilson, Colin, *From Atlantis to the Sphinx*, Virgin Books, London 1997

—— (Ed.), *Men of Mystery*, W H Allen, London, 1977

—— *The Occult*, Grafton Books, 1979

Wright, Esmond, *The Medieval and Renaissance World*, Hamlyn, 1979

Zuckerman, A J, *A Jewish Princedom in Feudal France 768–900*, Columbia University Press, 1972

Index